Praise for *Sanctuary*

Sanctuary is a heart-wrenching-and-warming story in gory and glorious detail—a love story of souls taking sanctuary in each other and in God. There's nothing like it in LGBTQ-affirming literature.

Ken Wilson, best-selling author of Christian books, including *Letter to My Congregation* and *Solus Jesus*

Set aside the "how to" guides and experience an authentic narrative from those who led their church to thrive in full inclusion. Wassink, Imborek, and Wassink share deep self-examination, as well as biblical and theological reflection. In this story of celebration, readers will find a model to lead a congregation to lovingly welcome all people.

The Rev. Dr. Sherry Parker-Lewis, United Methodist Elder, Michigan Conference

A small Midwest church makes the big leap from evangelicalism to LGBTQ inclusion in a highly readable book that can be a beacon for all who aim to welcome queer congregants.

Sanctuary weaves together the voices of two co-pastors and a gay parishioner from an unlikely place: a Jesus-centered, LGBTQ-inclusive church in Iowa. They reveal the church's rocky yet rewarding six-year evolution. In the process they lose some prejudices but keep their sense of humor while building a queerly dynamic faith community.

Kittredge Cherry, lesbian Christian author of *The Passion of Christ: A Gay Vision*

Sanctuary is deep and winsome and funny, and it tells a beautiful story. Actually, it's a lot of stories. It's the story of two pastors and a church that found their way to include and bless and celebrate LGBTQ people. It's a story of queer visitors and congregants and leaders who are no longer turned away as their full selves or merely tolerated, but are now embraced as friends and disciples and teachers in the way of Jesus. And I like to think this book tells the story of God, who is so glad that more of God's children are getting free. The authors write early on that God is still looking for a church home where she'll be safe. *Sanctuary* sounds like just such a home. Enjoy the story.

Steve Watson is the senior pastor of Reservoir Church in Cambridge, MA.

As a fellow pastor and friend, I find the journey chronicled in this book deeply moving. In a time when so many congregations, clergy, and leaders are grappling with the complexities of inclusivity, Adey Wassink and her team offer a compelling narrative recounting their journey toward becoming an open and affirming congregation. Through personal stories and reflections on the hurdles faced within themselves, their church, and their denomination, they provide valuable lessons on the emotional, relational, and spiritual costs involved in this pursuit. Yet, amidst the struggles and inevitable losses, they have emerged as a reconciling community committed to their mission, "We make space for every race, ethnicity, age, orientation, and gender identity. We welcome belief and doubt, devotion and exploration, while hoping to connect with God, one another, and our world as we do life together." I recommend this book to those navigating similar paths. It offers valuable insights and guidance with heartfelt grace and wisdom.

Rose Madrid Swetman, Associate Director, Center for Transforming Engagement

Sanctuary

Queering a Church in the Heartland

Adey Wassink, DMiss
Katie Imborek, M.D.
Tom Wassink, M.D.

For more information and further discussion, visit:

SanctuaryIC.org

Cover design by Rick Nease
RickNeaseArt.com

Published by Read the Spirit Books, an imprint of
Front Edge Publishing
42807 Ford Road
Canton, MI, 48187

Read The Spirit Books is an imprint of Front Edge Publishing, LLC. Since 2007, Read The Spirit Books has been publishing books that celebrate religious and cultural diversity. Our writers explore these themes each week in our online magazine which can be read and subscribed to at ReadTheSpirit.com.

Front Edge Publishing books are available for discount bulk purchases for events, corporate use and small groups. Special editions, including books with corporate logos, personalized covers and customized interiors are available for purchase. For more information, contact Front Edge Publishing at info@FrontEdgePublishing.com

Contents

This book is dedicated to the people of Sanctuary Community Church—past, present, and future—which celebrates its 25th year of existence in sync with the publishing of this book; thank you all for making our culture of transformation possible. You are the best faith community on our planet (and in our local galaxy (as far as we know)).

And it's also an apology to those of you who at any point in time had needed us to be further along than we were; we're sorry to you and sad for us.

Foreword

By Brian McLaren

Most people don't spend that many hours per week going to church as children. But the effect of those few hours can be disproportionately intense.

I accrued more "pew time" than most as a child. Our family was at church for at least three hours each Sunday (worship, Bible study, Sunday School, usually returning Sunday night for a preaching service). But even those hours were easily bested by the time I spent watching The Flintstones, I Love Lucy reruns, and Looney Tunes cartoons between Sundays. (For those born after 1980, those were big kids' TV shows of the 60s and 70s.)

Why have I spent so much of my time and energy through my adult life recovering from those few hours spent in church, and so little time and energy recovering from many hours of watching Looney Tunes, I Love Lucy, or Flintstones?

For those who join the church-oriented community later in life, church impact can be even more intense. These days, their lives are often divided into BC and AD epochs: Before Church and After Deconstruction.

Why does church involvement leave such a disproportionate mark on us, whether we're born into it or convert into it—for better and for worse?

There are many answers to this question, but among them surely is this: Churches typically tell us how things are with the most basic parts of us, including and especially our sexuality.

The cynical part of me sometimes thinks there is a kind of mafia-esque protection racket in how churches and other religious institutions work. They make us feel guilty and ashamed and then they sell us relief from guilt and shame. But the relief is temporary and conditional. We must come back next week for a fresh dose of forgiveness—and then a fresh load of guilt.

When I was a preacher, I did not see myself as a participant in this kind of spiritual protection racket. I was passionate and sincere about one thing: helping people become better people. But even that had its danger: Who was I to be so certain about what made a person better or worse?

That was especially true regarding sex.

I remember the first time a close friend came out to me about being gay. I knew he was one of the kindest and best humans I had met in my seventeen years of life. But I also knew that my church called his identity an "abomination." (Funny how that word had so much punch back then. Funny how the church could so easily cast stones at others and remove splinters from the eyes of others back then.)

I felt the tension in myself. I had no interest in homosexual activity, but my interest in heterosexual activity was surely enough to send me to hell many times over, especially having been taught that committing "adultery in one's heart" was as bad as doing the deed! My normal adolescent sexual awakening set me up to be sucked into the spiritual protection racket, with lots to feel guilty about every single day.

Not long ago, another gay friend told me, "One of the great gifts that gay folk offer the church is that by coming out about their homosexuality, they help everyone else come out about their human sexuality."

We're all recognizing that—whether with Catholic celibacy and moral and venial sin categories, or with Evangelical "pray away the gay" reorientation camps or purity rings, or with Pentecostals casting out the demons of lust and rebuking "the spirit of Onan"—our churches have done a lot of harm to a lot of us by making us feel ashamed of our human sexuality that is hardwired into us as biological entities.

In our sincere attempts to help people become better people, people like me have inflicted ourselves and others with a lot of pain, a lot of shame, a lot of trauma.

That's why I am so grateful for churches like Sanctuary and for pastors like Adey and Tom Wassink, and for sincere and insightful people like Katie Imborek. They're telling us honestly about the intimate pain that has been and is still being inflicted on people whose only crime is being sexual.

And thank God, Adey, Tom, and Katie also are telling stories of healing that pain, because they are living those stories.

They're modeling what religion should have always been good at, but too seldom is: repenting, which means rethinking or changing our minds.

The norms set up by human societies always label some things as normal and others as queer. Across cultures and over time, those norms change.

But often, whether it has to do with racial equality, gender equality, economic justice, or equality of sexual orientation—religious institutions are among the very last to change, which means that they are also the last to cease doing harm.

So here is a gift—a series of often humorous, often poignant, sometimes heartbreaking, and always well-told stories and reflections—to help us all rethink what is normal or queer, what is sacred or scandalous, what is bad or good.

We may just become better people in the process. May it be so!

Brian D. McLaren, April 2024

Brian D. McLaren is the best-selling author of a series of books about his decades-long journey from a leading national voice for evangelical Protestantism to an outspoken advocate for an inclusive Christian embrace of diversity and concern for the world's most vulnerable.

Good Luck With That!

Hello,

My name is Alden. I was referred to you by a friend of my husband, Adan. We are a beginning family looking for a church home.

Oh Alden, I thought, *good luck with that.* Alden was writing to me as the Senior Pastor of our evangelical church on April 1st, 2010. He continued:

I was raised pretty Evangelical and for several years after high school attended a Vineyard church in Iowa. This was a frustrating experience for me because though I loved the church and my relationship with Jesus, I was gay and the church was non-supportive.

But Alden, we're also a Vineyard church in Iowa, so what are you hoping for from me?

For many years I have sought spiritual things on my own. I was lucky enough to meet a wonderful man nine years ago and even luckier to be able to marry just last year. We foster children and are actively seeking to adopt. I questioned whether to even consider a Vineyard after my past experiences, but my husband had a friend who encouraged us to seek you out as she felt her experience with the Vineyard in Iowa City was different than what we described from our past.

Huh. So somehow, hidden within our conservative movement, our Iowa City faith community had nonetheless managed to emanate to someone a welcoming vibe.

I chose to step out on her recommendation and ask what your stance is on gay members, especially married gay members with children. Our intention is to find a home church that nurtures our individual spirits as well as our family.

Oh Alden, you are so so reasonable ...

It is important that our children will never have their family denigrated by people we bring into their lives and though we cannot control this completely we feel that at least in this arena we have this power. I believe in Jesus Christ as my personal savior. I don't believe the Bible is the literal word of God. I do believe the Holy Spirit is his Living Word. I do believe in ongoing revelation and the power of the Spirit to work in individuals and communities.

... an infinite string of cringe emojis ...

I state this in hopes you may understand where I and my family come from in searching for a church home. We hope to hear from you soon. Feel free to call if you feel an email is too distant.

Alden

Alden, we do! Our 2024 selves totally understand where your family is coming from in searching for a church home!! Because we now include Katie! And Kevo!! And Tim and Michael!! And Jill and Nicki!! And Jesse and Krystal!! And our Christian space is lovely and safe and queer!!

But all we can say on behalf of our 2010 selves is ... sorry. Sorry sorry sorry sorry sorry. Sorry that even before you ever met us, we had participated in harming you. Sorry that we had caused you to need to tell us of your trau-matization in our denomination, of your reluctant hopefulness to give our particular church a try, of your journey of spiritual loneliness that brought you to this moment. Sorry for your fear of your family being denigrated in a Jesus Christ Christian church of all places. Sorry for your need to declare to us your orthodox Christian bona fides, matched by your need to know in advance our queer ones. What other church visitor on the planet must run this gauntlet of insecurity and self-disclosure and bravery in advance of just walking through the front door? Sorry that you came to us five years too soon. Sorry that we were not ready for you.

But none of this apologizing will be enough for you, Alden and Adan and kids, because of course you won't hear it, and we can't not be who we were back then, and so you'll come, and be with us for a little while, and you'll like us, and we'll care for your children in our Kids' Wing, but then one day we'll turn around and you and they won't be there. Which is, we suppose, a little better than with Brinlee, who had written to us pretty much the exact same email at about the same time, but for whom our nice but veiled response let her know to stay away. But which was followed two years later by Katie and Paula and their two boys coming and then staying because we helped to save their gay marriage (at least for a little while), and so Katie is a co-author of this book. So yes, something changed.

We three—Katie, Adey, and Tom—are telling this story of the conversion of our selves and of our church from evangelicalism to inclusion. Because unlike many who have attempted such a feat, our church came out on the other side not just alive, but bigger, healthier, happier, and more godly (hey, three out of four ain't bad). While some people left, more came. We did not implode or plunge into the abyss. We lost duplicitousness and gained sanity. We became that most tenuous of things—an independent local nondenominational church—which turns out to be fun. We shed institutional scrutiny and gained kind and like-minded pastoring friends. And while, sadly, neither Brinlee nor Adan nor Alden nor many others along the way are worshiping with us now, we celebrate that Katie and Dustin and Dylan and Jill and Nicki and Kevo and Chris and Sadie are. Our congregation includes a substantial and growing LGBTQ+ community worshiping freely and seamlessly within the larger faith community that is Sanctuary Community Church. It's genuinely lovely.

Most of the events recounted herein stretch across seven years, from 2010 to 2016. We make audible in our storytelling at least twenty-seven distinct voices, including pastors and laity, adults and children, straight and queer, those who stayed and those who left, some local livestock and God, so that our telling is not just about, but is, our faith community. And though this book is situated within the stream of Christianity called "evangelicalism,"

Katie grew up Lutheran, Adey grew up and remains Jewish, and Tom grew up but no longer remains Calvinist, so the resonance of our story with Christianity writ large is expansive.

Some rough structure: Chapters 1–6 introduce you to the formative religious experiences of Adey and Katie and Tom, and how we three all met one day with a shared desire for queer inclusion in Adey's office, and how this lovely small meeting led to some really stressful and premature bigger ones. Chapter 8 is the funniest, with pregnant Paula trying to tell Katie's unknowing and fragile Grandma Imborek how she (Paula) came to be that way while Katie stares out the window. Chapters 10–14 describe us moving forward nonetheless, and how some of our formerly conservative parishioners experienced our transformation.

Chapters 16–19 describe everything that it took to leave (be expelled from?) our denomination, and so in Chapter 21, we have to come up with a new church name which the kids wanted to be Twinkler, but which the adults vetoed in favor of Sanctuary. In the remaining chapters, queer friends come and evangelical friends go; we at long long last, on Sunday, January 17, 2016—after Adey wrestles with the stupid cordless mic—Come Out!; everyone cries; and later that summer, as we grieve the Pulse nightclub massacre, we swap out our own terrorization for dignity.

The rest of the chapters present some more queer friends and liberated queer Christian thoughts.

We also intersperse three Bible storytellings which are not the typical LGBTQ clobber passage clobberings, but rather Jesus stories that reflect how we came to perceive him dismantling patriarchal systems of dominance with his corresponding liberation of gender-defined subjugants.

Also, at the end of Chapter 8, I, Katie, tell you that in 2021, so ten years after Sanctuary saved my gay marriage, Paula and I chose to get divorced. I tell you so that you're not surprised at the end of the book by an obscure paragraph hidden in the epilogue, like one of those movie reveals that forces you to go back and reinterpret every moment of the whole thing. I don't tell much about why, but I do describe how this occurrence, though tremendously sad, caused us all to realize that the meaningfulness of our story of inclusion cannot be that coming to Sanctuary makes everything for everyone turn out well—as if queer lives lived in Sanctuary will be spared the struggles of heterosexual lives—but rather that God lovingly and compassionately inhabits every aspect of every lived life.

A few final notes:

We have come to be more thoughtful than when we began this journey about how we use gendered pronouns to refer to God. But when we present thoughts and communications from our patriarchal past, we stay true to how we referred to her back then so that we don't sound better than we really were.

We often present actual communications—emails, chats, letters, recordings—to try to keep ourselves honest.

We try to be funny.

Which is usually to counteract chagrin from being honest.

We love our church.

2

We Were All Nervous

Katie Was Nervous

Katie:

"Sundays are so busy for us—let me check with my wife."

This was me deflecting Julie's invitation. It was summer of 2012, and she had been telling me about her church for six months—the kindness she had experienced there, the quality of community, the woman Senior Pastor. It's not that I wasn't intrigued, but showing up at a church just wasn't that easy. I was okay with the awkward exchanges and forced pleasantries that go with every first church visit, but, like Adan and Alden before me, my real concern was bringing my family into a space that might actually cause them harm. I couldn't exactly blend into the background with my wife, Paula, and our two young boys in tow. Would the smile of the greeter falter when he saw our family walk in? Could I bring my boys to Sunday school without having to worry about the debrief on the ride home—Momma, did God really say that being married was only for a man and a woman? Is it wrong that we have a momma and a mommy and no daddy? Would Paula and I have to sit through a preacher declaring that Paul's words in Romans 12:2, "Do not conform to the pattern of this world," were never as relevant as for today when one state after another was legalizing same-sex marriage?

What worried me most, however, was the possibility that these people would be kind and welcoming in a way that would make us want to come back. We would develop friendships and come to feel secure in the church's welcome only to realize that there was in fact an end game—their hope being that through our presence in their church and the powerful impact of their loving prayers, God would heal us and help us turn away from our "sinful lifestyle."

But I knew that children were supposed to go to church. I had been baptized into the Lutheran Church as an infant and confirmed in eighth grade after three years of weekly classes devoted to Bible study and memorizing *Luther's Small Catechism*. My mom picked up my great-grandmother every Sunday morning on our way because attending was a righteous duty, even if we arrived home late for the Chicago Bears' noon kickoff. And Julie knew that my marriage was in trouble. Paula and I were in the midst of getting separated, I was desperate for things to work, and Julie—much to my surprise—said, "I think these pastors would help you with that."

Throughout the long years of coming out, my connection to God had morphed from angrily pushing God away, to befriending someone whose name was invoked to persecute people like me, to believing that God had made me and loved me—all of me—including my sexuality. This last belief superseded my need to have church figure out theology for me; I felt assured of God's love for me and my family without any help from religious authority. But I knew there was more to church—or there was supposed to be—than just beliefs. So to satisfy my duty to my kids, and to quell Paula's Catholic guilt, and as a desperate leaning into the super-unlikely possibility that a Christian church might rescue my gay marriage, after the eighty-teenth time that Julie asked me to attend with her, I finally said, "Okay."

Per our usual, we arrived late. We thereby avoided the pre-service small talk and slipped quietly into the sanctuary. We kept our boys with us instead of bringing them to the Kids' Wing so we could make a quick escape if needed. I was initially put at ease by a young woman center-stage with tall black boots and purple streaked hair. But then as she began to lead the music and I noticed people had their hands in the air, I felt panic. *Shit!* I thought, *this is an evangelical church!*

Now I really had no idea what "evangelical" meant, I just knew what they had done to my people. I was co-director of a health clinic serving lesbian, gay, bisexual, transgender, queer, and questioning people. Evangelical Christians supported the "conversion therapy" that had traumatized so many of my queer patients. I remembered back in November 2004, when

George W. Bush swooped into the White House on the coattails of evangelical Christian voters who turned out in record numbers to ban gay marriage
in eleven states. And I had supported—and benefited from—the legalization
of same sex marriage in Iowa in 2009, but then had watched helplessly as
evangelical Christians led the ousting of the Iowa Supreme Court justices
who had perpetrated this atrocity.

And I recognized their music—peppy light rock, a little squishy lovey
towards Jesus, I'm bad but God is good and together we're gonna win. So as
the music rose, my fears did too. Now was the time to sneak out the back as
quietly as we came in!

But next to me was my friend Julie, smiling warmly. I looked into her
big brown eyes and knew how much she loved my family and me, and I
felt a tremor of trust that she wouldn't lead us astray. Paula and I were here
together, our kids were not freaking, and there seemed to be more small
children than adults. I hadn't yet detected any homophobic warning signs,
like cross necklaces or fish skeleton bumper stickers. And there was something there that we connected with—the worship, the thoughtful message
that seemed to bring the Bible to life, and the vibrancy of the congregation.
There was a palpable passion in the room. It was more of an experience than
a church service, and unlike anything I had felt before.

So we wanted to come back for another Sunday, which the pastors apparently wanted too because I found this in my email inbox a couple days later:

> Hi Katie,
>
> I can't tell what is welcoming and what is a pain in the neck, so
> you have to let me know. Next Sunday the church is hosting
> pizza with the pastors after church. If that is something of
> interest to your family, please join us. Also, would your family
> and Julie like to have a meal with our family?
>
> Love,
>
> Adey

Adey and I had met in church, and she was super-friendly. So I responded:

> Adey,
>
> Thanks so much for the email. We are on vacation currently
> in Estes Park, CO, and having an amazing time. The boys are

having so much fun seeing wildlife and being in the outdoors.
It is beautiful out here.

The truth was that Paula and I were working out the details of our separation, but I was far from ready to trust my mess to this woman who had
probably just pretended to be nice to me in the foyer of her evangelical
church. Before we could come to even one more service, Adey and I had to
really meet so that I could avoid the heartache of realizing too late that we
weren't fully welcomed after all. So I resorted to Alden's template:

> Adey, I have been thinking a lot about church and talking quite
> a bit with Paula about it as well. In fact, I was planning on
> emailing or calling you when I returned from vacation. We
> both have a really good feeling about Vineyard and especially
> are impressed with the children's programs. I was hoping to
> be able to sit down and meet with either you alone or all
> of the pastors and discuss not only your personal views on
> homosexuality, same sex marriage and same sex couples raising
> children, but also the sentiments of the congregation and the
> beliefs of the larger vineyard USA church as a whole.

I wanted to know it all, so I continued:

> I am sure that you can imagine the complicated relationship
> that gay folks have with religion and even faith. It is definitely
> something that we want and need in our lives, but I want to
> make sure that it feels right for our family. I want to make
> sure that the things our children will hear and be taught in
> our chosen place of worship will never leave them worrying
> about the validity or sanctity of their family. By no means do
> I want to ignore the seven passages in the bible that relate to
> homosexuality, instead I want to find a faith community that
> can actively have a conversation about them in a real way that
> aligns with today's world.

So that's me prefacing a church visit like so many of my queer friends: my
gay Christian history, my longing for church, me and my wife both feeling
good about your church which makes me really anxious, my theology in
brief—and will you harm my kids? I topped it off with: Are you and your
fellow pastors capable of having a real conversation with us about all this? An

actual conversation where we as adults converse respectfully about momentous things instead of you as God's expert either hiding what you really think
or telling me why I'm going to hell. I concluded:

> I sincerely hope that Vineyard Community Church is a fit for
> us. Everyone has been so welcoming and I trust the judgment
> of Julie with all of my heart :) I look forward to getting together
> soon.
>
> Katie

And Adey Was Nervous

Adey:

The same kind of nervous as when Gary Goldstein asked me out my
senior year in high school. I hadn't had many dates yet and I liked him and
we decided to go on a picnic. My one task was to hard-boil some eggs. But
when Gary came to pick me up, I couldn't find them. I emptied out the
fridge, looked in every cabinet, checked the stove, the sink, the toaster oven.
I mean, really! How does one lose a half dozen hard-boiled eggs? We went
out sans eggs and had a nice time, though their strange disappearance hov-
ered over our date like a foreboding omen of doom, which was confirmed
the next day when Gary passed me in the high school hallway with nary a
word. Days later, when my mom was getting out a pot to steam zucchini
and carrots, we found that after cooking the eggs, I'd left them in the water,
the water in the pot, and put it all—pot, eggs, water—back in the cabinet.

When Katie responded to me saying she'd like to meet, it was Gary all
over again. I was excited, hopeful, and way anxious. All I could think was:
Don't screw up the eggs! Katie and Paula showing up at church had not gone
unnoticed. When you have two hundred heterosexuals (supposedly) in a
room doing church and two women walk in holding hands with two little
boys in tow, believe me, you notice!

As a faith community, we had dispensed—or so we thought—with our
us/them mentality of mission where the "usses" in-the-know provided help
to the "thems" wandering and lost outside our special place. We had come to
realize instead that we were all thems. So we had been welcoming everyone
to our Jesus thing: friends, neighbors, co-workers, students, folks from every

background and walk of life … except for gay people. And lesbians. And those who were transgender, and queer, and, truthfully, any sexual or gender minority person. Which had become increasingly troubling to me in a city with a welcoming ethic as expansive as ours. While Iowa City might struggle to attain diversity in some aspects of identity, such was not the case with gender identity. We had a vibrant queer social scene backed up by supportive university and city governance, all of which swelled our city's numbers of LGBTQ people.

So what did it mean that none of these folks felt comfortable worshiping with us? In all other areas of identity our church was seeming to overcome the limited diversity of our local culture, but with sexual and gender minority identities, we weren't even close. If we endeavored to be a church of and for our city, we had problems. Which, it turned out, we did! Theology problems and otherizing problems and homophobia problems. Most in our church had inhabited homophobic cultures, which had then been sanctified by conservative evangelical theology. So I knew that problems existed within me and within us, but I knew too that we could not, without help from an enlightened Other, perceive what those problems were.

And that enlightened Other had to be a gay man or lesbian woman or transgender or bisexual or queer person, or maybe—dare we dream—two of "them." We had to have "them" at the center of "us" or we'd never become the full-throated community of faith that I was increasingly convinced God wanted us to be. I, as a woman aspiring to lead in our patriarchal denomination, had experienced the prolonged dysfunction of men determining the fate of women. So I prayed, "Jesus, send us folks from the LGBTQ community through whom you will teach us, shape us, and show yourself to us."

To which I quickly added: "And when they come, help us keep them." After all, Brinlee never came, and Alden and Adan had stopped attending. At the moment of Katie's email, no LGBTQ person had stayed—not one—and I felt terrible. Tom and I would take long evening walks down Newport Road, past sheep and goats and fireflies and corn and the setting sun, and I would cry—hardest on Mondays. Tom, then still conservative in his theology, would comfort me. "Don't be sad," he'd say. "If that's what the Bible says, it has to be good!" So at least then instead of being sad at God, I could be mad at Tom.

But by the time Katie visited church, we had begun to change. We had studied the handful of biblical passages of restriction and perceived their tenuousness as texts on which to base a practice of exclusion. Tom had become unsettled by the relentless championing of religions' outcasts by Jesus. I was insecure theologically, but my heart was 100% in because I knew that Katie and Paula were simply looking for a place to experience the living God just like I could. They wanted safety for their family in a church just like I did. They wanted to be helped by the Bible and to connect with Jesus just like I did.

So I had started loving Katie and Paula before we ever met, and my response to her email was immediate:

> Katie:
>
> I would love to do all you said.
>
> Talk alone with you and Paula.
>
> Talk together with the staff.
>
> Your questions are so important. We will be honest and open. I can't speak for your future here—though I can't wait to have conversations—but, I am thrilled you've had a good experience and so hopeful to walk this out together.
>
> Can you throw out some dates that work for you guys and I will arrange a conversation with our staff.
>
> Adey

Even Tom Was Nervous

Tom:

Which was a weird state of being for me. I don't often get nervous because, like lots of men, I never developed an amygdala. They're the little almond-shaped parts of our temporal lobes that are supposed to help us feel things and then to not freak out when we do. Which neurological deficit also hinders me detecting momentousness, particularly when people are involved. So that I did detect its possibility in this nascent little gathering was indicative.

My problem is that instead of people, I begin and end with the text. I love the text—meaning the Bible and its stories—particularly the stories of Jesus. He comes to life for me as he pings from fighting against pastors to blessing children to shooing away a beseeching crowd so he can grieve alone on a lakeside hill under midnight stars because his friend has just been killed. I still today see him and know him from the stories of him.

But living from the text turns out to be a profoundly inadequate rubric for life. I didn't always feel that way because I inhabited Calvinist and then evangelical Christianity, both of which deify the text. But then we moved to Iowa City and I took long walks with Adey down Newport Road during which she helped me see how much wasn't in there. Like people. Sure, the Bible has some people—Jewish people, and sinners, and tax collectors, and shepherds, and Brothers and Sisters in Christ. But then there are whole other classes of people who I was never going to encounter, like geography teachers or hairdressers or Dutch people or queer people.

Which last overlooked group would have been okay for me except that Adey and I, as I noted, moved to Iowa City. Queer people didn't exist in my growing up town of Holland, Michigan. Gay there was skipping happily across a springtime meadow, and queer was going out for dinner to an ethnic restaurant. We were instead Dutch and Calvinist and rigidly sexually normative. The only thing that changed in my subsequent evangelical church was that while we vaguely acknowledged the existence of nontraditional attractional tendencies, we suppressed them or policed them or cast those demons out!

But as Adey said, Iowa City is an LGBTQ+ haven. Not completely safe, but better than just about anywhere else in Iowa. Iowa City has been celebrating Pride openly for decades, with only four or five extremist Christians and their nasty signs protesting at the parade. Queer people were in Iowa City working and serving and loving and getting educated and leading and teaching and holding hands, and trying to go to church—sometimes our church.

Which made me nervous. In part because of unfamiliarity, in part because of its religious wrongness, but also because somewhere in my unawareness it registered that if queerness turned out to be lovely in the eyes of God, my whole constructed self would need to be dismantled. My theology, my conceptions of identity, what God cared about in human beings, who the Christian faith community was for and how it was meant to function, who and what sex was for, even my own sexuality! My most impressive house of a godly person would turn out to have been built on a foundation of sand, and so like my intellectually imprisoned compatriot Nicodemus, I would have to be born again. So I resisted God and my wife and the queer people who came seeking access to this place where I had power to exclude. Until I didn't.

Gusty was/is one of Adey's and my dearest lifelong friends from our church of origin who we watched suffer constraint and trauma across decades because her lesbian longings were not condoned in our sexually conservative church movement. But I found myself one day thinking: She practices Christianity way better than I ever will, and against greater odds—how could God not want a fulness of life for her, as God does for me, *just as she is?* And then there was yet one more walk down Newport Road when Adey was banging on the door to my heart trying to arouse my slumbering amygdala with the plight of yet one more *person*, and me feeling myself this time opening that door just a crack, just enough for me to think, *maybe.*

And then came Katie. Now just to state clearly—me repenting about my personal practice of injustice should not in any way depend on the quality of a person I encounter who is suffering that injustice. But ... Katie was so genuine and perceptive and aware and articulate ... and a doctor like me in the hospital I worked at, serving a marginalized people group like I was, but with a way more expansive sense of systems and justice. I, like Adey, had seen Katie and Paula and their kids coming to church, and had chatted with them just enough to detect what they might be able to bring to us. I had become strangely warmed to the possibility of our church being queerly transformed. I knew that I couldn't magnanimously figure this all out—that we needed them to awaken us. And so when Adey in a staff meeting told us that her communications with Katie were leading to a meeting in her office to discuss Katie's questions, I thought, *I don't want to be left out!* I didn't want to miss out on something big and wonderfully shattering because of my propensity to be intellectual or disapproving. I wanted to be there to make sure that I got to voice my affirmation for whatever heresy it was that we all together were about to birth into our church.

Katie

We scheduled our meeting for 10 a.m., September 17, 2012 in Adey's office. The night before the meeting, I prepared questions:

- Do you believe being gay is a sin?
- Will my two sons ever be taught that their family is somehow wrong or less than any other child's family?
- What is your interpretation of the Bible passages about sex and marriage with respect to loving, committed gay couples?

I arrived expecting just Adey, but all four pastors—Adey, Tom, David, and Leah—were there. I was even more surprised when their answers to my questions conveyed a sense of love and welcome. It felt like they each independently wanted to communicate their truly welcoming intentions towards me and my family, and that they didn't quite trust the others to do that convincingly enough. And like they each just wanted to be in the room for this moment. I felt the specialness of it all for me, but I also seemed to detect the specialness of it all for them. While I came into this crowded office with a big gay chip on my shoulder prepared to prove to them the hypocrisy of their communion invitation, I was instead their honored guest, met with kindness and welcome.

↜

But getting to that special moment in Adey's office had required each of us overcoming a lot from our personal and religious backgrounds ...

3

Tom

Tom:

"Arrghh!!" says Adey. "How can you be so heartless?"

"Because, honey, the Prophet Jeremiah says in our Holy Scriptures that 'the heart is devious above all else—it is perverse!' And I don't know about you, but I am loath to be perverse."

I thought that, but I did not say it, and so we're still married.

Newport Road is a bucolic country lane that runs past horses, sheep, and cows grazing the rolling Grant Wood hills just north of Iowa City. Adey and I would come out of our home's cul-de-sac, turn left onto Newport, and stroll together in the waning afternoon sun to disturb the tranquility of the local livestock with our fights about LGBTQ inclusion. This one occurred in the summer of 2007. As we walked Newport Road heading vaguely northward, the sun was pendulous, the corn buzzing, and the cows torpid, but we noticed none of it. We'd missed the turnaround markers. I think we were in Wisconsin.

What I did say to my wife was: "This has nothing to do with 'heart!' You just want the Bible to say something other than what it actually says!"

"I do not!" retorted Adey. We did a lot of retorting on those walks. "I know what those few verses say. I also know that I love Gusty, and Alden, and Adan, and I think God would want them in church just as much as he wants me. Or you!"

"I'm happy to have Gusty and Adan and Alden in church with me," I rejoined. "But we can't change what the Bible says just because it feels better. I don't want us capitulating to culture!"

It would take another ten years for me to realize how much I and my Christian forebears had been capitulating to conservative religious culture for over half a millenium. But on this day, Adey was right: my *No!* to inclusion was because I, like the Tin Woodman, had no heart. Which until this sunny stroll had been just fine! I had inhabited conservative Christian traditions—first Calvinism and then evangelicalism—that exalted the mind and impugned the heart, which worked out well for me because according to the Myers-Briggs Type Indicator, I have an **I**ntroverted-i**N**tuitive-**T**hinking-**P**erceiving (INTP) personality type, meaning that I have:

> No understanding or value for decisions made on the basis of personal subjectivity or feelings. I strive constantly to achieve logical conclusions to problems, and don't understand the importance or relevance of applying subjective emotional considerations to decisions. For this reason, I am usually not in tune with how people are feeling.

Whatever. Because I also embodied all the demographic characteristics that made me unexaminedly correct: white heterosexual male oldest son physician. And tall. My perceptions were presumptively true because I was the apotheosis of dominant culture so that whenever Adey, walking down Newport, pleaded the plight of people, I could, with the backing of the institution, play the trump card of cold-hearted Biblical Truth, and not have to feel bad about it. Nice!

Most of what shapes our thoughts resides happily in our unawareness until our wives can't take it anymore. As much as she made me mad, the only reason that I took the time to understand how my Christianity had caused me to be able to exclude queer people, and to then repent of that, was because, nevertheless, she persisted.

Cauvinist Psychopathology

Wassink is Dutch. I grew up in Holland, Michigan, surrounded by Zeeland and Graafschaap and Overisel, all of which we Dutch Reformed absconded from the Ojibewe, Odawa, and Potawatomi in the mid-1800s while ourselves fleeing religious persecution from the Christian Reformed Church in the Netherlands because of our progressive heresies. In spite of which uppitiness we Dutch nonetheless prided ourselves on a culture of constraint. Everything calm and in its proper container. One conversation at a time no matter how many at the table. Don't get too excited (things will get worse) or too sad (you're not dead yet). Clapping and shouting only when your team (Go Blue!) wins. And quiet tears only after funerals as you eat Jell-O salad and sliced ham on a buttered dinner roll washed down by half-strength Country Time lemonade in the church fellowship hall.

Yet despite a certain insularity, I had made a few non-Dutch friends in high school, including a family with a Jewish father from Israel, a Lutheran mother, and three Jewtheran kids. I remember the first time I and one of those kids drove down Dempster Street through Skokie, Illinois, on our way to being college freshmen together at Northwestern University. As I passed within hallooing distance of my future wife's childhood home, I perceived it to be a strangely high-tech place because of all the signs for "gyros," which I knew only as those spinning devices that stabilized missiles.

So when Adey came into my life a few years later, we went all in with the My Big Fat Jewish Wedding paradigm. Adey's family was boisterous, affectionate, and expressive. More arguments than people at the dinner table, each louder than the next, a symphonic crescendo of kosher passion. Adey's father, the first time I met him, kissed me full on the lips.

In spite of which I continued to prefer Calvin over Moses for my theology, *even though he* (Calvin) *was not Dutch!!* Adey's intransigence caused me to resentfully reexamine everything—Jesus, queerness, and myself. Which we Dutch just don't do! Particularly the "myself" part. But off to Wikipedia I traipsed to understand my heritage, where I quickly realized with chagrin that a living and vital part of "myself" turned out to be this guy from days of yore wearing a smart person beanie cap in his portrait, which hung illuminated in the foyer of my growing-up church.

John Calvin was born "Jehan Cauvin" in Noyon, France, even though all Dutch people who have anything to do with church believe that Calvin was Dutch. I asked my Reformed compatriot Megan Bomgaars the ethnicity of Calvin: "He was Dutch!" And her husband, Ben Roos: "Dutch!" Adey: "Dutch!" David, our executive pastor, said, "French! Though I only learned that after seminary when [smart friend] Alvis told me. Before that, I thought he was Dutch." I myself had wondered whether "John Calvin" was an anglicized moniker pared down from Jaan VanCalvinDykemaVanMaaaauuw so as to conserve vowels. But "Calvin" turns out to be just the latinized version of

"Cauvin," who then lived his French life in, of all places, Switzerland! Which is where rich people go skiing in their bank vaults!!! It's all so hedonistic, so not Dutch, a spiritual 23andMe moment: *Wait, I'm religiously **French** by descent?*

Cauvin, I further learned, came to renown as a leader in the 16th century European effort to wrest Christianity away from Catholicism known as the Reformation. In this endeavor, he contributed to many laudable theological advances in domains such as church polity, the Bible, the pope, sainthood, and even how sinners got saved. But his theology was dark: the complete and utter depravity of every human being; every individual soul sent irrevocably towards either salvation or perdition by God's capricious and implacable will; the complete inability of human beings to initiate or do anything good or substantial, with God as the one and only Doer. All of which laid a great foundation on which to construct in me the practice of otherizing.

The thing is, I thought I had successfully deflected all that. It would be difficult for me, for example, to overstate my nostalgia for my growing-up church's Sunday morning bulletin because it was so central to my mastering the art of dissociation. Sixty minutes of using the visitor card ink pen to scrawl squiggles and symbols and tropical islands—which were the easiest to doodle because the sun shines down from upper right corner, and birds are just two inverted swooshes, and palm trees are way simpler than deciduous, and waves are upside-down birds—every Sunday morning as the Calvinism flowed from the pulpit. I was particularly pleased on Sundays with few bulletin announcements because of the increased white space. Probably most cave paintings are just the cavekids doodling during antediluvian church services, and it's a skill (dissociation) that I still gratefully employ during most of my secular meetings.

Then on Wednesday evenings, in our church's fellowship hall basement with its gray-white linoleum floor and accordion room dividers, I was learning (not) through the Heidelberg Catechism about my church's systematic take on my fate, Part I of which begins with: **Misery.** *Question: How do you come to know your misery? Answer: The law of God tells me (Rom 3:20; 7:7-25).* I filled my gridded catechism card with shiny stars of memorization, but I tried to make it like studying the periodic table of the elements for the midterm exam where you store all the information on a USB brain thumb drive that you then unplug and lose in your messy frontal lobe desk drawer right after the test.

Capitulating to Culture

Furthermore, by my 2007 trudge down Newport Road with Adey and the cows, I had for over twenty years been a Vineyard Christian, which was both evangelical and pentecostal, and so putatively smarter and freer than Calvin. But—curses!—Calvin 500 years prior had anticipated my evasive maneuvers and so had commandeered this sketchy unevangelical substance called "culture." There are many things from my Dutch culture that I treasure: a love of water, and more precisely of the cleansing power of a morning swim in a cold lake in the green woods; modesty, family, the farm; cheese, frugality, cheese, and a strange lust for speed-skating gold medals every four years; and of course the cultural triumvirate of clogs, tulips, and windmills. All good. But my "I will not capitulate to culture" riposte to Adey would turn out to be ironic because I was so deeply and unknowingly embedded in a culture that produced my rejection of a culture.

"God commanded us to suppress every human affection for the sake of religion," asserted Calvin. And he had defined "affections" broadly: choice of clothing, dancing, playing cards, how you named your children, dinnerware selection for a banquet, and certainly anything and everything that in any way touched on sexual behavior. Singleness into adulthood, pre- or extra-marital sex, separation, divorce, provocative dress, toe-revealing shoes, public quarreling (retorting?) between spouses, prolonged widow- or widowerhood, same-sex sex—these offenses and more were publicly decried and forcefully suppressed through a politically empowered clergy that could punish offenders with fines, public humiliations, physical punishments, banishments from the church and city, and executions. All of which tools Calvin employed liberally.

The most renowned execution over which Calvin presided was in 1554 of Michael Servetus, a Spaniard who had criticized Calvin's theological writings, and who had then unfortuitously fallen into Calvin's hands while passing through Geneva. Then in the spring of 1555, Calvin had his clergymen preach that a spate of arrests of young men for homosexual sex was an indication of moral depravity arising from the corrupt influence of Genevan families opposed to Calvin's political aspirations, which preaching produced in the elections of that year a slim Calvinist majority. The opposition marched through the streets in protest, but sensing their imminent demise, two of the lead protesters fled Geneva and were banished, while four who remained were decapitated and then quartered, with their body sections displayed for public viewing around town and in the nearby countryside. In the fall of that year, the Calvinists executed eight more opposition leaders—the final tally would be twenty-seven—sentenced fifteen to death-in-absentia, and punished thirty-six through beatings, banishings, humiliations, jailings, fines, and deprivations; all this in a city of about 15,000. Calvin used the money he appropriated from his fled and executed opponents to fund the construction of his new theological school.

How this culture was propagated forward to me is both described and exemplified through the book, *Reformations: The Early Modern World*, a history of the reformation published in 2016 by Carlos M. N. Eire, the T. Lawrason Riggs Professor of History and of Religious Studies at Yale University, and a past President of the Society for Reformation Research. In Reformations, Eire brings Calvin to life as a "sage, a prophet, and a holy man, a model of genuine devotion and Christian sobriety." *Reformations* glosses Calvin's violence and perpetuates the Calvin mythology:

> Calvin's and Geneva's success became a myth larger than history … and as Calvin's fame grew along with Geneva's, the myth became a paradigm. Five decades after Calvin's death, John Winthrop, an English disciple of Calvin, would have Geneva in mind as he prepared to sail across the Atlantic to establish a Puritan outpost in the New World … So it was that Calvin's spirit sailed to America, long after he was dead, … and so it was that Geneva became embedded in the American consciousness.

And in mine. I remember as a teen hearing the hazy buzz of a distant lawn mower starting up *on a Sunday afternoon*. We all, in my house, were immediately tense because someone new nearby was not Christian. I felt a tug to follow the heretical sound to their home and whisper to them why they'd be safer waiting until tomorrow when my parents and God wouldn't disapprove. My mother's parents felt permission to play cards only when they, well into their adulthood, saw Christian Reformed pastors playing rummy at a summer church camp, and my mother in turn fought against her parents for the right to wear makeup when she went to college. The sale of liquor on Sunday was not permitted in Holland until 2008, and is still prohibited in our sister city of Zeeland. And no one ever ever ever, in my city, ever, still to this day, talked about sex, ever, though we all somehow knew that masturbation was shameful—truthfully that orgasm was shameful. And so sure, we didn't execute homosexuals anymore—kudos to us!—but only because they didn't exist. We did not even have the words in our Dutch lexicon for the unimaginable construct of queerness. So I was confused when, one college summer, I suddenly broke off a relationship with a male friend in the same way that I had abruptly ended relationships with female friends who out of the blue had asked me, *Are we dating?* Which objectively we were, but which I was too unready for commitment to acknowledge. More than twenty years later, only after I had come to have lots of gay male friends and had slow-danced on stage with a man at a Taylor Mac concert, did I realize, "Oh, that's what was going on!"

And so I carried Calvin forward. I had come into this telling of my story humorously aware of some of the foibles of the Dutch—emotionally rigid, afraid of introspection; tall, blond, urbane. We were flawed, sure, but not catastrophically so. But then I listened to my Black and gay friend Chris with his PhD in queer theology from King's College, London, preaching on a Sunday morning from our Sanctuary Community Church pulpit about how my Dutch Reformed Church compatriots in South Africa realized *in 1996* that apartheid was bad, Chris afterwards saying to me with chagrin that he would never have preached that had he known I was Dutch. Suppression of affections—of my Tin Woodman heart, and now through me of your queerness—had been in the religion of my youth all along, foundationally insinuated into the fabric of my conservative Christian thought, lurking there all these centuries later, potent with threat … *in that basement … in our Vineyard … walking this road …* It was another 23andMe moment, but darker: *Wait—I'm religiously **violent** by descent?*

Tom is Violent By Descent

All of which contributed to the parallel truth that much of my retorting at Adey was just from my anticipatory weariness at the thought of doing the work. I had grown up Calvinist, and then she and I had both inhabited our current evangelical denomination for over twenty years. We were leaders in the movement, pastors of an Association of Vineyard Churches church, and intertwined relationally with lifelong Vineyard friends. Smart people at the top had wrestled with these troubling queer questions so that we wouldn't have to, and staying true to their answers required much less effort than doing thinking ourselves that might lead us to challenge them. And more loomingly, if their answers turned out to be wrong, they would be through and through wrong. Not just, *Oops! mail merge left you off the invite list*, but rather our entire rubric for constructing the guest list would turn out to have been irredeemably corrupt. So it was much easier, on that hazy Iowa summer afternoon, to claim my lineal role as the Empowered Heterosexual Male of the Establishment, and just say no.

4

Adey

Adey:

"Arrghh!!" said Tom. "What are you so afraid of?!"

Well, I thought to myself as the sheep watched warily from the field, *this is a turn of events!*

This Newport Road retorting occurred probably in the fall of 2009. Seemingly yesterday, it had been me trying to convince Tom to soften toward welcoming, with him getting all Bible-truthy at me about why that was just a capitulation to culture. But then ... he did! It was disorienting. He listened to me, and opened his heart, but rather than engaging in a lengthy and halting process of transformation, he instead just flipped his inclusion switch from "off" to "on." In his personal Bible study, he suddenly saw that Jesus was radically welcoming to those whom religion excluded and he quickly became convinced of that as a necessary ethic for our gospel message.

So with me now being pushed instead of pulling, it really was the right question: *What was I afraid of?* I ticked quickly through my list: I'm afraid of stress. I'm afraid of conflict. I'm afraid of the pain of loss when my good friends leave my church. I'm afraid of the cost to you and me, honey, from these daily arguments. And of the cost to our pastoral team from our weekly staff meeting inclusion "discussions." I'm afraid that the church I've grown from ten people in my living room to this vibrant community of over three hundred across the past ten years will implode ...

The horses nickered from across the fence.

... I'm afraid of what's happening to our understanding of the Bible. I'm afraid that all our conservative longtime church attenders who understand the importance of giving will leave with their money. I'm afraid of how damaged our church will be when we have to leave our Vineyard movement. I'm afraid of being alone. I'm afraid ... I'm afraid ... I'm afraid ...

"Honey," said Tom, "where'd you go?"

"Sorry," I said. "I'm afraid of standing in front of Jesus having gotten it all wrong."

So there was my Bucket-O-Fears, with fear of making a God-sized mistake trumping them all. Tom still had fears too, though he'd apparently worked through at least a few of them by this particular afternoon. And so had David (our Executive Pastor), and our church. Some of our fears were personal, some theological, some cultural. Some of them were the fears that come to everyone when a stable structure changes. Brooding underneath it all, we discovered, was a fundamental and pervasive mindset of just plain fear that we had inherited from our Judeo-Christian religion, with mine originating in the Judeo part.

Jewish Fear

My Jewish grandparents came to America around 1900, escaping pogroms a la *Fiddler on the Roof.* I was born in Skokie, Illinois, just twelve years after the end of World War II, with its slaughter of six million Jewish people. Skokie in those days served as a refuge of sorts for Holocaust survivors; one in six of my neighbors had numbers burned into their arms. I learned from a young age that there were big horrible annihilation-type things in the world to be afraid of, especially with antisemitism still rampant. Jewish people, in my youth, could not attend the country club in the heart of our village. The Williamsburg subdivision in the northeast corner of Skokie prevented Jews from buying a home there, though every Halloween my friends and I would sneak in, cloaked by our costumes. The elevator in my college dorm had "k-i-k-e" etched into the metal. "What will we do?" said my father when, in 1977, the National Socialist Party of America threatened to march through the heart of our town.

Jesus snuck into my Jewish bedroom of fear in kindergarten. Sharon and Jill, my best friends from grammar school, were playing at my house one afternoon when they told me they wanted to teach me a song. I liked to sing, so hooray! Sharon said, "You need to get down on your knees to sing this song." So we got on our knees. Jill said, "You need to stretch out your arms to sing this song." So I stretched out my arms. And after we belted out together our love song to Jesus, I said, "Let's go sing for my mother!"

My mom was sitting on a couch in the living room reading a magazine. She was super-pleased, the way moms are when you're about to do something lovely. Sharon, Jill, and I got down on our knees, stretched out our arms, and belted out our love song to Jesus. After they left, I asked my mother what was wrong. She said, "Honey, little Jewish girls don't sing love songs to Jesus." Thus my first reprimand for trying to live into an impermissible blending. For our LGBTQ+ friends, it would be queer and Christian, or male body and female soul and Christian, or fluidity and Christian. For me it was Jewish and Christian.

I went to Hebrew school, learning 613 commandments instead of the paltry ten for Christians, and was *bas mitzvahed* at age 13. I still love the Hebrew prayers I grew up reciting, and I was moved by the call from the synagogue to support Israel by purchasing trees. But while others found God in the synagogue, I did not, which was distressing because I needed God. I struggled with low self-esteem, was plagued with shame, and me and Johnny Lee were "looking for love in all the wrong places." After college, I became successful in my business, with money and boutique clothes and boyfriends and drugs, but it all felt empty. I couldn't make sense of two Kennedys being killed and Martin Luther King Jr. being killed, and rioting in my city, and feeling every day those four elevator letters now etched into my soul.

So at age 24, after my synagogue's Yom Kippur High Holiday service, I went searching for God at the Morton Arboretum with my friend Rhonna. When that mostly didn't work, I tried, in rapid succession, a guru and vegetarianism and yoga and Sedona. And then one particularly low day at work I did something that I hadn't done since Sharon and Jill. In my office, next to my desk, I got down on my knees and I said:

> God, I need to know if you are real. If you are there and you
> hear me, can you let me know that Mickey is okay?

Mickey was a guy I had dated who I hadn't heard from in years and worry about him had just popped into my head. When I got home from work that evening there was a message that someone named Mickey had called. Soon after that, on my way home from a business meeting, I was driving the numbingly flat Illinois I-55 with the sun setting and I was starting to doze. There were no cars anywhere nearby, so I asked God:

If you're real, give me a car to follow.

Within seconds there was a car in front of me and one behind me with the drivers occasionally waving to each other through me until I got to my exit and they disappeared.

So I kept saying, "God, if you're real …" and God kept indicating that God was. But I was also becoming increasingly worried that this might-be-real God might be Jesus. My closest friend had just come to believe just that, and thought I should try Jesus out too, which was an insanely terrifying idea. There was no representation of God that for this Jewish girl from Skokie could have been worse. The Judaism of my youth forbade it. My Jewishness was absolutely incompatible with Christianity's Jesusness.

The night before I gave my life to Jesus—and just to be clear, I'd never read or really even seen a Christian Bible. The closest I'd come to encountering the gospel was through watching the movie *Jesus Christ Superstar* when I was 18. Like Mary Magdalene, even though Superstar Jesus was stressed out by crowds and never got off the cross, I fell in love with him, but totally as a hunky hippie movie star, as opposed to some sort of God-being to whom I would devote my life.

Anyway, the night before I "gave my life to Jesus," I tearfully said something like, "God, for the first time since I was a little girl, I know you are real. I believe you are here and you are listening to me. I believe you know me and call me by name. So I need to know who you are. But please, please, please don't be Jesus." I took a breath: "But if you are Jesus and you prove it to me, I will give the rest of my life to serving you. All you have to do is send a Christian man to my office tomorrow and have him answer these three questions." And then I asked God three specific questions about how a Jewish woman from Skokie could also be a Christian.

The next day Nico walked into my office. Nico was an Italian man I'd met a couple weeks earlier at a party, and when I'd learned he was Christian, my only thought was: "Wow, Christian guys can be cute—who knew?" Nico asked me if I'd like to go out for a drink later that day. He met me after work and we walked without talking to a restaurant. We sat down and ordered drinks. Nico looked at me and said, "Adey, I am a Christian and I believe that God speaks to us today. And last night while I was praying, God told me to tell you these three things." Then Nico answered my three questions in order.

No Longer Alone

My coming-to-Jesus was the worst of times, and the best. For my Jewish family and friends, out of the entire universe of possible wrong choices, I had made the wrongest. Becoming a Christian was not me just drifting away or becoming agnostic. I was rejecting a precious gift of identity that had cost them everything to preserve for me, and which they envisioned us joyfully sharing as we moved forward through life together. I was choosing instead an identity that my family and friends perceived as explicitly un- or anti-Jewish.

One friend wrote to me that my actions made the six million Holocaust victims die in vain. I had other friends who, upon conversion, were mourned as dead by their parents through formal funerals. My family was not so drastic—they did and do still love me—but they were traumatized, and going forward something was different. I think I became to them not-Jewish because there was no imagination in my culture for a person being Jewish and connected to Jesus.

My recompense for this loss was my church community. It was 1981. Cute Italian Nico, as well as my recently converted best friend, both attended what was then a small independent evangelical charismatic church that in about three years would join the Vineyard denomination. I started going to a small group there that began partnering with World Relief to help settle Indochinese refugees, and I loved it, loved it, loved it! I think I, as a wanderer, as someone who had never fit in, and who had just been jettisoned into loneliness, jumped at the chance to help anyone who tugged at those heart-strings. Through World Relief, I met incoming refugees at O'Hare airport, brought them to their apartments, showed them how to use the El to get around town, drove them to get documents, carried furniture upstairs, held babies and played with kids. And led Bible studies. Yes, a-little-bit-Christian Adey led just-off-the-plane Cambodian friends through the Lord's Holy Scriptures. And they were the loveliest engagements with the scriptures ever experienced by humankind, anywhere, period.

My sweetest moment—one of the top ten events of my entire life that captured perfectly in a microcosm my simultaneous expulsion and wel-come—was going to a movie with these friends on Christmas Day, 1984. I had started the day alone. My family was not one of those that celebrated Hanukkah as a stand-in for Christmas, so no Hanukkah Bush for this Jewish girl. And my new Christian friends didn't yet know me well and so weren't aware of my plight. But as I was flipping through my home VHS library and ordering takeout, I got a call from a young Cambodian friend: "Adey," he said, "we know it's Christmas and you're probably busy, but if you're not, there's a movie we'd like you to come see with us tonight."

"Okay!" I said. "Where and when?"

And so I went with my newfound family on Christmas Day, 1984, to see *The Killing Fields*. Yes, a movie about the Cambodian civil war of the 1970s, itself a spillover of the Vietnam War, with the film prominently featuring the notorious Killing Fields of the Pol Pot regime that contain the bones of two million slaughtered Cambodians. Not exactly *It's A Wonderful Life*.

But it was their story. My Cambodian friends, up till that night, had been unable on their own to summon the will to tell me their stories. But after someone else had told me their story, their tongues were loosed. So there we were, not even waiting till dinner or an apartment, spilling out onto the State Street sidewalk in Chicago's Loop, with big white movie-quality Christmas snowflakes wafting earthward under a darkening sky, our hair wetly matting down, with friend after friend talking over each other to me, telling me story after story after story of lost relatives, forced travel, expulsion from villages and homes, harrowing escapes, and the gratefulness to be here together, all of us sobbing in a huddle.

I felt profoundly privileged. Their travails reminded me, just a bit, of the little I knew of the story of the first Christmas for Jesus and Mary and Joseph. And it was my best Christmas ever because I was not alone anymore; through welcoming others, I had come to belong.

The Slippery Slope

If only my story could end there! Loveliness and inclusion and purpose and a community. But while it had turned out that I had now, in my church, entered a space where Jewish and Christian was okay, I pretty quickly came to embody a different intolerable blend: woman and leader, which would pave the way for my encounter with the *most* intolerable blend: queer and Christian.

Within a year of my *Killing Fields* Christmas, I was hired by my church to be a liaison between them and World Relief. Two years later I was invited to join the pastoral staff. I became a trained counselor and so gained a niche of expertise. I became an oft-invited speaker at retreats for other churches and at Midwest regional meetings of Vineyard pastors and leaders. As that rarest of commodities in my denomination—a female pastor—I was soon participating at the regional level on committees and task forces and at conferences.

Which was all fine with everyone as long as I was safe, which meant as long as I was not *THE* leader. It's like I was plutonium—powerful and valuable as long as I didn't spill out of a safe container. If I were to get out into the world on my own, all hell might break loose! But if a man were over me, organizationally, then patriarchy and the cosmos were not threatened. Which also made my denomination leery to give the forever stamp of approval to my pastoring through the Christian validation ceremony of ordination. While all the men pastoring in the way that I was were ordained, my denomination put that affirmation of me on indefinite hold.

Tom and I moved to Iowa City in 1996, and while he trained in psychiatry, I started and built our church. When in 2000 I went to our denomination to make our church official, I was given the thumbs up, but instructed to have Tom named as the Senior Pastor. I and a few other female leaders worked for nearly a decade to overturn the woman senior prohibition, which we celebrated in 2006 when our denomination permitted a local church to give the title and function of Senior Pastor to a woman. But oh at what cost! Years of discord and strife at levels local, regional, and national. Me functioning as a lightning rod drawing to myself a lot of patriarchal rage—which turned out to be not just about femaleness, but also about homosexuality.

Wayne Grudem, a conservative evangelical theologian important to the Vineyard, was an ardent alarmist in our day for *The Slippery Slope*. It sounds now like the next Lemony Snicket book, but boy was it real. Grudem decried the descent into hell certain to follow on women's empowerment in a 2006 book that read like a CDC Situation RED warning of an impending pandemic. The road to perdition, according to Grudem, ran thus:

1. Abandon inerrancy of scripture
2. Endorse ordaining women (that would be me)
3. Abandon mandating males as the heads of our families (sorry Tom!)
4. Exclude clergy who are opposed to women's ordination
5. Approve homosexuality as morally valid in some cases

6. Approve homosexual ordination

7. Ordain homosexuals to high leadership

Take one timid step into that chain of contingency and the homosexuals would soon be lasciviously running everything.

All that traumatic history flooded me as Tom and I walked along Newport Road. My desire for LGBTQ+ inclusion posed what I knew would become another monstrous threat to the unity of my beloved institution. *What was wrong with me? Why couldn't I just be content with my empowered femaleness?* Two miles up the road, we passed an apple tree dangling over its owner's fence and ate some forbidden fruits. Tom's "What are you so afraid of?" had roused the God-voice that the Christianity of my denomination had put in my head: "Are you willing to compromise Me for the sake of 'loving' people?"

And to my very masculine deity I answered, feebly, "Yes."

5

Katie

Katie:

If Adey was afraid of getting it wrong, and Tom of capitulating to culture, I was afraid, as I contemplated us all coming together, that their fears would win. By the time we all met together in Adey's office, I had come to believe, all on my own, that the God of the Bible loved me, just as I was. But I needed to find a Christian community that believed the same thing. *Would this be that place?*

My queerness has been with me from as far back as I can remember. As a child, I had not been into the kinds of clothes, toys and activities that were expected of little girls. By the time I was able to vocalize my displeasure—around the age of 2—I refused to wear the dresses my mom kept buying for me. My third Christmas morning, I threw across the room the Cabbage Patch doll my loving grandmother had waited over four hours in line at the local Kmart to buy. And my career aspiration was solidified after watching the '85 Bears win Super Bowl XX: *I was going to play in the NFL!*

I didn't feel like I was a boy, or identify as such, but I sure wished I could do the things boys did. And I realized at an early age that I was attracted to other children of the same sex. This initially was simply a confusing awareness of feeling "different." But by the time I was 11, I knew there was a name for someone who had the feelings I had for other girls. I was raised attending a conservative Lutheran church. While I don't remember a specific sermon outlining the evils of homosexuality, the utter wrongness of being gay just seemed to permeate my culture. The few people in our community who were rumored to be "that way" were talked about in hushed whispers, as if what they were was too terrible for the ears of children. My family members talked about the "sin of Sodom and Gomorrah" and chuckled if a waiter was thought by my dad to be "a little light in his loafers."

So in sixth grade I made a promise to myself and to God that I would never act on my feelings. I would bury this inconvenience deep inside and focus on doing the "right thing." It seemed like a challenge, and I was good at challenges. My diligence and hard work had already paid awesome dividends through my ability to please my parents and teachers and sports coaches. This would be no different. And it worked! I did not ever act on the steady stream of crushes I had on girls throughout my adolescence.

But to hide my identity within myself, I also had to internalize my world's homophobia. The two went together, like bad roommates—myself and my hatred of myself living within me—which hatred I spewed onto the gay world outside of myself. By the time I was in high school, I made it known that I was disgusted by people who were gay. My senior year of high school, my best friend and I emblazoned an anti-gay message on our softball team sweatshirts. I took part in bullying the only two girls in our high school class of five hundred who were brave enough to come out of the closet.

The shameful irony of this is not lost on me. As a physician, I have dedicated my career to caring for patients identifying as lesbian, gay, bisexual, transgender, queer and questioning. I am aware that more than 80% of LGBTQ students report being bullied in school, and as teens they are up to three times more likely to attempt suicide as their heteronormative peers. I grieve over the pain and trauma I caused to those questioning or trying to live out their authentic identities. I cringe when I think of how scared, broken, and ashamed I had to have been to have projected my own self-hatred onto others as part of the scapegoating mob.

Then came my undoing. As a freshman in college, after only a few weeks on campus, I met Paula, the woman who would become my wife. Over the course of several months, I went from thinking she was super cool, to wanting to spend every waking minute with her, to trying hopelessly to calm the butterflies in my stomach at just the sound of her voice. I remembered the promise I had made years before—but this time I was powerless to resist. I would lie awake at night anguishing over my desire to stay true to my word to never act on my feelings, while knowing that these feelings were not something I had sought or manufactured—they seemed to arise unbidden from my innermost being. As much as I was trying to outrun them, suppress them, or scare them into the darkness, they persisted. I spent lots of nights next to Paula, as "friends," me doing battle with my internal angst long into the night and her snoring softly the second her head hit the pillow.

It gradually became clear to me that my ideal Genesis 3 bone-of-my-bones magnetic attraction love interest would not be an opposite-gendered "helper" but a same-gendered partner who no less completed me. Ultimately, it was my understanding of God's love for me exactly as I was, and of my having been created by that same God, that provided me with the strength to further pursue the deep connection I felt with Paula. This was not something I had chosen, this was who God made me to be. I was gay.

As I've clung to this truth, I often turn to Psalm 139:

> O Lord, you have searched me and known me.
>
> You know when I sit down and when I rise up;
>
> you discern my thoughts from far away. …
>
> Where can I go from your spirit?
>
> Or where can I flee from your presence?
>
> If I ascend to heaven, you are there;
>
> if I make my bed in the depths, you are there. …
>
> For it was you who created my inmost being;
>
> you knit me together in my mother's womb.
>
> I praise you, for I am fearfully and wonderfully made.
>
> Wonderful are your works;
>
> that I know very well.

I resonate with the psalmist as I realize that God already knows my thoughts, my identity, my proclivities. God created the core of my being and it is wonderfully made. It's like I work up the nerve to come out to God: "God, you might want to sit down because I have something important to tell you. It's good and I'm so happy, but I'm worried that you might be upset. I am still the same person that I've always been, and I want you to remember that, but—*deep breath*—God, I'm gay." And God answers back, "I'm sorry it took so long for you to be able to tell me that. But I have known it since forever, and I have always loved everything about you."

But while I found God's love, the world that God had supposedly made was still opposed to me. I had no lesbian couples to look to as models for my relationship with Paula, for pursuing a career, for having a family, or for what just living normal life could be like. My hero was the most famous lesbian in the world, Ellen DeGeneres, who had just come out on her TV show—which was then cancelled. So I took inventory of the things I would be giving up for Paula: marriage, children, friends, family, perhaps even the career I wanted. And definitely church. My assurance in God's love for me, though real, was fragile, and would not withstand Christian anti-gay rhetoric. But I had never in my life felt this way about another person, so I made my decision.

Paula joined me in my cramped closet, in which dark space we spent the next several years of our togetherness trying desperately to keep our relationship hidden. At college, I joined a sorority whose sole reason for being was to help lesbian me find my opposite-gender match at one of the fraternities. I dated men just to quiet the rumors that circulated when Paula would come to campus to visit. My mom found out my secret and sent me to a therapist who, much to my mom's chagrin (were she to have known) said in our first session, "You are normal and will continue to be so regardless of where you land with your sexual orientation—straight, bisexual, lesbian, queer." Which just made me more anxious.

But then Paula and I came to Iowa City to give life together a try—and it turned out to be for us a magically queer place! It's like there was no closet here, or we were all in the closet together, only instead of it being cramped and dark and shameful, it was bright and honest and joyful! For the first time in my life, I met gay people who were completely out—to their families, their colleagues, their employers. They were successful doctors, lawyers, and teachers. Many of them had long-term and healthy relationships. For the first time in our lives, Paula and I walked down the street holding hands. My mind was exploding. At times I could physically feel my shoulders relax, and I had a newfound comfort in my own skin. Over the next decade, I became a physician, married Paula in a beautiful ceremony blessed by family and friends, had two children, and helped create my beloved health clinic. One by one, those things I had thought I had to give up were being realized. Except for church. For Paula and me, our parents had required us to attend church to appease their cultural religious mandates, and so we did the same to our kids, which kept not working. I felt recurrently drawn to what I kept anticipating would be the love of God in there, and then I'd be away from the last one long enough to forget the harm that I actually experienced, and sometimes I'd have to go because of my family, so I kept dragging Paula and the kids to try it yet one more time, which was always horrible. David Gushee, a Christian ethics scholar, writes in his book *Changing Our Mind* that "the least safe place to deal with sexual orientation and identity issues is the Christian church." It totally set me up to be afraid of Sanctuary.

⌐⌐

Adey: Yes, Katie, you and Paula had some pretty horrific experiences together in church before you came to us, right?

Here's part of a conversation in which the four of us—Katie, Paula, Adey, Tom—went back together to a couple of memorable pre-Sanctuary church experiences for Katie and Paula ...

Katie: Oh my god, yes. We both remember being together at a holiday Mass—it's what we Lutherans called the service—with all the family around us. Even my totally devout but aging Grandma I, with her frail heart and weak ears, was there. And because there were so many people at Mass, the priest was asking for money. It was that sort of situation in which you are turned off in so many ways. I was sitting there like: Are you seriously talking about the offering because there are all these people in church who only come on a holiday? This is why people do not go to church. I remember looking around me: All these great people are gathered here! And this priest thinks it's a golden opportunity to guilt them about money?

And then he began to talk about homosexuality as a sin, marriage being one man and one woman. He used phrases like, "let us not bend to culture" and "the failure of society."

Paula: What I remember is wanting to walk out. I remember saying to Katie, "Did I just hear that right?" As the priest continued talking, I was shocked. Did he just say that?!

Then I was thinking: I want to leave right now—but Katie's Grandma I [Grandma Imborek] is right next to me and this sweet lady, who is old with many infirmities, is going to literally die if I walk out. Well, at least she's going to be really upset if I walk out. I suppose I could have made up an excuse like: "My tummy hurts!" But I didn't move. I couldn't leave. Nothing happened. The service continued. Then, as we walked out of church, Katie and I both said, "Wow, that was really uncomfortable."

Katie: I recall our saying together: "Wow, that was crazy." Then I said, "If that ever happens again, I will walk out of church." I was not prepared for it;

I had never really thought about it—but I felt like I realized that I did not need to stay and would not listen to that ever again. If it happens again, I thought, I will just walk out.

Paula: And then? We never talked about it again that day.

Tom: I hear that from a lot of people—that specific thing—that you are caught by surprise the first time it happens, but the prohibition against making a scene is so strong that you just sit there and take it silently. One Sunday afternoon in 2013, our daughter Cassie called us. She was a freshman at college and had gone to the church of a friend who, she knew, was conservative. In the middle of the sermon, with no real connection to the content of the message, the pastor launched into an impassioned anti-homosexuality riff.

Adey: Cassie had a spiritual panic attack—flushed, unable to breathe, heart racing. She was thinking: *I've got to get out! I've got to get out!* But she couldn't. She was sitting next to her friend who had invited her. Cassie was respectful, not a disrupter. She didn't get up and walk out. Then, afterward, she sobbed on the phone with us because she'd betrayed Katie and Paula by not getting out.

Paula: That's how it can happen. You do not go into church thinking: Someone is going to offend me today.

Katie: And if you stay, what do you do as the service continues? Can we—or should we—compartmentalize after an offensive sermon? After that, can we stand up and sincerely sing the next song? Join in a prayer? Or did this pastor just ruin all of that? After all, this guy in all his clerical garb stood up there and, representing himself as a mediator to God, attacked me and my family. How is my ability to worship and my connection with God not affected after that? At that holiday Mass with Grandma, we actually went up for communion even after what the priest had said!

Adey: I understand. In a situation like that, everything you choose to do—or not do—is a statement. And maybe your whole family is watching. Maybe Grandma I is right there with you. And it happened again, didn't it?

Katie: Yes, there was a second time—even though I had said that if it happens again I am going to walk out of the church. This was some years later. We were already married and had two children and, at that point, even Grandma I knew about us. This time, it was a baptism in a Catholic church with my extended family and I had been asked to be godmother, so I had to go.

It was just after Pope Francis had said about gay people: "The key is for the church to welcome, not exclude, and show mercy, not condemnation." And he said, "If a person is gay and seeks God and has good will, who am I to judge?" Our friends were shocked, like: Did the pope just say that!? But the pope had not changed the church's basic teachings or rules and regulations. That meant there were lots of priests around the world who were rushing to reassure conservatives that the church still condemned LGBTQ people.

So, those global events were unfolding around us, but I thought: Attending a family baptism as a godmother is such an honor! Of course, I have to go. And there were about thirty of us there for the baptism. What could go wrong? But at the service, this priest also thought he had to stress that marriage is still exclusively for one man and one woman—and then blah, blah blah. And my reaction was: I said I would walk out if this happened again—*but I'm the godmother!*

Paula: I left with Parker [Katie and Paula's oldest son].

Adey: In the middle of the baptism?

Paula: Yes, but there were thirty of us, so it just looked like I was going to the bathroom.

Tom: Well, I'm still impressed that you walked out—but I'm also unnerved that you had to go through this again—and again—over the years. Did anyone say anything to you about what the priest said?

Katie: No. I did bring it up in the car as we left. I said, "Does anybody want to talk about this—because I'm offended!" But everyone was just laughing about it.

Paula: I wasn't in that car.

Katie: I know. I was in the car with Mom and Dad. I was angry. Then I said bitterly, "I'm glad the Catholics are so welcoming! And they want to make sure we are all really clear on what it means to be kind and loving to gay people. That they think we deserve respect but never should be married." My mom said, "Well, this is actually a pretty progressive step for Catholics." I was not wanting to hear that! What I had hoped to hear was something like: "That was really crappy. I'm sorry." But I never heard that from anyone that day.

~

Katie:

So Lutheranism and Catholicism did not set up my queer self to have a good anticipation of any form of Christianity. But I had, nonetheless, at the insistence of my friend Julie, and because of my desperation, decided to give Adey and Tom's church a try. But I really had no idea what I was getting myself into.

6

Adey and Tom Go
to Vineyard

Katie: "Guys, what *is* evangelicalism?"

Tom: Katie asked Adey and me this question some time after she had settled in and felt safe with us. Her real wondering was: "Why had the -ism that your church was coming out of so come to hate me?" Which was a puzzler. Our Vineyard church was first of all evangelical. Consensus tenets of contemporary evangelicalism include: the necessity of personal conversion or being "born again," the authority of the Bible, and the directive from God to spread the Christian faith to others. Some also include as a fourth the pursuit of justice for those who are oppressed, to all of which we in Vineyard had added Pentecostalism.

None of which explained Katie's revilement. Evangelicals describe their gospel as "good news" that presents how God lovingly rescues lost souls through Jesus. And Vineyard's welcoming of the previously excluded Holy Spirit seemed a precursor to the kind of inclusion we wanted for Katie. Adey and I had found Vineyard to be genuinely liberating and life-giving, so what was the problem? Why did Katie's queerness turn our lovely good news into an instrument of hate?

Before becoming a pastor, Adey had been a therapist who often worked to bring relief to women who had been sexually victimized. In my practice as a psychiatrist, I spent a stretch of time trying to help military veterans troubled by combat-related trauma. So as Adey and I matched Katie's question up against our experiences of evangelicalism, it came to us both: Evangelical

Christianity functions by producing and then relieving the anxiety of God-based trauma. But while Adey and I could access the relief components, Katie—for as long as she remained queer—could not.

Evangelicalism

In 1737, the brothers John and Charles Wesley traveled from England on a mission trip to evangelize the American penal colony of Georgia. They felt that they mostly failed, and were also chagrined by the superior faith in God of Moravian Christians when threatened by storm-tossed Atlantic seas. These and other perceived deficiencies caused both brothers to grow "deeply anxious about their spiritual condition." So Charles prayed ardently and was rewarded in May of 1738 with a God-interaction that brought him relief from his sense of doom. Three days later John, while listening to Luther's preface to the book of Romans, felt his heart to be "strangely warmed." "An assurance was given me, that he [Christ] had taken away my sins, even mine, and saved me from the law of sin and death." From these experiences of God-threat and Jesus-relief the brothers founded Methodism, a precursor to evangelicalism.

Meanwhile across the pond, Jonathan Edwards, a leader of American evangelicalism, preached on July 8th, 1741 one of the most iconic Protestant sermons ever: "Sinners in the Hands of an Angry God." In Sinners, Edwards famously declaimed to his listeners that:

> God that holds you over the pit of hell, much as one holds a
> spider, or some loathsome insect over the fire, abhors you, and
> is dreadfully provoked: his wrath towards you burns like fire …

So little Jonny dangled spiders over fires while I, as a kid, zapped ants under a magnifying glass. But Edwards went on to believe that this was how God treated humans. His sermon is 7,192 words of relentless invective that was central to a lauded New England revival that summer. His goal was to induce in the listening sinner a state of guilt-ridden existential terror—a melting or dissolution of the reprehensible self—that would set the stage for a profound rebound into assurance. Charles Finney, a nineteenth century American evangelical leader, famously installed an "anxious bench" at the front of his church for those parishioners successfully undone by his depiction of the peril of their plight. For nineteenth and twentieth century

evangelical Baptists, the cycle of dissolution and reconstitution for a parishioner might be played out many times across the years because the divine
assurance of baptism was never truly safe from the threat of God's wrathful
response to human perfidiousness.

From American evangelicalism came fundamentalism, birthed out of
an existential threat to Christianity from secular culture. Responding to
Christianity's waning influence due to science, and to the cultural destabili-
zation produced by World War I, "Fundamentalism" was first articulated in
a series of pamphlets published in the 1910s called *The Fundamentals*. These
pamphlets raised the alarm about cultural entities that, if allowed to infect
American culture, would provoke the vengeance of God toward our nation.
Fundamentalists countered threat with threat, which for them came from
fabricating the monstrous other. One historian writes:

> This view ... led to 'the paranoid style' often seen in American
> political thought. The fundamentalists ... were disposed to
> divide all reality into neat antitheses: the saved and the lost,
> the holy and the unsanctified, the true and the false. Moreover,
> their common sense philosophical assumptions added the
> assurance that they could clearly distinguish these contrasting
> factors when they appeared in everyday life.

Twentieth century fundamentalism thus identified and scapegoated
(expelled) one monster after another—communism, intellectualism, science,
evolution, feminism, abortion, modernism, civil rights, liberalism, socialism,
alcohol, hippies, ... and even the Holy Spirit. Yes, the biblical essence of
God's own being, one third of the Holy Trinity, came to be perceived as a
threat by this very influential Christian voice, and was expelled from it. But
as Joni Mitchell sang about a Hawaiian jungle paved into a parking lot:

> Don't it always seem to go
>
> That you don't know what you've got
>
> Till it's gone

What we expel today often turns out to be the good that we want to take
back tomorrow.

Pentecostalism

The Holy Spirit is presented by Jesus and the Bible as that being of the Christian triune godhead (Father, Son, Holy Spirit) that most directly comes into contact with human beings. But the Holy Spirit has a troubling Jeckyll/Hyde identity. There's the nice Spirit, called by Jesus the "Counselor" or "Advocate," that takes the form of a dove wafting down from heaven and alighting gently on sincere believers to produce in them the "fruits" of the Spirit like generosity and kindness and letting the one-item shopper go ahead of you in the checkout line. But then that same Spirit brews the potion of Pentecost and sploshes onto and into us with fire and wind that triggers tears and babbling and bodily movements and chaos.

Evangelicalism's relationship to the Holy Spirit was thus ambivalent. Physical manifestations of an encounter with the Holy Spirit were highly sought components of eighteenth and nineteenth century evangelical revivals and awakenings, seeming to both signify and contribute to the undoing of a repentant sinner that would precede their conversion into a saint. And the Spirit also produced much desired miracles like healings and deliverances. But the attendant disinhibition, both of individuals and of the church writ large, unnerved evangelicals, so that by the early 1900s evangelicalism either rigidly controlled or literally demonized Holy Spirit manifestations.

Which just diverted the desire for experience into its own stream. In 1906, an itinerant holiness preacher, William Joseph Seymour, who had trained in Topeka, Kansas under Charles Parham—the champion of Holy Spirit induced speaking in tongues—was invited to lead a small church gathering in an abandoned African Methodist Episcopal Church building at 312 Azusa Street in Los Angeles. Seymour's preaching there ignited the Azusa Street revival. Attenders of his gatherings experienced the sudden and irrepressible irruption of an expansive array of Holy Spirit manifestations and religious ecstasies, many of which were extremely bizarre. The outpouring stretched across days and weeks, and crowds began to come—some hopeful, others critical—swelling nightly revival services that continued for three years. Many who came were overwhelmed by their experience of God, which they then took back to their home congregations.

Thus was Pentecostalism born, which much of Christendom had apparently been craving. By the end of the twentieth century, Pentecostal denominations numbered over seven hundred, with more than five hundred million members. Core features of Pentecostalism came to include a conversion event, a second purification event leading to holiness, the baptism of the Holy Spirit as evidenced by speaking in tongues, and then additional empowerments such as being able to prophecy and to pray with power for sick people to get well. Pentecostalism packaged these tenets in an emotive, voluble, and expressive practice of Christianity.

But despite the packaging, Pentecostal theology never drifted far from its conservative evangelical roots, with strong adherence in particular to the authority of the Bible. Of note for our story, both evangelicalism and Pentecostalism identified homosexuality as a forbidden depravity that would activate the threat of God's wrath. It's not that, as the schism played out over the first half of the twentieth century, re-merging the two streams wasn't tried. However you dichotomize the antipathy—head vs. heart, subjective vs. objective, constraint vs. freedom—opposites are attractive. Chaos is reassured by reason and thinkers like to feel. The charismatic renewal of the 1960s was one such episode of merging, when many head-forward Christians "rediscovered" Holy Spirit experiences that they then brought back into their denominations. But well into the second half of the twentieth century, mainstream evangelicalism mostly kept the threat of Pentecostalism at a safe distance, which is where, for us, Vineyard came in.

Adey and Tom Go to Vineyard

Because in 1974 the Holy Spirit strummed an evangelical guitar on a California beach … and a movement was born. Or so went the Vineyard origin story we told ourselves about ourselves. A Jesus movement pastor named Ken Gullickson—the strummer of said guitar—launched his church with charismatic practices out of the evangelical Calvary Chapel group of churches. He named his surprise church "The Vineyard" and was soon leading multiple similar congregations in and around Los Angeles.

John Wimber was also then in LA, having led hundreds to faith during the Jesus Movement of the 1960s. By 1977 Wimber was pastoring a burgeoning Calvary Chapel church in Yorba Linda. But Wimber, like Gullickson, desired unfettered Holy Spirit activity in his church—his ministry had been triggered into growth with help from Lonnie Frisbee, an acid-tripping gay (suppressed) Pentecostal hippie preacher—and so in 1982 Wimber also left Calvary and joined Gullikson's Vineyard Movement, which he soon came to lead.

So whatever our theological roots, we were direct descendants of anti-establishment Christian hippies who surfed the wave of the Spirit and shrugged "what are ya' gonna' do?" as God busted us free from one religious rigidity after another. We were launching, from within our corner of evangelicalism, Holy Spirit inclusion.

Adey:

Thanks to Nico, I started attending my Evanston church in 1981, and then made first contact with Vineyard in 1984, when I and a few of our church's leaders did our version of an Azusa pilgrimage to a conference called "Signs and Wonders" in Anaheim, CA. I can still see the first evening: contemporary soft-rock music filling a cavernous reclaimed warehouse space ... happily entranced worshippers singing and swaying ... and then a rotund, middle-aged man with flaxen hair and beard dressed in tropical garb walking casually from stage right to the podium and saying, with an affable smile, "Hi! I'm John Wimber." I experienced him as theologically astute, deeply spiritual, and hilariously funny. He was confident but not arrogant, and authentic without manipulation. He taught all that week on "Signs and Wonders," part of his call for reactivating within evangelical and denominational churches the kinds of beyond-natural occurrences that Jesus seemed, in the gospel stories, to so readily produce. He'd finish every message with a moment of dialed down quietness and then say, "Come, Holy Spirit."

I encountered in that room what I continue to believe was the Spirit of God. People were crying, laughing, and swooning—and I was right in there with them. I came into a deep God-connection unlike anything I'd known before. Someone had at last given a name to the God-being behind my come-to-Jesus experiences and so I was now able to communicate more directly with this attentive and loving friend. From that first Vineyard encounter on, when I was alone, I'd quiet myself ... take a measured breath ... whisper, *Come, Holy Spirit* ... and there He was ... I was no longer alone. The God of the universe took up my insecure invitation and was immediately with me, letting me know how much He loved me.

Tom:

Which was lovely ... for Adey. I, like her, had started coming to our small Evanston church in 1981. The people there sang songs as if God was listening, and studied the Book as if it was helpful, and so even though they were chatty and sincere and casually dressed, and had church in someone else's building, at four o'clock in the afternoon, I nonetheless slumped in a stairwell during a break in my first two-hour service there, thinking: "If God was in the room, this is what you would do!" Three years later I was sitting in the front row because our pastor, returned with Adey's recon team from crazy California, was bringing crazy back. He started with, "We're doing things a little differently today, so why don't you all stand up," and then he said,

Come, Holy Spirit.

We all waited for eight, or maybe nine, silent seconds ... until first a sniffle ... then a sob . . . and then everyone laughing, crying, swooning, "manifesting." Pandemonium! Except for me. Not this white male Dutch Calvingelical INTP. No no no. Uh uh. I was standing in my own very private eye of a Pentecostal hurricane. Don't get me wrong! As much as I feared it, I desperately wanted it, whatever "it" was, for the sake of the experience and the validation from God and the participation in the group. But it didn't happen to me, and I was not going to manufacture it. So I stood grinning sheepishly and feeling left out.

Thus began twenty years of a love/doubt relationship for me with Pentecostalism. I don't know if I ever, across my three Vineyard decades, had what would be considered by experts to be a bona fide Holy Spirit experience. I would occasionally ... sort of ... feel *something* ... a little. I became an official commiserator for those who didn't experience God but nonetheless *believed*. Because I did believe! It was, strangely, my intellect that kept me in. Whatever my hardness of heart, I was desperate for God to be more than a human thought construct, and Vineyard, with Wimber at the helm, produced language and practices that for the first time, at least for me, permitted the possibility of coming into contact with God's real and present Spirit.

So Adey and I, from early on, were all in. We pilgrimaged to Anaheim, traveled to Vineyard conferences across the country, and huddled with friends around a Radio Shack cassette tape player back home listening to Wimber teachings. We modeled the Vineyard approach to praying for healing in all the groups we led, and helped train interested congregants from nearby churches. We first became interested in each other while helping teach Vineyard stuff to parishioners of the local First Presbyterian Church— us in the back of the room misbehaving in a budding love kind of way while our dearest friend spoke. And because our church, with Adey and me as central participants, soon came into leadership in the Vineyard movement, we saw firsthand what it took for our religiously anxious evangelical movement to pivot to Holy Spirit inclusion.

We got, for example, a new theology. Evangelicalism restricted Pentecostal activity to either the past or future, but "Kingdom of God" theology asserted instead that the Bible permitted Holy Spirit stuff to happen now. We developed educational materials and training events to help diverse individuals and organizations connect with our new reality in their own time and way. We thoughtfully anticipated the myriad discomforts our parishioners might experience as they tried to engage with our new beliefs and practices. In the 1995 book *Empowered Evangelicals* that recounts Vineyard's formative years, a longtime Vineyard leader gave his take on what was required for Vineyard to fully embrace "Come, Holy Spirit:"

> The conversion from a more typical evangelical background to this new synthesis took us several years. Along the way, we found that many of our assumptions … needed radical reassessment. Other areas … had been so neglected that they were entirely missing from our church's practice. Fears, discomfort, cultural biases, and legitimate theological questioning all needed addressing as we moved forward.

So lots of discomfitures that were subjected to radical reassessment for the sake of Holy Spirit inclusion. And then we turned around and did the same thing for women! Sort of.

7

A Female Senior

Adey:

Way back in 1984, after pastoring for just over a year, my Evanston church had become eager to "ordain" me. I didn't know what that was—the act of making something ordinary? This Jewish girl had never planned on becoming a Christian, much less a reverend, but pastoring, it turned out, was in my kosher blood. So doing a ceremony in which my church friends and fellow pastors, with God presiding, made my newfound vocation official—*hooray*!

But then in the March/April 1984 issue of *Vineyard Reflections*, the Vineyard's then official magazine, John Wimber published a letter titled (ironically), "Liberating Women for Ministry and Leadership," the central sentiment of which was:

> I believe God has established a gender-based eldership of the church. I endorse the traditional (and what I consider the *scriptural*) view of a unique leadership role for men in marriage, family, and in the church. This ultimately reflects the hierarchy of the Trinity: 'For this reason I kneel before the Father, from whom his whole family in heaven and on earth derives its name' (Eph. 3:14,15). Consequently, I personally do not favor ordaining women as elders in the local church. I encourage our women to participate in any ministry, except church governance.

Well, slam. And just in case I felt the un-feminine temerity to protest, Wimber attached a footnote: "For a more theological and biblical discussion of the basis of male eldership, I heartily recommend *Recovering Biblical Manhood & Womanhood,* edited by John Piper and Wayne Grudem" (Wimber 1994: 5). Heartily. Piper and Grudem were our guiding fundamentalist academics, having schooled us in the "hierarchy of the Trinity," which put God the Father in charge, the Son second, and the Holy Spirit proceeding from and subordinate to them. This trinitarian chain of authority provided the theological basis for a rigid hierarchy structuring all earthly relationships too, with immutable aspects of identity determining one's social strata. Based on gender, for example, heterosexual married males were bequeathed the strata just below the deities, with power and titles and privileges galore, with women—and truthfully everyone else—somewhere below getting none of those things.

So despite coming into being during the 1960s–70s free love hippie Jesus movement, when second wave feminism was sweeping through secular culture, the Vineyard began with a traditional evangelical stance on gender. My permissible roles, as delineated by Saint Paul in the Bible, were constrained by my female body. A woman was not suitable for leading/teaching the church writ large, or more specifically, men. She could teach/preach if her subjects were children or women, or really any marginalized population like heathens or prisoners. She might even be able to speak to men as long as the speaking wasn't "official," like with the woman having authority or a title. And no matter what, it was helpful when a woman spoke—especially if from a stage—to have a man with authority visibly and protectively nearby. God and God's system were apparently quite fragile, with the whole thing threatened by conflagration if feminine me uttered unchaperoned words from behind a podium.

But the problem was that I and many women were actually quite good at all the various components of speaking and teaching and pastoring and LEADING, without triggering the conflagration, and the men knew it! My church had, after all, wanted to ordain me, and Wimber's *Reflections* communication was a response to male fragility activated by his promotion of a woman to Senior Pastor after her Senior Pastor husband had died! So the men muddled: Wimber advocated for blessing and release for women so that they could be free in the movement to function in the full range of ministry, with the exception of governance. He stated that while both men and women could "eld" (?) according to their gifting, the office of eldership (?) was reserved for men only, and ordained men in particular. He felt that opening up functional elding (?) to women would be liberating and that the absence of title and recognition should not be problematic. And in fact, many of us women were celebratory. Wimber's guiding ministry ethic of "everyone gets to play" stood in contrast to the more rigidly codified gender-based roles found in our surrounding fundamentalist milieu.

The ultimate trouble with this system would not just be that all entities who were neither divine nor male were suppressed, but also that the structuring principle of hierarchy itself was divinely originated. Hierarchy issued directly from the very being of God, and resonated pre-consciously with human nature. We struggled to engage even conceptually with the possibility of different structuring principles such as equity or serving or love because hierarchy was so endemic. Which meant that the only way forward for women was to finagle the rules, as opposed to tearing this temple down and building up a new one. So I, as an insecure new pastor who didn't want to cause trouble with her leader, her movement, or her Father God, heartily agreed to put the whole ordination thing on hold, which worked fine until …

Iowa City

Tom and I moved from Chicago to Iowa City in 1996 for him to do a two-year psychiatry research fellowship through the University of Iowa's College of Medicine. Because of our kids, I had not been able to continue as a full-time pastor for at least the year prior, and so there was nothing vocationally hindering me from departing. And I was, after all, subordinate to Tom. And I did love him.

The plan again was for a two-year sojourn, because Iowa is just as fly-over to people from Chicago as it is to those from LA or NYC. But as Tom was driving the U-Haul across the plains with one kid next to him, and me driving with three in our car and one in my tummy, Tom tuned in to Iowa Public Radio. A local woman was describing how her husband had graduated from the University of Iowa shortly after World War II, but then instead of moving as planned, they stayed because they couldn't find work anywhere else, and now forty years later their kids were having kids in Iowa City and, *Isn't that wonderful?!* "I am not paying attention, God!!" shouted Tom. "See my fingers in my ears! La la la la la la! We are doing our two years in Iowa City and then moving on!"

But like the Hebrew people in Sinai, we haven't been able to find our way out. For the first two of our now twenty-five-plus years here, my primary relationships remained four hours back across the corn fields. Tom and I, near the end of year one, were walking alone one night with diminished income and no place yet to worship on a Sunday, and he said "Not very well" in response to my "How's your fellowship going?" in response to which I sort of melxploded (melted and exploded): *I gave up my beloved emeritus-pastor-for-life status in my come-to-Jesus church for "Not very well"?! Please start doing better quickly or we're going back!* So he did. He was awarded a small research grant and published his first scientific paper. And disconcertingly, he came to realize that he liked, and could probably come to love, the academic world of our new town—the intellectual freedom, openness to questions, thrill of the unknown, at the center of which were the people—secular liberal colleagues become friends.

And while Tom was working at the hospital, I was getting to know our neighbors, and our kids' friends' parents, and inviting them into our home for food and conversation and—for any who were interested—Jesus stuff. I lived and breathed meeting people, and asking questions of meaning, and connecting us all helpfully to Jesus, and forming a community of safety built around that. By somewhere in year two, I had gathered a group of twenty to twenty-five religious misfits who were meeting in our living room on Wednesday evenings doing something vaguely Christiany.

Byron would roll in at 7:15 for our 7:30 start time, the son of nearby Mennonite pastors, with a huge shaggy beard, a promontory of a body, gregarious bear hugs, and no tolerance for confinement, religious or otherwise. Jenny and Jeff were young and super artsy and also leery of religion, but they loved our home and our group and our children. They helped film, in our backyard, a fairy tale spy adventure starring our five kids and their five capes that won the Oscar that year for "Best Backyard Film of Kids with Capes." Jenny, a good Nazarene, was there with her husband, Tim, who called me his "Rebbi" and played guitar in our "band." Vivienne, our beautifully spirited next-door neighbor—the only one from that original group who stayed all they way with us through to who we are now—would occasionally drop by. I don't have any recollection at all anymore of what we actually did for an hour and a half on a Wednesday evening—I just feel fuzzy warm with love whenever I remember.

So yes, I was heading straight into pastoring heresy all over again *because I couldn't not do it.* Just like I couldn't not be a female. Magnifying the trouble, by the time I came to instigate this new "church," I was in no way being missional to Iowa City. Vineyard pastors from other Iowa cities who'd hear of our fledgling church would console me soulfully, like I was a naively addle-pated saint, or Iowa's Jonah—*it's spiritually dark there ... they have an abortion clinic ... and Principalities of Liberalism and Science ... We'll pray for you!* But I was not a spiritual savior rescuing the denizens of liberal hell— that was the task of the new evangelical church transplanted here from the college town to the west. I just genuinely loved whatever it was that we were becoming. And Tom and I both realized pretty quickly that even were we to transport our Evanston church to Iowa City, our misfits would never visit twice. We also realized that we ourselves might no longer be able to go back there because we were turning into our new friends! Starting to attend their meetings and use their words and perceive things like identity and purpose and the nature of love as they perceived those things.

Nonetheless, when midway through his second year (1997) Tom was offered a psychiatry job in Indianapolis, and a Senior Pastor friend there begged me to join the staff of his growing Vineyard church, I shouted, "Thank you God!" as I packed our bags. Though I loved my misfits, I had by now endured four years of medical school and five years of residency and I was ready for a husband with a real job and a me with a real job. But Tom had met some researchers in Iowa City with whom he wanted to do yet one more year of indentured servitude ("fellowship"), so I retorted a telephone across the room at him, and him a tray of lasagna at me, and then he prayed.

Tom:

"God," I remember saying to God, "I think you have it in mind for me to stay here, which means that Adey is being ungodly when she says we must go. But—just stating the obvious—she is way more godly than me. So if you have it in mind for me to stay, you need to make it so that she wants to stay." I was driving around the next day when I heard, as clearly as I ever have, God's voice: "Spend the money, dummy!"

I understood immediately what God meant, and that it would work. One of our misfit couples had given us some money to spend on trying to start a "real" church. I had, however, saved the money and felt like a responsible adult as I envisioned giving it back to them when we moved away. But when God called me dummy, I remembered Jesus telling a story in which a slave who buries money instead of investing it is berated and tossed out by his master to some forlorn place where there is weeping and "gnashing of teeth." I don't know how to gnash, so I went home and said to Adey, "God wants us to spend the money so you can build your church here."

Adey:

And I said, "Yes!" I had apparently desired more deeply than even I knew to do our church our way with the new friends we were gathering. The point of which for our inclusion story is that my Senior Pastor friend in Indy was much more tethered to Vineyard and its gender conservatism than me, and so going there would have functioned like inclusion contraception. I would not have become there a female Senior Pastor, nor would we, I don't believe, have become converted to inclusion had we left Iowa City.

How does one operationalize this most essential aspect of my and our church's transformation? The necessary first step for us becoming inclusive in the way that we are today was to get out of our parent church, and thereby out of evangelicalism. The necessary next step was to not dive back in. But we did not want to leave, and eighteen months later we would have jumped back in in a heartbeat! We had no ability to perceive the way our container constrained us while we were in it. We did not have a grand vision to birth something new that was motivating us to leave when we left. We had no awareness of how much we would come to rue how deeply evangelicalism had infused us. We could not even perceive it as something distinct from us! We just loved it, and thought that it was good and true and godly. We only became who we are now because we, out of necessity, against our own will, and mostly unaware of what we were actually doing, had to leave our beloved thing and begin building a new thing.

Early Arrivals

Our first church service in Iowa City was on Easter Sunday, 1999, in the upper room of the Q Bar (now the Blue Moose). The Upper Room gave the venue a spiritual zing, and though it was the only time we ever met there, years later folks would say, "Oh, you're that cool church that meets in a bar!" Our first regular location was a basement room of our city's Mercy Hospital—elongating hallways, garish lighting, labyrinthine. Our core group was Tom, me, our five children, and three other couples—so Wassinks 7, others 6. The "Kids' Wing" was a corner of the room cordoned off using accordion room dividers and pastored by Larry the Cucumber.

Six months in, we'd grown to fifty-ish and moved to the Robert A. Lee Recreation Center in downtown Iowa City, from whence we lived the Moby Dick stage of small church development—all our music gear crammed into a rattly duct-taped white whale passenger van that we unloaded before and stuffed full after every Sunday service, and then parked illegally somewhere for the week. After ten years, we were ready for a place of our own. We searched for three more years, almost signed a contract twice, and had essentially given up when two of our members said, "You should check out this building in Coralville [next to Iowa City]." We went and looked: high ceilings, unfinished interior, and ample parking. Sold! We put up walls and bathrooms and lights and speakers, waxed creative in the Kids' Wing, and in December of 2009 we held our first service in our new home.

Our Vineyard evangelical/Pentecostal blend was both conservative and progressive enough to attract Christians from a wide range of commitments. One of our earliest arriving families, coming to us during our Mercy Hospital days, was Anna and Mark and their children. Mark, like Tom, was a scientist, and Anna was a national leader for multiple worldwide evangelical ministries. They would come, as time ticked forward, to lead small groups and Bible studies, Mark would serve on our board, and Anna would teach sometimes on Sundays. They would become friends and spiritual partners, and would bring into the church a steady stream of evangelical Christians. They would champion equality for women and support our eventual departure from our denomination. But they would also stay true to their evangelical gender-identity commitments, and so would lead out our inclusion dissenters sixteen years later on the verge of our church's *Coming Out!* service.

At the same time came George and Marilyn. George had just been surprise-fired as pastor of his Mennonite congregation for being willing to remarry divorced people. He was on the front end of realizing how much his freedom-loving spirit had been crushed by Christian conservatism. He and Marilyn would also become our dear friends, leading Adey and me again and again into the magic of the American Southwest—the Grand Canyon being George's true home—in which we would discover together caves hidden behind the waterfalls of Havasu, and trek the Virgin River narrows, and one night swim alone in a moonlit Glen Canyon lake with looming red rock walls encircling our private Eden. George and Marilyn would become the spiritual godparents of our church. They would lead the way in welcoming the marginalized because George could not ever again abide a place that was not fully inclusive, being always aware that no matter who was newly welcomed, someone else was still on the outside looking in.

We welcomed Luke and Tracy from a conservative Vineyard church in downstate Illinois, and Mim from an arch-fundamentalist background, but also Bill and Katie with lots of happy queerness in his family, and Dylan and

Erica who loved the youthfulness of our church but were baffled by how queerness made us anxious. And as we slowly grew into a motley community of about five hundred attenders, our evangelical ambivalence about sexuality made the gendered-ness of our journey fraught.

John Wimber had passed away in 1997. This sadness for us nonetheless opened the possibility of a loosening of his strictures on women. His replacement only stayed with the job for two years, but his departing request in 1999 was that the *next* national director revisit the restrictions on women, which the next next did, asking a national board member to develop a proposal addressing ordination. That proposal, while not producing a national level policy, advocated for the autonomy of the local church in appointing pastors, including Seniors, and was approved in April of 2001.

But we weren't yet, as a movement, all in with that fledgling policy, because at about the same time, I went to apply for admission of our misfits as a bona fide church to the Vineyard. I approached our Midwest regional director, who said to me, "Yes! Of course you and your church will get in. But for now," and I could feel his grimace over the phone, "for now, Adey, on the application form, could you just put Tom's name on the Senior Pastor line, with you as a staff pastor? We both know the truth, Adey, about your role in the church, and one day we'll be able to say it right, but for now?" And Tom signed his name.

Women and Slaves, but *Not* Homosexuals

But then that same year femaleness was delinked from homosexuality. Grudem had predicted in his slippery-slope dictum what none of us could permit to be the case: that Christian empowerment of women would lead to Christian empowerment of homosexuals. Because if it did, we were done before even starting. We all—meaning us heterosexuals—knew that homosexualism was worse than feminism. LGBTQ people could not ever be permitted to minister in the church from within their fully expressed selves, so if our freedom led to theirs, we women would need to continue to be constrained. We needed God to treat them differently (worse) than us, so hooray for William Webb!

On May 30, 2001, Dr. William Webb, an evangelical scholar, published a book called *Slaves, Women & Homosexuals: Exploring the Hermeneutics of Cultural Analysis.* In his book, Webb presented a Bible interpretation rubric in which God's response to culture's response to people distinguishes the groups that God advances from those he constrains. If God is nicer than human culture to a particular group, then we should advance their rights, but if He is meaner, we should implement constraint. Webb demonstrated, through his rubric, that the God of the Bible loosened up the restrictions imposed by biblical "culture" on both slaves and women while being more suppressive than the ancient Near East toward homosexuality. Webb's book was logical and scholarly and had diagrams, and we were convinced! Here's what I wrote in a paper while, at that time, pursuing a graduate degree from Fuller Theological Seminary:

> When I encountered Webb's *Slaves, Women, & Homosexuals*, and read the principles behind how he called us to read scripture … I thought I had died and gone to heaven. I did worry—what if Webb and Giles and Stackhouse and Keener had simply found creative ways to justify me and others like me? What if they'd just caved in to contemporary liberal culture, as Grudem feared? But for years I had apologized for being me [a female pastor]. I still bristle when strangers ask me what I do. I work to hold my head up and not to diminish the privilege God has invited me into.

Oh God. I am so about my own fate that I can't even perceive what this would have meant to queer people. They were nonexistent to me. And the message is horrific: *If we can keep queer people out, we women are in!*

But it works, because in 2004—so exactly twenty years after the initial impetus—I became formally ordained as Senior Pastor of Vineyard Community Church of Iowa City. The event was joyful and represented a real advance in empowerment for me and for women in our movement. But Tom was ordained at the same ceremony. His ordination was good and right and valid and an accurate representation of Tom's commitment and abilities. But the symbolism was unmistakable—my ordination was made safe by Tom being ordained at the same ceremony. And just like the original delay of twenty years, my being reordained in a ceremony just for me as solo Senior Pastor of Sanctuary Community Church didn't happen for another twenty years! (A Moses-like forty for those doing the math.)

In 2005, Bert Waggoner, the next next National Director, led one more series of conversations on the issue, framed around thorny questions, like:

Can women speak at our regional and national leadership conferences? Can male egalitarians speak at our National Conferences? Can we encourage conferences that empower women at any level of ministry? Can we write articles in our denomination's magazine *Cutting Edge* on successful women pastors and preachers in the movement? Can *women* write such articles? Can women become area or task force leaders if gifted to do so? Can the national leadership speak positively concerning what women are doing in leadership? Were our educational systems free to train women to be pastors and national leaders?

It's just so distressing to reread these questions that we women waited anxiously for the anxious men to answer. But they're exactly what we, a decade later, carried forward into our questions about homosexuality:

Can gay people lead groups?

Get baptized?

Take communion?

Hold hands in church?

Teach and touch our children?

The National Board issued this statement in 2006:

In response to the message of the kingdom, the leadership of the Vineyard movement will encourage, train, and empower women at all levels of leadership both local and trans-local. The movement as a whole welcomes the participation of women in leadership in all areas of ministry.

Hooray! ... except:

This decision is not a dictate passed down from the national leadership. Pastors continue to be free to handle these issues according to their convictions within the context of their local churches. It is simply a description of how we will act toward women in leadership as we endeavor to lead the Vineyard movement in the U.S. at the national level.

So the movement now supported women advancing into all levels of leadership, but individual churches were not required to adhere. Some churches began training and encouraging women to serve at all levels according to their gifting, but seventy others left the Vineyard, nine explicitly because of the new stance on women, with many of the others for which this motivation was likely. In 2008, Waggoner brought together a small group of women leaders, including myself, to discuss the implementation and effectiveness of the new policy. The meeting gave rise to the National Women's Task Force, on which I served until 2013 when my burgeoning views on homosexuality forced me to bow out.

So: How did Holy Spirit inclusion, and then female inclusion, presage queer inclusion? Not optimistically. Holy Spirit inclusion was the formational event for Vineyard. Our choice to include the Holy Spirit forced us to leave our parent institution and become a new thing, our own thing, to become Us. This birthing event was joyous, preserved in celebratory origin stories, and produced a unified and pervasive Holy Spirit culture. While those who came to us later weren't forced to adhere to Vineyard-style Holy Spirit inclusion to belong, it wouldn't have made any sense to come if you weren't going to do that. Our practice of Holy Spirit inclusion was why you would choose to join us.

Female inclusion came later. It was not core to Vineyard identity; it was instead secondary and nonessential. The process to produce female inclusion was a contentious fight that left many people angry, that was not celebrated in song, and that was only minimally successful, because while the rules had changed, culture had not. I completed a doctoral dissertation from Fuller Theological Seminary in 2012, and as part of my research I found that the representation of women in Vineyard regional and national leadership settings had not gotten better, and had perhaps even diminished, subsequent to the publication of the Vineyard's national statement in 2006.

And so the likelihood of LGBTQ inclusion in Vineyard? Please. The traumatic memories of "championing" female inclusion were what provoked my Newport Road "Not again!" chagrin with Tom as I became taken over by the plights of my queer friends. Queerness would be much less cared about and much more troubling to our religiously conservative institution than femaleness. And so queer inclusion would become Sanctuary Community Church's formational event in the same way that Holy Spirit inclusion was Vineyard's.

8

Grandma I
Doesn't Know

Katie:

While Adey and Tom were dawdling in getting their church ready for me, I needed someone *now* to tell my Grandma I why Paula's midsection would soon be expanding. Grandma Imborek's maiden name was Kovach, her mother's maiden name Stiglitz, and her stepfather's last name Blazevich. Her parents had emigrated here from Croatia, and she was born in East Chicago, Indiana ("The Harbor", as my dad called it) in 1921. Grandpa Imborek was born in 1916 in another industrial Lake Michigan town, Saginaw, where his parents had emigrated to from Poland with the last name of Imborski, which his father changed to Imborek in 1918 when he couldn't find work because of discrimination against Polish immigrants.

Grandma I was a fabulous cook of pierogis, kapusta, sausage and kraut, nut rolls and kolaczki cookies. In northwest Indiana, my relatives still serve fresh Polish sausage—very different from smoked Polish sausage—as the traditional holiday delicacy. And Grandma I was very Catholic. She sent her two children—my dad and my aunt—to Catholic school. She attended Mass with friends every single Sunday, in Polish, without fail, for her entire adult life. She prayed the rosary ceaselessly in our house. Grandpa I died from Alzheimer's in 1996. Grandma I lived until 2011, passing away when she was over 90 years of age. So the stories that follow happened in my pre-Sanctuary world, with me, Paula, Adey, and Tom talking them through over dinner one night …

⌒

Katie: Did you know that once you are over 65 you do not have to go to church every week? Because my grandma's priest told her that once. That is what Grandma I would always tell us: "You know what? I don't have to go to church every week because I'm over 65." I said, "Really Grandma? It says in the Bible—" "No! The Father said so."

She was so devout. Before meals, she would take some "host" that had been blessed by the Father from the top shelf of her cupboard, the white Styrofoam kind where you just break off a piece, and pass it around. She would pray her rosary daily and had a Bible and daily devotions book on the TV stand next to her chair from which she would watch the Cubs every day.

But here's the thing—she prayed her rosary at our old house underneath the huge pictures of me and Paula at our wedding that were hanging in the living room! She would sit there, under those pictures, in her chair, and she would pray her rosary in the morning and she did not know that we were married. I said, "Mom, I think we should tell Grandma that Paula and I are married." And my mom said, "No, no." I was like, "But, our pictures are on the wall."

Adey: Like a professional wedding picture?

Paula: Yes—I am kissing Katie on the cheek. We are both wearing wedding gowns.

Katie: My mom said, "Oh, she can't see very good. You know that she can't see, she has really bad macular degeneration." I was like, "Okay."

Paula: We wear matching rings, and the family says, "Oh, she can't see." We talk about our wedding when we go to Uncle Ron's, "Well, you know, her hearing is not good." I'm thinking, "She's alive, people." And so now I'm pregnant with Parker, which would have been 2006, right? We are going to Uncle Ron's, which is Katie's uncle's house, for Thanksgiving. For some reason I was always the one that would pick up Grandma I—"Paula, can you go get Grandma I?" So by the time of this Thanksgiving, we are already married, but we have not told her because, it seems, she is deaf and she is blind.

Adey: What state did you get married in?

Paula: In Illinois. In Chicago.

Katie: Yeah, that was a complicated story too. We had a commitment ceremony in '05. We were not legally married—everyone around us made it clear that this commitment ceremony was not a legal marriage. We could not have a wedding cake, our invitations could not say, "The Wedding," Paula's parents were maybe not going to come, we probably should not kiss, we should maybe high-five. There was a lot going on. Though it was a great day actually, when it was all said and done.

Tom: We had our mini version of that with Adey being Jewish but getting married to me in a Christian ceremony. There were so many "nots": we had to have it outside, not in a church; we could talk about God but not Jesus; and our primary living memory of the ceremony comes from the video that shows her mother with an unchanging expression of pain. I had the thought recently, "You know, that video image of your mother's pain colors our whole memory of the wedding."

Paula: Our videographer was videotaping from behind me, and my mom's face was in the background, and yes, the same pain. We made the videographer switch the angle to show Katie's family.

Katie: She had two cameras, so she sent us the first draft and we said, "Go with the different camera angle because we cannot handle it, we just can't watch it."

Paula: So, anyway. Grandma I does not see the wedding rings on our fingers, she does not see the 3 by 5 foot picture of us—

Katie: —while she prays her rosary—

Paula: —but it's now over a year later, and I am about to have a child running around. So clearly this is the time to tell Grandma I, you know? "So, Katie, how are you gonna do it?" "Well, you're gonna tell her!" "What do you mean I'm gonna tell her?" "Well, it's your news to share, you're pregnant." I was like, "It's *our* news—are you kidding me? You're gonna make me tell your grandma?" and I look at Katie's mom and her mom is like, "Yeah, I think so, Paula." I am like, "Oh my God."

So Katie is in the back seat, we go and get Grandma I, we have a ten-minute drive from Grandma I's house to Uncle Ron's house and everyone was saying, "You better tell her before you get to Uncle Ron's because she won't be able to hear you because of all the other noise that's going on." So, I am driving, and I am waiting and waiting, not sure how to bring it up and then I was just like, "So, Grandma." She was like, "Yeah?" I was like, "I've got some good news." Then she said, "Oh, you're getting married?" And I said,

"No, no, no. I did that with your granddaughter a couple of years ago and we haven't told you about it ..." No, I did not say that—I just thought it.

I actually said, "No, no, I'm pregnant!" and she was like, "No, you're not pregnant." I then tried to stick my barely noticeable baby bump out as far as it would go and insisted, "Grandma, I am pregnant." "Well, I did not know you had a boyfriend." I was like, "No, I do not have a boyfriend."

Adey: Katie, are you in the car listening?

Katie: Yes, I am in the backseat thinking, "Why did we think it wasn't gonna happen exactly like this? Why did we not prepare for this? Of course these are the logical questions that you ask when you are 90 and you have all these assumptions." So I am just intently staring out the window.

Paula: I look in the rearview mirror, thinking loudly, "Can I have some help?" and she was giving no eye contact, so I am still on my own. This was really going downhill fast. Then I said, "No, I do not have a boyfriend." I thought, Oh my gosh, she thinks I got knocked up at a bar or something. So, I was like, "No. So, Grandma, I just felt like it was the time in my life to start a family, so I wanted to have a baby." She said, "I don't get it." "Well, I went on the internet, I bought some sperm—"

Adey: Oh my god, is that what you said?

Paula: Yes! And then Katie finally spoke: "She went to a doctor." That is all Katie said the whole time, just to make sure everybody knows that I went to a doctor to get inseminated.

Katie: It was bad.

Paula: Grandma said, "Well, okay." And that was our ten minutes. I said, "Oh look! We're here at Uncle Ron's now." So, I walk into Uncle Ron's and everyone asks, "So, how'd it go?" I was like, "Horrible," and then sometime later Grandma I asked, "So, is Katie just gonna help take care of the baby?"

Adey: So, did she ever know?

Katie: Well yes, but it took time. Parker was born in '07. My dear Grandma I comes over right after Parker was born, holds the baby, gives Parker an afghan that she had been keeping for my first child, and asks my mom questions like, "So, I have this china that I am waiting to give to somebody and I am kind of waiting to give it to Kate when she gets married, what do you think?" and my mom would say, "I think you should just give it to her now, I think that's fine."

So I kept feeling, "Guys, Grandma knows. Why does everybody act like she doesn't know? Grandma knows." But I kept being surprised, even though it kept going exactly like anybody else from the outside looking in would expect. I thought we were going to give her the information: "Katie and Paula are together," but we somehow always ended up somewhere totally different.

Then two years later—two years!—in '09, came the Iowa Supreme Court ruling in support of marriage equality, and we got married the very first day that we could because we were just worried about it potentially being repealed, so we got married at the courthouse. We had a party four months later, a big party, a potluck, it was great, we had four hundred people that we had invited. All of our Iowa City friends were there, we had people come back from high school, and my folks and Paula's folks came.

And we invited other family members, including my uncle Eddie who was in our family by marriage—his wife had passed away, but we were still really close. So I am getting my hair done at the stylist for this party, and my brother calls me, and he says, "Kate, Uncle Eddie just totally threw you under the bus!"

I am like, "Man, what are you talking about?" He says, "Dude, you better call Mom. Uncle Eddie just told Grandma I that you and Paula are together!" I was like, "What?"

So I call my mom as I am getting my hair done and I am like, "What the hell?" She says, "Okay, Grandma I called Uncle Eddie and said, 'What's going on in Iowa? You're going to Iowa, Robbie and Bob are going to Iowa— what's happening there?' and so, Uncle Eddie says to her, 'Well, don't tell anyone that I told you, but Kate and Paula got married and they are having a reception.'"

Then—oh my god—she was so upset that no one had told her.

Tom: She still hadn't known by then?

Paula: Apparently not, but she did now!

Katie: Yes, and then she was like, "Jesus this and Jesus that."

Adey: Like in a good way? Or upset?

Katie: Pretty upset, sort of worried for our eternal salvation. So then I call her, and I am still at the frickin' stylist.

Tom: Was there anybody else at this point who did not know, or was it just Grandma I?

Katie: Probably just Grandma I, because Vonna, the woman who cleaned my mom and dad's house, had told Grandma B—who is my maternal grandmother—a couple of years before. What you can learn from Katie and Paula's coming out story is: "You should tell people because they find out." I remember poor Vonna crying because she's thinking, "Why wouldn't Grandma B have known? Everyone else knows. I have seen Katie and Paula a thousand times—clearly everyone knows they are together. And so then Grandma B was in hysterics—

Tom: But now you are on the phone with Grandma I, the last person who remains in the dark?

Katie: Yes. It had only been a couple of hours, so she had not had much time to, like, digest this. So she is crying, and everybody is already in Iowa—nobody can even make it better and pick her up and just bring her because everybody is here; we are having the party that night. So, she says, "I just feel like I'm the last one to know." And I say, "Grandma, my dad told me not to tell you. I'm sorry. I wanted to tell you but they said that it would upset you, that your weak heart would fail."

Then I think that she just said, "Well, are you happy?"

And I said, "I'm so happy. Paula's amazing and Parker's great."

Grandma I had always loved Paula. She would do that grandma thing where she would slip you $10, and she would slip Paula $5, even though I was 27 years old, and Paula is 30. So, she really did love Paula and probably just felt that Paula must be this orphan who does not have a family to go see every Thanksgiving and Christmas because she comes to our house every time.

So then she said to me, "Well, you know, I have been thinking about this, and I feel like I talked to Jesus and he said that everything is going to be okay." So she had come to this sort of "It's okay" place with God where she felt that she was at peace.

And that was it. We never talked about it again, and we would see her all the time. We would go home, and we would see her; she came when Will was born—and she was money with babies, just really loved them, held them, sang to them in Polish, the whole bit. Really loved them. She was great.

Tom: I do not know how to say it differently—was she willfully ignorant of the two of you being together, or just actually could not conceive of it?

Katie: I have thought about that too, Tom, because I kind of worried that we were pretending that she was clueless just because she was old, when she was really more intuitive than we gave her credit for. So, my initial narrative was, "She knows, guys, we're kidding ourselves." But she, I think, legitimately did not know. And so, was she just in denial or was it just that she had no imagination?

Adey: It feels deeper than denial, because you describe so much evidence for what was going on.

Katie: This was the grandma that in 1983, or '84, whenever the Cabbage Patch craze was, when people were beating each other to a pulp in Kmart to get a Cabbage Patch doll—and God knows she went to Kmart, for sure, she shopped there all the time—she stood in line at the Kmart and bought me a Cabbage Patch doll for Christmas and I opened this thing up and I threw it across the room and I said, "Me hate dolls—me boy!" You know? So the evidence was twenty-five years in the making. There was a lot of evidence saying, "Maybe this is a possibility." But I do not think she ever knew someone—

Paula: I am sure she never knew anybody, right?

$\backsim$

Tom:

The story of Grandma I is funny in the retelling, but the humor is dearly bought. Katie is beloved, but carries within herself a flaw that must be kept secret because of the threat it poses to Grandma I. The threat is not actual—Katie's queerness has no real impact whatsoever on Grandma I's well-being. The threat is instead knowledge-based: if Grandma I learns of Katie's queerness, and learns that Katie is living true to her queerness, this knowing will be so violative of Grandma's Christian norms that she will experience an emotional/spiritual implosion, and perhaps will actually physically die.

But Katie keeping her queerness a secret is a form of death for her. She must suppress a core aspect of her identity, and then participate in the bewildering practice of secret-keeping, being constantly reminded of the trouble she's causing because the entire family has to keep track of what is known by whom, and why some are entrusted with the knowledge while others are not. Which all turns out, in the end, to have been completely unnecessary! Grandma I resolves her existential angst over Katie's queerness through a brief conversation with Jesus, and a couple questions to Katie, and that's it. Henceforth, "she was at peace."

So why was such a deep, but apparently unfounded, sense of threat deposited by the family onto Grandma? Why was it never checked out? It's a common occurrence—a person in the family, typically older and with a long practice of religion, is imputed to be unable to tolerate the revelation of queerness in a beloved younger relative. *We're okay with it*, the rest of the family says, *but not Grandpa X*. And Grandparent's intolerance cannot be challenged because it's understandable and Grandparent is beloved and fragile. So everyone else in the family can claim being nice and tolerant, while the system still upholds that queerness is a problem. It's like a double-scapegoating. The queer person is scapegoated for being queer, but then the rest of the family puts their own intolerable intolerance of queerness into a hapless elder, who is unknowingly expelled from the circle of knowing. Grandma I was the only relative not in Iowa for the wedding.

This wedding story also presents the oh-so-common jumble of ceremonies for queer couples. There's perhaps a commitment ceremony whose validity is undermined at every turn, then a civil affair in front of a stranger *quick!* before the open window of gay legality is slammed shut, and then a few months later a party. But with God never quite fully present, Her invite lost in the mail—*where's my table assignment?*—God alluded to, maybe, but certainly not lovingly presiding. Our queer couples can have been with us for years and still not have felt God's blessing of their union. Even the gay wedding lexicon—"union," "partner," "civil commitment," "judge," rather than marriage, wedding, bride, groom, husband, wife, pastor—can seem sterile, not as romantic or celebratory as heterosexual affairs, leeched of the sexuality and sex that's supposed to be at the center of the whole thing.

⤳

Katie:

Paula and I stayed married until 2021—so until five years beyond Sanctuary's *Coming Out!* Sunday celebrated in Chapter 25—but then we got divorced. Sanctuary helped to save our gay marriage for a little over ten more years from when we crossed its threshold, but then, when we decided with finality that we needed to not be together anymore, Sanctuary helped us navigate separating. Which was both the right thing for us to do, and awful! Not just because of the pain of extricating, but because gay Christian marriages could not be allowed to fail! We had worked so long and hard to make them possible, and scowling conservative Christians were itchy to have been right about our moral turpitude making us unable to sustain such unions, and here now was me, Miss Activist, playing right into their hands!

As if the fidelity and longevity of theirs were superior. Which nonsense is actually how our occurrence, though regrettable, helped us better understand the true mission of an inclusive church. Sanctuary is a Jesus-centered faith community that welcomes, at every moment, the entirety of our identities and choices and joys and struggles. And queer lived lives, it turns out, experience most of the same joys and struggles as not queer lives. We just needed a church, and a representation of God, that believed that. So our message is not and cannot be that because Sanctuary is now inclusive that all queer lives go well here, any more than that all straight lives go well here. Our ethic is instead that all the joys and travails of everyone who avails themselves of this communal God-space are attended to equally with non-judgmental love.

‿

Adey:

But at the time of Paula's nascent bump there was not such a space of loveliness for her and Katie to enter into because, as Katie noted at the beginning of the chapter, Tom and I were "dawdling" …

9

The Slipping Begins

Adey:

One winter evening in 2008, I gathered Tom and David and two biblically erudite friends, Alvis and Evan, in the fireplace room of our house. David and his wife, Ali, had started coming to our Vineyard church in 2001. David grew up in Indiana, studied philosophy as an undergrad here at the University of Iowa, and then had worked for a few years on staff for Anna's evangelical college ministry. He left that ministry unhappy with its motives, methods, and fruitfulness, but still went on to pursue a masters in divinity from North Park Theological Seminary, of the Evangelical Covenant Church. As a degree requirement, David began a summer internship with us in 2006. He was passionate and smart, he loved people and pastoring, and both he and Ali had emerged from some pretty horrific evangelical experiences (Chapter 14) with still a deep belief in the possible goodness of church. So I stretched his internship one month more, and then another, then another year, scheming for something more long-lasting to emerge from his stint with us.

"Do you think," I asked the gathered men, "that gay sex is sin?" It had been twelve years since we had left our Chicago evangelical church, nine years since we'd started our own, and four years since I'd been ordained, however imperfectly, as Senior. Tom and the cows knew of my queer angst, but it had taken this long being away from our parent church to work up courage to openly ask queer questions to others. I still believed in the consequentiality of sin as a thing that would provoke God's wrath, but I was no longer convinced that being queer itself was sinful. I now wanted to hear someone I trusted theologically (sorry David and Tom!) take the next step and say that they didn't think homosexual sex was sin.

The five of us huddled conspiratorially close in the fireplace room of our home. I remember the chair in which I sat, an overstuffed puffy brown thing that *pssshhed* as I sank down into it, enveloping me in its aged brown crackled leather, bought from Big Lots long ago, with the reclining mechanism now glitchy and the footrest unstable and the whole thing trembling until we could afford a replacement (our metaphor for evangelicalism). And my memory, which it turns out is mine alone—Tom remembers our chair but not the event, and neither does David, though they were both there—*or maybe the whole thing was a dream*—has Evan and Alvis pondering in that male intellectual squinch-faced finger-to-chin kind of way ... for a beat ... before one of them says, while the other nods affirmingly, "No, Adey, I don't think gay sex is sin. Probably not God's best. Probably not even God's design. But also probably not sin." So—yes! Score one for my slippery-slope-to-LGBTQ-perdition team. Even that tepid qualifier-laden "probably not" which would drive me over a cliff today seemed in that room revolutionary and subversive and hopeful.

Tom:

I preached later that same winter a sermon from the John 8 Woman Caught in Adultery story (renamed by us in Chapter 27 of this book) in which I suggested that Jesus' central message, instead of "go and sin no more," was him standing between the accusers and the accused, creating a zone of protection for her from the religionists. Our parishioners knew in advance that this teaching would represent by proxy some of our current thinking about LGBTQ welcoming. The move in the direction of kindness as a contrast to conservative disapproval was detected and appreciated. We heard later that some of our way-ahead-of-us parishioners came to that Sunday anticipating that they'd have to leave the church, but then realized that maybe they didn't have to depart just yet.

Adey shortly thereafter pressed on me and the cows yet again that maybe the clobber passages were not substantial enough to justify our prohibition of gay sex. This was the day when, for the first time, on the return leg of our Newport Road walk, about fifteen minutes from home—the clouds scudding and the cows cudding and the corn leaves rustling in the hot wind—rather than me hearing my internal *Capitulation to Culture!* alarm blaring, I thought to myself: *well, maybe.*

And that was all he needed. The next day I found Jesus in my rapidly queering text deluging me with his waterfall of inclusion. Not just one story, or a fringe person from an obscure section of Mark eleventeen, but *every single Jesus story*, with him relentlessly and intentionally centering those on the margins. The question for me rapidly became not: *Was Jesus maybe okay with one tepidly safe form of including?* but: *How could I not previously have perceived AT ALL what Jesus was relentlessly doing??* With Jesus also muscularly pushing power—theologians, pastors, priests, government officials, royalty, wealth, family—out of the frame. It came to present itself as a rubric: When I am confused about who Jesus would currently champion, whether in a dispute or in culture writ large, I just need to identify the ones being castigated by Christianity, and there's my answer.

Adey:

In December 2009, a church member wrote to me about a Jewish friend of hers who had become a Christian and who had just been fired as a pastor for coming out as gay, and who had then fantasized in a blog post about his dream church:

> Adey, I can't help but think that the church he dreams about is the church you and Tom have planted. His description sounds like the church we are and the one we are growing into—this is the church I want and I think we all want. I wish he lived in our town so he could come to our church. I think our church is the church for a gay Jewish Christian democrat evangelical.

In 2010, I wrote to a friend, "i'm becoming more openly heretical by the hour. lovely new gay couple coming regularly to the church and in a small group. i'm so pleased!" Which new couple was Adan and Alden. Alden's email had come to us on April Fool's Day, 2010:

> My name is Alden. I was referred to you by a friend of my husband, Adan. We are a beginning family looking for a church home.

Leah, a staff pastor—she of the purple hair leading music on Katie's first Sunday visit to our church—had forwarded me his questions, saying:

> Here's where the rubber meets the road. Would you guys like to respond to this?

which I sent anxiously straight on to our pastoral staff:

> I'd like to hear from you all before we send an email.

and after hearing from them, I responded to Alden:

> Tom and I would love to have coffee or dinner with you and your spouse and get to know each other. please let us know if you are coming to good friday or easter so we can find you and welcome you to the community.

I'm like the anti-Alden. He's direct and self-disclosing and wants truthfulness up front. But while I sound nice, I'm veiled and want to delay saying to him what's actually the case about us for as long as I possibly can.

So my advice to you, Oh Reader, is to click "Yes" when your email program asks: "Do you really want to permanently delete this email?" Because to reconstruct this telling we unearthed our actual communications from the long ago, and everything we found in our digital trash cans provoked "ouch." In the unchallenged rosy glow of remembering, we have always been, in our hearts of hearts, compassionate toward the excluded, unrattled by external threats, and way ahead of our regressive Christian peers theologically. But through our archival excavations, we heard ourselves being afraid not just of Alden, but of conservative friends, progressive friends, our denomination, the need to belong, secular culture, Christian culture, God. And we saw ourselves "progressing" so very gingerly through all the half-hearted precursor stages of inclusion about which we are now so indignantly impatient in others.

But in spite of my non-response, Alden wanted to attend Beginnings, an intro class to our church that concluded with a discussion of what we considered membership to be, which we hadn't yet formulated for queer people because each individual baby step toward inclusion triggered its own storm of irresolution and anxiety. So I wrote to my pastoring friends for help, but they were all over the place, as was my staff. David was "quite uneasy" with progressing even though he was now good friends with my lesbian friend Gusty. Sonya, another of our staff pastors, felt "uncomfortable" if membership included affirming or blessing homosexuality, but also "uncomfortable" if forbidding membership would cause gay people to not come. I was worried about sin and indulging but wanted to go forward, and Tom was both viscerally aversive to inclusion and "ready to go forward for sure" and sending to all of us a Jesus-welcomes-an-outsider story a day. David didn't like Tom's Bible stuff, Leah wanted a conversation about *what does it mean to be a member anyway?* and at the end of it all, Sonya said: "I am overwhelmed with differing angles, ideas, questions, and opinions and need time to sort it all out."

I wrote to a pastor friend the morning of April 7th, "my staff is going crazy. no one knows what to do," and to my staff that afternoon:

> I don't think we will get kicked out of the Vineyard if we invite folks into membership. I just think we need to walk into it with our eyes open. We will be criticized by many. But I think if we do not want to invite folks into membership we need to stop preaching on God's radical inclusiveness, or at least figure out what exactly we mean.
>
> It's never that I'm settled that membership makes sense. It's more that I'm settled that having gay folks as part of our community will enrich us and we them and mostly make space for Jesus in their lives.

My Inclusion-Man husband responded:

> Last night at staff meeting, I was caught up in the intensity of the abstract future possibilities and all the anxieties they'd create. This morning I thought, of course we'd welcome these folks as members of our community. How could we not given what we believe about Jesus and how far we've already walked down this road in our preaching and thought? How could we turn back?
>
> I really think many more of our people would be much more upset with us if we turn back than if we go forward. And who wants to go back anyway? Forward is an adventure. And even though I can quickly become anxious again thinking about all the questions and challenges that going forward might bring, I do believe it's the right thing to do.

To which I responded a half hour later:

> I think I feel worse going backwards than forward, but, I feel as though I'm on shaky ground and will be grateful for more conversations with pastors (I'm an external processor and I need to process a bit before I settle). My gut says go forward, and I think for well thought out reasons, but, I'm shaky ...

None of us can recall whether Adan and Alden came to that Beginnings class, but they worshiped with us for a season. They brought their foster children to our Kids' Wing Children's Church. They enjoyed the Sunday service and chatting with folks afterwards. Until they didn't. They had a growing family, they were busy, they had their own life challenges. Their not staying might have had nothing to do with our traditional theology, or with them being the only gay people on the premises. Or maybe "safe" to them meant something different, something more complete, than it did to us. But whatever we were or weren't to them, they, unbeknownst even to themselves, nudged us forwards ...

The Meeting

In 2009, gay marriage is legalized in New Hampshire, Iowa, and Washington, D.C. Katie and Paula get married on April 27, 2009, the first day Iowan couples could. On August 4th, 2009, a federal judge strikes down a voter-approved gay marriage ban in California, then a federal appeals court strikes down that striking down, then an appellate court in Dallas rules that a Texas ban on same-sex marriage does *not* violate Equal Protection and so could stand. In September 2009, Tyler Clementi commits suicide after a video of his sexual encounter with a man is streamed over the internet. In October, a California judge orders the government to stop enforcing "Don't Ask, Don't Tell" but then an appeals court blocks that decision. And in November, two of the three Iowa Supreme Court justices who had voted to legalize same-sex marriage are removed from office in judicial retention elections due to the anti-LGBTQ activism of conservative Iowa Christians. Iceland legalizes gay marriage in June 2010, with the first Icelandic couple to avail themselves of their new freedom being the prime minister Jóhanna Sigurðardóttir (pronunciation: ˈjouːhana ˈsɪːɣvrðarˌtouʰtɪr) and her wife Jónína Leósdóttir. Iceland is so cool.

In the midst of this national and international foment, we invited our church leaders into ours. David, Tom, and I had talked one-on-one about

LGBTQ welcoming with many of our church's leaders, and Alden and Adan had provoked conversations amongst our staff. But I now wanted us all to have the conversation in the same room because if we were possibly going to welcome, the "we" had to be not just me and Tom, and not just our staff, but our church *together*.

So on May 7th, 2010, we wrote that our next leaders' meeting would be "a unique one—we're going to begin a conversation about homosexuality and the implications for our church life and practice." We scheduled it for Sunday morning, June 6th, before church. It was probably better attended than most of these things. I vaguely remember us taking our seats—padded stackable chairs arranged in a circle in the Toddler room. Legos and SpongeBob strewing the floor; coffee, OJ, and pastries on paper plates. Summer evangelical chatter, and then the hushing that says, "What are we talking about again?"

I probably gave an intro—probably some statements about the broader Christian context, our desire for all to connect with Jesus, our high view of the Bible, the increasing and very real presence of beloved LGBTQ individuals in our personal lives and our church. Probably gave an instruction about hearing from each other rather than teaching, and sharing personally as opposed to theologically. And then I asked my question: "Okay, let's just go around—share with us where you're at on this topic." And my church friends went, one by one, around the circle ...

George, kind and loving, saying that he wanted us to welcome everyone, "and if the Bible says otherwise ..." **Anna**, also kind and loving, but worried about Compromise and Slippage and "that we not lose our Commitment to the Authority of Scripture." **Sonya**, coming from a liberal-Catholic then secular background, baffled by just the possibility of exclusion in the Christian church, but intimidated by the evangelical intellectualism in the room. **Barrett**, husband of Sonya, raised Christian conservative but now inhabiting the secular business world, who for the life of him cannot comprehend how excluding is even a consideration. **David and Ali** are there, kindred at that time theologically with Anna but also bringing a metric ton of unprocessed LGBTQ-related Christian trauma. **Tracy**, a conflicted progressive wannabee, telling of her conservative home church that was life to her, but "my very best friend from high school just came out to me last week, telling me that he had hid himself from Christian-me the whole way through school, which feels awful, and so now I just don't know." **Luke**, Tracy's husband, also wanting to be kind and welcoming, but is the son of super-conservative Christian parents who are powerful pastors of a large Vineyard church. **Bill**, whose father and uncle and cousin are gay, and who like Sonya will later say that he is made to feel dumb by evangelical intellectualism, but who just doesn't get *what's the problem*? Next to Bill a **Pray-the-Gay-Away couple** and their **faith theology mom** who are helpful in church in every imaginable way but who believe in hard truths and the painfulness of the "good news" …

How could so much diversity of LGBTQ thought come from fifteen hetero Iowa Christians? Raw unprocessed thoughts and feelings tumbling out, many of us discovering ourselves as we spoke, lots of it triggered and anxious and directed at a specific person across the circle, me watching in growing dismay, not able to halt the proceedings for necessary interventions—*Tracy, do you feel like Anna just consigned your friend to hell? Anna, how does it feel to be vilified for questioning liberalism?*

So I just tallied up the wounds: Ooh, that'll take a long time to heal … Ouch, she'll never talk in a meeting again … Uggh, I'm sure this is Tom's fault … Lots of hurt without any clearly discernible benefit. I don't have any recollection of how we closed the meeting, just kind of a numb shuffling away to bagels and church, Tom on his way out muttering loudly, "We are never having a meeting like that again!"

The Staff Meeting

But we had not the luxury of recuperation because at 9 o'clock the next morning *The Meeting* spilled into *The Staff Meeting*. There we were—me, Tom, David, and a couple others, with agenda item #1 being *What the hell just happened?* and #2, *What do we do now?*

David knew. He's an enneagram 1, a person of principle, "conscientious and ethical, with a strong sense of right and wrong." But the enneagram warns that for 1's, "when moving in their Direction of Disintegration, methodical Ones suddenly become moody and irrational." And this was a time of disintegration. What I vividly remember is David lividly shaking his Bible at me and shouting *"But the Bible says!!"* What David said it says I don't remember, but I'm pretty sure it was not favorable to sexual freedom for LGBTQ Christians.

David followed up in an email the next day:

> … my passion was, I think, for a couple reasons. First, I think it was the course of the conversation, anxiety building over time. I didn't do well managing my own anxiety, and it leaked. I hope not in too inflammatory a way. When I feel like my view is

being misrepresented, I feel like I've "lost" the argument. And here, too, I'm aware of my driven need to be "right," which I am working hard to pay attention to and surrender. I apologize if that came out just bad.

He's sensitive and self-aware and apologetic, until:

> As far as the roles of homosexuals in the church, I would place absolutely no limits. And personally, I would work hard to get the church to be at a place to be able to receive homosexuals as such. In other words, I would not want the church to place any restrictions against individuals on account of identity. This assumes that homosexual persons in leadership are, like all singles, abstaining from sexual activity (and repenting when sin occurs).

So, lovely lovely lovely *wham*! No sex for homosexual persons, and say sorry if you do! David's relational angst-ridden introspection was why I loved him and had a glimmer of a hope of a possibility that we would make a great team. But I knew that for us to move forward together, we needed to talk about *how* we communicated as much as *what*, so I joined the fray:

> I believe our process is really important. David, can you tell me where you get messed up with me and or Tom? We have so much love and have loads of respect for you. But, it seems you have something in mind about how we see you …
>
> Love to you both, Adey

But before David could respond, Anna sent me her thoughts about yesterday's *The Meeting*. She had compared, in *The Meeting*, our church's reluctance to preach about the wrongness of homosexuality to our reluctance to preach about the wrongness of divorce, and so was following up:

> I was trying to express my concern that we might be afraid (or avoidant) of teaching all parts of scripture, knowing that some passages might make homosexual couples uncomfortable (e.g. Gen 1-2 or Romans 1). What I am trying to express is that one of the tensions we face is the tension of creating an environment that is hospitable and welcoming while at the same time teaching "the whole counsel of God." I could have

used a different illustration like teaching about materialism knowing that it might offend folks with extravagant cars or teaching about the exclusivity of the gospel knowing that it might offend relativists or universalists.

In one sense, we always face this tension as we decide what and how to teach. The presence of homosexual married couples pushes the tension because homosexuality is so public and has been chosen as an identity.

Pretty much every brooding evangelical concern with gay sex is there: the "exclusivity" of the gospel (?), the volitionalness of being gay, an expansive moral purview that encompasses queer sex and the wealthy and divorced people and relativists, and then the weighty responsibility given to us evangelicals of communicating to everyone "the whole counsel of God," as if we know what that is, but which counsel's successful communication is proven by having produced discomfort. Over the ensuing days, as conversations spilled out between us about these and other queer evangelical concerns, I felt underneath it all increasing discomfort with a more central puzzle: *Why us?* How did we as evangelical Christians come to have standing amongst humankind to control sex? Unmarried sex, divorced sex, same-sex sex. We knew from our Christian tradition that God expected evangelicalism to oversee the sexual activity of others, but it was a really problematic and unpleasant part of our mandate, and we were starting to wonder ...

David Says Sorry

The next day David wrote to us all:

Hi friends,

I realized that in the midst of our conversations regarding homosexuality, I think I've lost sight of the whole point of doing church together. I've become more preoccupied with "being right" than with seeking the truth (or Truth, i.e. Jesus) together and loving others well along the way. Forgive me. I've been an ass. I know it leaked quite a bit the other night at our staff meeting in particular. Especially to Adey—I'm so sorry. Please let me know if we need to talk through it some more—I'm totally open to hearing from any of you. Thanks in advance for your patience as I grow up. much love,

David

Did I mention that I love David? He is perfect and you may not try to hire him. I retrospectively worried that I had somehow used his post-lividity chagrin to goad him into repentance. But when I showed this to him these many years later, he was happy: "I sound pretty good! My 30-year-old self is mature—I like him!" And he added:

> My conversion back then was not a conversion from exclusion to inclusion; it was a conversion to a whole different way of thinking about church and community and people, a conversion to process being just as critical, or more critical, than arriving at the right answer. I'm leaving behind the idea that any church community has the right answer.

David would officially join our staff as a pastor six months later.

So that was us in June, 2010. *The Meeting* then *The Staff Meeting* then some moralizing—or not—all whisked together with repentance and relational angst and truthiness, and baked in the oven of ... I don't know. Maybe not the best metaphor, but it sure felt like being in an oven, or a cauldron, or a pressure cooker. Trying to advance queer freedom out from under our evangelical overlords, but really not knowing how to proceed. What, I wondered, were the odds of us making it?

10

Reverend Doctor Lesbian Barbie

Gusty: u there?

    me: buy me a rev barbie

Gusty: i thought you might like that!

Adey:

Augusta ("Gusty") was my dear comrade in progressive heresy for nearly two decades. We had come into leadership at our Evanston Vineyard church in the late 1980s and had bonded because of our parallel pioneering, me as a woman leader in a conservative church movement, and Gusty as a *lesbian* woman leader in a conservative church movement. But while I got to live into myself, Gusty could not. She could not be gay. To be true to her talents and passion in our church, she suppressed expression of her sexual desires, embraced celibacy, received healing prayer, and did all the emotional and psychological bullshit that I and my hetero church leader friends pressed onto her. She had nonetheless been expelled from the church of our youth for same sex flirtations in 2006, had wandered for a few years trying to figure out what came next, and moved to Iowa City to be with me and our church early in 2010.

Gusty and I had simultaneously started at-a-distance graduate programs at Fuller Theological Seminary, commiserating with and encouraging each other as we advanced our heretical causes in that strangely progressive con-servative place. On April 8th, 2010, so a week after Alden's email, Gusty had

shared with me a blog post describing how a female episcopal priest from
Kent, Ohio, had created Reverend Barbie, a blonde plastic clerical figure
whose bustiness was concealed under a cassock, surplice, and a wealth of
other vestry garments.[1] Gusty and I, supposedly writing deep thought seminary papers, were off and running:

> **me:** i want to present the article at my women's conference.
> funny
>
> **Gusty:** what article?
>
> **me:** what you sent me. can i also get a rev barbie of color? and
> i want a not-skinny rev barbie. Let's drop out and make
> pastor barbies

Seeing the sexualness of Barbie—the apotheosis of patriarchy's feminine
ideal—cloaked in clericalism caught our fancies. My mind leaped from
myself to specific women in my Fuller cohort to all women trying to bust
free from racial and body and gender imprisonments in this culture of men:

> **Gusty:** there is so much craziness out there … you also need an
> asian and latina if you are going to be inclusive … and
> don't forget lesbian barbie!
>
> **me:** lol lol
>
> **Gusty:** i'm thinking this is how I will fund school.
>
> **me:** i want a lesbian barbie
>
> get me a lesbian barbie
>
> lots of money in lesbian barbie
>
> for sure
>
> **Gusty:** me too … she better be wearing a baseball hat though to
> be authentic
>
> oh my gosh … can you imagine!!
>
> **me:** we want her outdoors stylish,
>
> huh
>
> who could that be?

1 onfaith.co/onfaith/2010/04/07/reverend-barbie-the-plastic-episcopal-priest/7198, beautytipsforministers.
com/2010/03/28/the-genius-of-the-rev-julie-blake-fisher/, and religionnews.com/2010/04/05/
barbie-gets-ordained-and-has-the-wardrobe-to-match/.

Gusty: maybe you can bring lesbian barbie to your next staff mtg to help talk about the gay issue.

you could pattern lesbian to look like me just don't show Vineyard people!

me: LOL

i got to go read walter wink [our theologian of the moment]. did you like his stuff?

Gusty: that way I could get double royalties … we could make lesbian rev phd barbie

me: wow!!! quite a market i'm sure

Gusty: oh you mean you don't want to spend the afternoon doing this? Yes … did not get through all of wink, though he feels sane.

me: no i mean i need theology to justify my humor.

are you kidding i could spend days

Gusty: oh i get it. lol

The call and response of chat is always a bit out of sync, but the themes are there. We were so ready to blow up the narrow confines of Christian gender norms so that we could legitimately exist, but still so anxious. Beyond Barbie, we had also become aware of an ongoing attempt in a particular cultural setting to connect a religious practice of shamanism with Christianity, which we devolved into our own syncretism:

me: o. i thought maybe sham(e)ism.

was making a joke

ha ha ha ah

dummy

Gusty: ok, shameism … that is funny. let's make our own theology … shameism

me: yes!!!

all our own

Gusty: we can be the first shameists

me: lol

Gusty: anyone who does not admit to shame cannot be saved.

    me: lol

        you type faster and so you get the one liners before me

        stop that

Gusty: they definitely can't be leaders …

        maybe not members …

    me: well they can't lead other shameists

Gusty: can't take communion …

    me: :)

        let's write a book and see if we get rich

Gusty: we could make our bible start with … what book?

        yes … i think we are on to something big here. tell everyone
        that to swim in shame is their salvation

    me: we are in. finally a club that wants us

Gusty: yes … one that we can dominate!

    me: i'll call later

        yes we are the best

Gusty: k.

    me: bye

Gusty: bye!

Though we displayed confidence to the outside world, we clung to each other to stay afloat in our shared sea of shame. Shame about being the wrong kind of people, about having our insides so heretically incongruent with our exteriors, about not conforming, about making men confused and uncomfortable, about swimming illegitimately in someone else's private pool of privilege.

A month later:

Gusty: u there?

    me: going crazy. Didn't know an assignment due a few days
        ago :)

Gusty: uh oh ... but i might have to talk later. Read stupid blogs about gay stuff that totally depressed me

me: you didn't tell me you needed to talk.

oooowwwwww

sorry

Gusty: It always shocks me to read people who think it is not compatible to love Jesus and be gay.

ok back to your work. back to my trinitarians ...

me: look at you queen of intimacy.

i say, ooohhh sorry and you say, back to work

hmmnm

Gusty: i am queen aren't I ... ooh, didn't mean that either.

just didn't mean to pull you into convo when you need to work!

me: :)

Gusty: so lets touch base later

me: come and work til 3 and then we'll walk

Gusty: its like we are aliens from another planet that has nothing in common with the rest of humanity. ok - thanks!

Gusty and me taking on the world, conquering gender-based prejudice, while every day being beaten down by The Man. Gusty would connect me to gay-friendly thought leaders and writers like Chad Holtz, Andrew Marin, Tony Jones, and others, and we'd be mutually cheered! But then we'd be smacked back by the rageful Grudems and Pipers and the less overt but still condemning leaders from our own movement. There was *no* safe space for her—not with me, not even with herself—because even within our humor-shielded cone of commiseration, neither of us were sure. All of which meant that Gusty and I had to work really hard, just like me with my staff, and the staff with our leaders, and the leaders with our church, on our us-ness:

Gusty: Do you feel bad about the conversation? *[I have no idea what this conversation was]*

me: well, he was nice and it was unclear where he lands … so i felt like i was talking like i know what i'm talking about or where he lands and

i have no idea …

more that i get messed up when i talk cuz i can't tell what i

feel/think. not about gay issue, but about my engagement with the issues!

maybe i know my angry engagement and can articulate, but, not my mature engagement.???? :)

Gusty: Ahh … i can't tell so I think im nervous about voicing an opinion so I don't mess you up!

me: maybe when you don't voice i get messed up. easier to engage and fine having diff response. but when you are quiet, i ramble like an idiot!!!! and then feel crazy :)

Gusty: K … i just know I'm probably feeling lots of angst and worry so feel ashamed because I know you are trying to not displease the Holy Spirit and I'm not so sensitive to that these days!

me: do i put you in a weird place? i'm sensitive to not wanting to mess you up and you're sensitive to not wanting to mess me up. lol

i just love you regardless.

My God did we make the Godhead fragile! In our evangelical Christian world, it wasn't just me or Gusty or our leaders or theologians, but Jesus too, and the Father, and the Holy Spirit—all these Big Religious Heterosexual Male Deities—who were freaked by any whispered hint of our disquiet surrounding the LGBTQ plight. One cryptic Pauline reference to God experiencing humanlike sadness—*don't grieve the Holy Spirit*—comes back to us heavy and ominous and laden with threat, and somehow related to queerness! It's like God is a cantankerous old-timer deriding our entitlement—*I never got to choose my orientation! Just shut up and use your gonads in the way I intended or I'll take 'em away altogether!* How did we so lose our minds?

Tom:

During her Fuller years, Adey would spend two weeks each spring and fall on campus in Pasadena. I'd fly out to her on Thursday and back to Iowa on Monday. We'd go for the weekend to the redwoods or the back side of the Sierra Nevadas or up the Big Sur coast. But one of these weekends found Adey and me eating dinner with Gusty somewhere near L.A. The weather was California nice—breezy, warm, softly bright. Iowa and Evanston, and Vineyard, and conservatism, were orbiting some other sun. We were peaceful and alone with just ourselves as we chatted after dinner.

Gusty had become … interested in someone. She asked Adey and me, "If I found someone I loved, would you marry us?"

We both said, "Yes, we would!"

I think we were all a bit surprised by the ease of our assertion. And our noble sentiment, to be clear, would remain sentimental for years to come. But Adey's harangues down Newport Road had flipped my Jesus, and now here a flesh and blood lesbian woman friend in front of us who more faithfully loved Jesus than we ever would, had worked their magic. We could not for the evangelical life of us perceive displeasure from Jesus in blessing a love relationship for Gusty.

Love the Innocent Victim

Here's our first Jesus story. We came to see his person and agenda quite differently as our turn toward inclusion unfolded. He was more attuned to systems and privilege than we had previously perceived, tearing down temples of the status quo at every turn. He relentlessly centered innocent victims while marginalizing power. We pay close attention to how we think the Jesus interactions might have been experienced in the moment by the participants—what they would have felt and thought and remembered—as a window into meaning. So we start not by looking for a solution to a problem, or an answer to a question, or a singular lesson, but rather for the effect that Jesus seems to have wanted to produce on the human beings present in the moment.

Why Wasn't I Invited?

Religious people looking from the outside in at the revelries of Jesus are often stricken with ambivalence. Every one of his parties is heretical and wrong and violates all that's decent—*call the police!*—but they look so fun. And at every one there's the nagging whiff of a hint of a possibility that God might just be in there.

So with this story. Just returned home from an awesome road trip with God, Jesus and his friends whoop it up while the religious experts glower indignantly from the other side of the public square. One of them finally calls Jesus out—*Hey, how can you exclude me from your party while letting those sinners in?* Jesus answers with a question that turns the examiner into the examined, and then tells a story that turns all notions of goodness and Godness inside out. And at the end, there's violence. 😈

Luke 10: 17-37

The friends came back ecstatic. "Jesus," they said, "when we channeled you, we dominated!" Jesus said, "I know! While you were out, I felt the whole corrupt system shatter. I have given you power so that you can crush every threat that comes your way without you getting harmed at all. Snakes, scorpions, whatever! You could walk over them barefoot and come away untouched. But," he added, "don't lose your heads over your new power. Be excited instead about your inclusion with God."

Then Jesus, caught up in it all himself, shouted out: "Father— God of Everything—what is most awesome is how you've concealed that you are doing from the best and the brightest but revealed it to infants! Just exactly how you planned it all along."

"And I know that this is true," Jesus said, turning to his friends, "because God has entrusted me with All Things. You see, no one really gets who I am except for God, and no one really gets who God is except for me and those I help to see—like you! You have no idea how many royal and religious men wanted to see what you are now seeing, but didn't, and wanted to hear what you are now hearing, but never did."

Just then an Expert in Theology interrupted, standing up to test Jesus by saying, "Teacher, what must I do to have this God-quality of life come to me?" Jesus said, "How do you read what's written in the text?" The Expert said, "'You shall love the Lord Your God with all your heart and with all your soul and with all your strength and with all your mind, and your neighbor as yourself!'" "You have given the correct answer," said Jesus. "Do this and you will live."

But wanting to justify himself, the Expert said to Jesus, "And who is my 'neighbor'?" Taking up that question, Jesus said: "A man was going down from Jerusalem to Jericho when he was ambushed by bandits who, having both stripped him naked and beaten him severely, went on their way leaving him half dead. Just by chance, a priest was going down that road; but when he saw the victim, he passed by on the opposite side. Likewise a pastor came to that spot, but he too crossed to the opposite side and kept on going.

By contrast, a Samaritan who was traveling came upon him, and when he saw the victim, he was moved by compassion. So he approached him, put oil and wine on his wounds, and bandaged them. Then he set the man on his own donkey, brought him to an inn, and took care of him. The next day, he took out a few hundred dollars, gave them to the innkeeper and said, 'Take care of him; and if you spend more than this, I'll pay you back when I return.'

Of these three, which one seems to you to have become a 'neighbor' to the man ambushed by the bandits?" The Expert answered, "The one who showed compassion toward him." Jesus said to him, "You go and do likewise."

∽

Jesus had sent seventy-two Jesuses-in-training to nearby towns on a trial run of doing Jesus things, and those things had gone well. So the Jesus teammates, now back together, are high-fiving and strutting touchdown dances while deriding the suddenly shorn-of-horns Satan and his minions. Even Jesus is excited, but in the typical Jesus kind of way: "God, I thank you because you concealed these things from the intelligent and educated, yet revealed them to infants."

Ouch.

When Jesus dispenses praise, no one escapes unscathed. Intelligence and education—meaning here religious education—do not appear, according to Jesus, to get you into whatever God-Thing is being celebrated, even though children get in! The word of diminishing that Jesus uses, "infants," to identify his friends has connotations of baby, immature, uneducated. *Hooray for us!* shout the disciples … *we think*. The infants are seeing and are therefore blessed, while the "adults" are blind and left out. And it is precisely who gets into the big God-Thing and who does not, even more than the thing itself, that most exhilarates Jesus—a good start for a story about inclusion.

And so the Expert in Theology intrudes:

> Just then an expert in religious law stood up to try and trap Jesus by asking, "Teacher, what should I do to obtain eternal life?"

So two intertwined agendas. First is "I": What should "I" do—in contrast to *them*. The Expert sees that the disciples have latched onto a connection to God that represents his much sought after eternal life. He definitely wants what they have, but can't for the life of him discern how they've qualified for it, so his question: *Teacher, what must **I** do to obtain this most sought after thing that **they've** somehow got?* But the Expert is not just personally curious. He's also, the author tells us, setting a trap for Jesus. We're not privy to how Luke knows this, nor to how the question contains a trap. Whether eternal life existed, much less how you got there, was a charged question of controversy very much in play at the time, so maybe any answer from Jesus could have been twisted against him. But rather than answering, Jesus parries the question with a question: You're the Expert—what do you think?

And it works! The man, given the opportunity to shine, steps up to the lectern and gives a good, full-throated, complete, sonorous, educated answer:

> "You are to love Adonai your God with all your heart, with all your soul, with all your strength and with all your understanding; and your neighbor as yourself."

And, according to the Teacher, he's correct:

> "That's the right answer," Jesus said. "Do this, and you will have life."

And so the Expert smiles. He gives Jesus a collegial nod, steps down, and strides magnanimously from the courtyard. Everyone exhales the tension of the confrontation, and the celebrants return to their revelries. Except that he doesn't, and so they don't. Jesus, after the Expert's answer, seems good to go. But the Expert? Not so much. It's confusing. The Expert is exonerated and has impressed, yet he persists:

> "And who is my 'neighbor'?"

The air quotes come from the Complete Jewish Bible. Not all translations have them, but they help me hear the Expert's hint of sarcasm: *"neighbor?"* But puzzlingly, the Expert is himself raising this question about himself. Jesus, after all, has not used the word neighbor; he hasn't yet, in fact, produced any meaningful content at all. Helpfully, Luke is again in the Expert's mind: *He wanted to justify himself.* It's as if the Expert feels himself to be on trial, but then becomes the prosecuting attorney and says to the judge, "I now call to the witness stand—myself!" And he asks himself a question to which a 3-year-old could produce the correct answer:

Q: Who is my neighbor?

A: Umm, the person next to you.

Right? It's not hard. *Neighbor: a person in close proximity to you.*

But apparently this man has developed an alternate definition of "neighbor" that he can employ whenever he does not want to love the one who is next to him. Because instead of diminishing what it means to "love," he's modifying "neighbor," making it 99.9% likely that his preferred definition for "neighbor" is based not on geographic proximity but on identity proximity—religion, wealth, ethnicity, or some sweet spot at the convergence of all of these. The Expert has welcomed into an exclusive club known as "My Neighbors" all those who are like him, while excluding most everyone else, and he wants Jesus to help him justify that practice.

To contend with which, Jesus tells a story. But he's not been paying attention, because his story answers the wrong question. His story transmutes *And who is my "neighbor"?* into "Which person behaves as a neighbor to a needy not-my-neighbor?" Answering is again easily in our 3-year-old's wheelhouse: "The one who helped." But it's the wrong question! The Expert poses his question assuming that he, from his own stable identity, is selecting an acceptable neighbor from amongst a few possibilities. But in Jesus' story, the stable identity is that of the needy victim of violence. Jesus centers on someone who is not the Expert, and then asks the Expert to imagine three people who encounter this brutalized other and to choose, based on their responses, which one best exemplifies God's ethic of neighborliness. So rather than answering the question of the Expert—*Who is my "neighbor"?* Jesus instead asks the Expert to answer a completely different question: *What constitutes Godly neighborliness toward an Other who is not-my-neighbor?*

Jesus ratchets up the confusion with a second form of messing. The Expert would expect to be the hero of any story in which he appears—as would his townspeople—due in large part to all the awesome components of his identity: male, intelligent, educated, wealthy, religious, heterosexual, probably married, elite. But Jesus does not permit that identity to be a hero in the story. It is instead a practice of Jesus to force those who consider their identities to be heroic to come to perceive reviled identities as being just as capable of heroism, and to enter into those reviled identities. To his disciples who want to learn to pray he says: *Imagine a widow* ... To elite men of the religious establishment: *Imagine a woman who's lost a coin* ... *Imagine a farmhand who's lost a sheep* ... To self-righteous pastors: *Imagine a tax collector* ... *Imagine a sinner* ... *Imagine an embezzler* ... And so to this Expert in Theology:

Imagine a Samaritan.

While the Samaritans and the Hebrew people had in the distant past practiced religion together, they had long ago parted ways. They had each in the eyes of the other come to worship Yahweh in the wrong way in the wrong place, they had married the wrong people, and they had made political and military alliances that betrayed each other. To outsiders, Judeans and Samaritans were nearly identical, like religious twins. But for the rivals themselves such identicalness was intolerable, so each had turned the Other into a monster. Which unfamiliar Other Jesus now wants the Judaean Expert to inhabit.

I experienced a taste of this while listening to my wife and some other women from our church talk about Mother God. Adey had brought together in a friend's living room about twenty of our women parishioners to talk about their growing dissatisfaction with their inability to see themselves imaged in God because of the patriarchy of, well, of everything. One friend after another—Ali, Katie, Sonya, Adey, Megan—described the constraint and limitation they felt in having God depicted through exclusively male terms and images that implied that femaleness could not embody God.

Because therapy has been helpful to me, I mostly just listened. As a result I, for the first time, perceived the unbalanced genderedness of the Father-Son-Holy Spirit (that's evangelically also a man) triumvirate of Maleness. I began to detect more of the feminine/maternal/woman/female in God. I imagined talking to God in new ways that my friends were describing, and I had an immediate sense of God opening to me desirable aspects of her being that I had kept at bay by my self-serving commitment to her maleness.

So, lovely for me. But what Cory and Megan and Adey were also wanting from me was that I stop using my power to constrain for others permissible conceptions of how Goodness might be imaged within the Godhead. To stop packaging God in exclusively male containers. Females and femininity, and non-binary bodies and fluid genderedness, can profoundly image God and please God and contain Goodness.

So to the Expert, Jesus suggests as a candidate for heroically embodying Goodness a Samaritan. Jesus is saying that a Samaritan can be "moved with compassion" to produce care for victims in a way that faithfully fulfills God's definition of neighborliness *just as well as anyone else*, including an Expert in God's religion. A Samaritan is a God-loved type of human being through whom God joyfully and effectually loves other human beings. And to Adey and me and our conservative heteronormative church, Jesus was saying:

> There once was a trans person who came upon and cared for a young woman beaten and left for dead by the side of the road …

Violence

So, we could now be done with this story. Jesus challenges the theological expert back then as I think he would challenge evangelicalism today. We Christians are invited to imagine ourselves as Them not just to produce empathy with their sad plight, but also to cause us to perceive the goodness of God that is in them but not in us, and that God wants to be expressed and emulated through them in our midst. That would be a nice closing thought.

But remember earlier how Jesus was ready to be done with the conversation, but the Expert in Theology kept him in it? Well, I was ready to be done with this story, but someone kept me in it, a central someone, a someone who has no name. The gospel writer is describing a conversation that occurred in a public space. A crowd watches, riveted, as their Big Expert tries to assert dominance over the outsider Jesus. To counter, Jesus zings a story back at the Expert in which a central character, the one who provokes all of the story's action, is:

> A man stripped naked, beaten severely, and left half dead by the side of the road.

Wait—*what?*

A man stripped naked, beaten severely, and left half dead by the side of the road.

How did I miss that? How is it that I haven't yet paid attention to that man stripped naked, beaten severely, and left half dead by the side of the road? To that nameless man, that innocent victim of violence, dropped by Jesus in front of the Expert and the crowd. That's gotta mean something, right? Or at least produce something beyond content, like, I don't know, a feeling of shock or horror, or an audible gasp!

In the Sunday school lessons of my youth, the man stripped naked, beaten severely, and left half dead by the side of the road was a non-person, dismissed as the foil Jesus used to make a point. *Everyone listening to Jesus knew that the Jericho road was dangerous,* we were taught, as if that explained something, sort of implying that the man's victimization was at least in part his fault. But this story is not the Jesus AAA travel guide to the highways and byways of Judea. Jesus is centering a person. And as such, he could have brought into our public square dozens of non-brutalized persons who nonetheless tugged on our heart strings: an elderly man at a crosswalk, a traveler looking lost, a single mom carrying out her groceries, fans of the Cleveland Browns. If the point was, "Be nice to mildly troubled people who cross your path," Jesus would have done better placing someone less charged, like without nakedness and bludgeoning, at the center of his story.

And he would have known that! Because beyond all the miracle stuff, Jesus was a savvy orator. He would have known that once you utter certain words, like naked or bloody or dead, listeners hear nothing else. He often talks about pleasant things like flowers and birds, but elsewhere he says, "Eat my flesh and drink my blood!" He knows what he's doing:

> A man was going down from Jerusalem to Jericho when he was attacked by robbers. They stripped him naked and beat him up, then went off, leaving him half dead.

Jesus is showing us not just how to be neighborly, but also forcing us to face the real presence of violence in our midst, and our aversive reaction to that violence. All the religionists in the story, when they encounter our nameless victim of violence, recoil and cross to the other side of the road. And all victims of violence know this—that just by having been victimized, particularly if the victimization is perceptible, they are stigmatized. They become humans from whom the rest of us recoil.

Our problem is that we treat these words of violence from Jesus like a jellyfish. We lift them up out of their context and plop them onto the beach for examination, where they turn to harmless gelatinous mush. When floating in the saltwater depths of their oceans, the words are beautiful and structured and tentacled and poisonous. Once on shore, however, they collapse from three dimensions to two, becoming squishy things that we jiggle with our toes. And while there are lots of potential contextual oceans to give shape to these words of Jesus—first century Judaism, eastern Mediterranean culture, Roman rule—threatened male religious power is front and center. And once you let that be the case, this open air confrontation from two-thousand-plus years ago shifts from being a sweet lesson on neighborliness to something far more sinister and explosive and seething and destructive, something like an old time Western showdown, the sheriff and the outlaw (which is which?) staring each other down flinty-eyed, hands twitching at their verbal holsters, tumbleweeds blowing by, children scurrying under porches, high reedy music on the soundtrack ...

Let's go through it one more time.

The religious establishment sees a group of unqualified reprobates reveling in favored status with God and cries foul. The Reveler-in-Chief says to the establishment's sheriff—there, there, just keep doing what you and your friends have been doing all along, and we'll all be fine. But the sheriff feels, underneath this sardonic mollification, seismic tremors of destruction threatening to crumble the structure of his life, and so he yells, "Don't mess with my temple!" To which the Reveler-in-Chief retorts, "To protect the sanctity of your precious temple, you beat innocent victims to a bloody pulp and coldly abandon them in the ditches, recoiling from them in disgust when they sully your path, when you should instead be healing them and bathing them and carrying them and feeding them and housing them and paying their exorbitant medical bills. A 3-year-old child would do better than you! And now you want to kill me too!"

"Damn right, you blaspheming renegade," snarls the sheriff. "Now's not the time, but we'll get you. Watch your back because we're gonna string you up."

The Parable of the Brutalized Innocent

So, "The Parable of the Good Samaritan"? That moniker would seem to be yet one more obscuring misnomer courtesy of the patriarchy. Because while one man seethes hatefully, his victim lies dying. But it does what we who think of ourselves as good religious people want it to do—splits our violence off from us by helping us avoid having to see our system's indifferent murderousness. But don't be fooled: rage and threat on a cosmic scale are in that public square. Jesus scathingly indicts the failure of all the revered religious groups of his day to practice God's most fundamental rule describing how human beings are supposed to love each other. Meanwhile, a godless Samaritan loves a victim extravagantly, and shines. The qualified experts are denied the goal of their religiousness—eternal enjoyment of favorable standing with God—while the Samaritan is in.

And this outrage, I think, stokes the revilement that the conservative church directs toward LGBTQ individuals. This isn't just about me permitting people who are different from me admission to my religious club. This is about Jesus burning my club to the ground. I mean—if our religiousness does not get us in, then what have we been playing at? If queer people can enter the kingdom *as queer people, easily*, then what's the point of all our righteousness? It's hard enough for heteronormative people to qualify for admittance (or so we've been told). But the revelation of Jesus shows all our effortfulness to be vanity as he crumbles the walls of our beloved structure to a pile of dusty rubble: *intolerable!* We must instead expel the reprobates and kill Jesus.

As I read it, I do not think this confrontation ends amicably. The Expert does not protest Jesus's story of murder and mayhem as a metaphor for his attitude—*Hey, that's a bit harsh. How about "A senior needed help crossing the street?"* I imagine he hears Jesus saying to him, *Let's not pretend*, and he responds, *Okay*. As many have noted, the Expert cannot even bring himself at the end of it all to say "Samaritan," to acknowledge that such a one could be human, much less in the image of God.

But for the sake of hope, maybe some of those listening from the crowd heard. Perhaps some of those watching thought for the first time: *A Samaritan as Samaritan can please God—who knew? … Who are the neighbors sullying my path? … Who will help me when I've been beaten and left for dead by the side of the road?*

12

Church as a Tormented Teen

It was at *The Meeting* and *The Staff Meeting* that our church turned 13 years old developmentally. We couldn't for god's sake continue as a little toy replica of our evangelical parents, but who we were becoming was gangly and unfamiliar, with the sensibilities of our parents continuing to erupt out from within us against our very own heretical selves all the time. And we were desperate to control which identity was being expressed at any given moment. What voice would speak from our mouths would hinge completely on whoever was, or was imagined to be, listening.

～

Adey:

Here's me writing to David in late 2010. I had just listened to one of our members describing how he had explained us to his conservative pastor father:

> I'm sure we came off as those crazy intellectual, liberal emergents in Iowa City!!!!
>
> Ahhhhhhhhhhhhhhhhhh
>
> It's fighting an uphill battle. I can't control the kids. :) But we are not liberal! Emergents … intellectual … hmmm … well we do ask lots of questions, but, I think that's ok!!! :)

Ugh ...

Ahhhhhhhhhhh,

Heretical in IC

We tried so hard to control the descriptors of our identity. Intellectual sure, emergent maybe, yes we ask questions—*just don't call us liberal!* Fantastical or somatical or marsupial—but not liberal! Because conservative Christianity had created a monstrous entity called "liberalism" rife with sin and perversion and godlessness that we would be stamped with the instant we were nice to a queer person. And my *ahhhhhhhhh* was not even from experiencing anything directed directly at me, but from my imagining being confronted by a conservative pastor who I'd never met!

Tom:

A woman named Brinlee sent us an email of queer enquiry. She was single, in her early 30s, and looking for a church. She straightforwardly identified herself as lesbian, so before attending our church, she, like Alden and Katie, wanted to know our LGBTQ beliefs and practices. We still didn't have them yet—LBGTQ beliefs or practices—but I wrote to her confidently:

Dear Brinlee,

Thanks for your e-mail! Sorry it's taken us so long to respond— we're just getting caught up with normal life after Easter *[I hadn't known how to respond, so I had procrastinated]*. To answer your question, yes, gay people would be fully welcomed into the life of the church. The way you would experience that is that we are just welcoming *[I have no idea what this means; I'm just wanting to do the least amount of explaining that will still entice Brinlee to come]*. We, as a faith community, tend to resist taking formal positions on issues such as homosexuality and Christianity. We find that those usually are either divisive or serve to pigeon hole us into a stereotype that doesn't reflect who we are *[or they're accurate but produce a bad outcome]* and that deflects attention away from what we see as the central purpose of the church.

We welcome everyone in because we all equally need Jesus, and he certainly went out of his way to make sure that everyone who wanted could access him. Our primary goal is to help everyone who comes connect with Jesus, be transformed by him, and then go out and influence the world on his behalf *[so yes, I'm giving a mini teaching in response to a simple request for information]*. I'm sure this doesn't answer all your questions *[or any? or maybe it does]*, but maybe it's a start. What would be great is for you to come and check us out *[that never happened]*, and then my wife and I would be happy to get together with you and talk more *[neither did that]*.

Sincerely,

Tom Wassink

Uggh. While believing ourselves to be welcoming, we were still much more theologically conservative than we appreciated, anxious under the imagined gaze of our evangelical parents. What we say sounds sort of true and sort of noble, but the sort of "sort of" that lets you know we're hiding something. What I presented to Brinlee was an ethos of being above the fray, of not wanting to be co-opted by any of the many vituperative cultural combatants. But really we're just not yet comfortable with what we're coming to believe. We try to get by on kindness and effort, but our flummoxed-ness is brought into sharp relief when we have to actually explain ourselves to … anyone—parishioners, visitors, pets, the mirror.

But we try anyway because we know that if we can just get one homosexual person to come and stay *on our terms* then we're good! We can tell ourselves that we are welcoming without having become liberal. We'll heroize Brinlee with adulation and testimony opportunities while we bask in our rosy-glow awareness of how kind and righteous and validated we are.

The lie to all of which is revealed when, a few years hence, on the other side of our church's grand *Coming Out!*, we emblazon *Welcoming and Inclusive* at the top of our Values page on our website and put a rainbow sticker on our front door and tell any questioner before they even ask, "You are completely welcome here … no restrictions … we bless marriages and ordain!" because we've come to understand the necessity of this clarity for LGBTQ visitors.

But while Brinlee did not visit, David at right around the same time sent out this to us:

> btw, Ali went to a wedding of two women on saturday. They have a small farm, and the wedding food consisted of all local farm fare served on compostable plates. The service, Ali said, was beautiful and deeply spiritual/religious. She said it

reminded her a lot of our own wedding (!). She sensed God's presence during the service, which was both comforting and disturbing.

A Summer of Anxiety

Tom:

Then, in 2011, I had a Summer of Anxiety. My freedom-hungry soul was in torment. While my intellect had progressed, I needed to flip my viscera too from evangelical constraint to liberated queerness. Late one night, when visiting my childhood home in Michigan for a few days, I felt the atoms of my body wanting to explode out from me like the Emperor's enema'd Death Star. I said to Adey, "Let's go for a drive," and we somehow ended up in the parking lot of Maplewood Public Elementary School, where I was good little Tommy from kindergarten through sixth grade, playing kickball and doing my Scholastic Guided Reading. There I shouted my guts out for a while:

F--- you, Maplewood Elementary!!

F--- you, Holland Michigan!!

F--- you The Netherlands!!

F--- you Reformed Church in America!!

F--- you Calvin!!

F--- you Dutchness!!

F--- you tulips!!

F--- you Evangelicalism!!

I felt a little better, and was able to sleep that night. Adey drove us back to Iowa the next day, with me hyperventilating most of the way. Then, encouraged by Adey and David, I started seeing a spiritual director who is a retired Lutheran pastor. My first time with him, I blurged angst-ridden self-derision for about twenty minutes. When I took a breath, he said,

"Let's light a candle."

He did, and we were quiet, with our eyes closed, for about three minutes. He brought us back to awareness with a calm Lutheran-sounding prayer, opened his eyes, and said to me,

"You know, Tom, that God loves you. Just as you are."

"Yes, I know that."

"I don't think you do. There are so many 'shoulds' in your talk. So much about you that needs to be fixed. But God doesn't need anything about you to be other than what it is right now, at this moment. You are not a project to God. God's not waiting until you're better or right. God loves you completely, right now, if you never change, just as you are. The question is, do you?"

Well, when he put it that way … I did begin at that moment to let go just a little bit of my belief in God as a being who used threat to produce adherence. I've continued to see my Lutheran spiritual director every month since.

But Our Church is Ready

Adey:

In the fall of 2012, one of our young liberal (!) progressive parishioners sent me this:

> While I think it would be totally awesome to make it known that we welcome every person from every walk of life with open arms, I do worry that the Vineyard would get pigeonholed as "that church that has LGBT people" and the greater message would be buried … but I'm sure you all have thought of all this. That said, I would still support such a stance!

These dizzying sentiments—we have certainly now become, in our greater Iowa City community, "that church that has LGBT people," and "the greater message" is what exactly?—set the stage for the September 2012 arrival of Katie and Paula and their two boys. I sent some anxious questions to our good friend and compatriot in heresy Ken Wilson three weeks after we had met with Katie in my office because Ken was the icebreaker in whose wake we were following. He had started a church in Ann Arbor, Michigan in the 1980s that, like our progenitor church in Evanston, would eventually join the Vineyard. Like Adey, Ken had become a leader in the movement, with the two of them serving together for a few years in the 2010s on the steering committee of The Society of Vineyard Scholars; Ken was also a member of the National Board of Vineyard USA for his final seven years in the denomination. Which termination came because problematically, like us—though about ten years ahead of us—Ken had become disquieted by his and our denomination's LGBTQ exclusionary practices, which problem he compounded by talking about his disquiet and presenting papers about his disquiet at regional and national meetings and conferences. In the midst of and because of which we became friends and co-conspirators. Ken would leave Vineyard in 2014, about a year ahead of us, to launch the fully inclusive Blue Ocean Church of Ann Arbor, now pastored since Ken's retirement by co-founder and dear friend Emily Swan. But in 2012, as we were beginning to reap the consequences of our own disquiet, Ken was really the only credible person in our orbit who we could turn to for help. So I asked him some anxious questions:

> Ken, hi there,
>
> We have some folks worshiping with us who are gay. A man, and a married lesbian couple with kids. We are wondering what serving looks like in Ann Arbor. For instance, are your gay couples teaching in Sunday school? Are they leading small groups?
>
> Thanks Ken,
>
> Adey

Me asking the same questions about Katie that had been asked about me by men seemingly only yesterday. We also began probing again the sentiments of our members. Not all in a big hellish group this time, but one by one. We felt committed by then, as a leadership team, to becoming inclusive, but we wanted to know as much as we could about what we'd encounter from our folks. David, Tom, and I identified our core group, divvied up who would talk to whom, had the conversations, and then began to report back, all of which took a couple of months. I was nervous, but Tom was optimistic—and he turned out to be right, which made me hangry (happy and angry) as I wrote to Tom, David, and Leah in early November of 2012:

> Tom was right again, and I hate you!!!
>
> Talked with Emma. They have no ceilings … she doesn't feel the need to understand all the theology. She has a best friend, gay,

who got married and her life became better in every way and she became a better person, friend, etc. It compelled Emma ...

So, here is the list of folks I've talked to so far, all of whom have no ceiling:

[long list of families].

We still need to chat with [four or five families with conservative commitments who we knew were going to disagree].

So no surprise *No's* and a united core with whom to move forward. Which was good because Katie and Paula's lives improved, which they attributed to church, and so on Sunday, November 18th, 2012—less than three months after Katie's meeting with us in my office—the two of them attended an introduction to our church class, with Paula responding to the end-of-the-class questionnaire by saying that she'd like to become a member and serve on three Sunday morning teams and give financially and invite her friends and volunteer in the Kids' Wing and help with our service efforts and help with the teen group, and Katie saying that she'd like to become a member and join two Sunday morning teams and give financially and invite friends and volunteer in the Kids' Wing and help with our service efforts and launch a "Diversity committee if/when you want to tackle LGBTQ issues." I cried back then when David showed me their responses, and then I cried again when I read them for this writing.

But Katie Wonders If It's All Bogus

Adey:

Katie trusting us was reflected in direct and vulnerable questions that soon followed. I gave a message on a Sunday in December of 2012 that in some way referenced both homosexuality and addiction that launched an email conversation the next day:

> Adey,
>
> Hey, I had to breakdown your sermon again in my head, it was just so moving for me. I want to figure out how to reconcile who I KNOW that I am with what so many like me have been told by so many who speak for the "church" about the

"sin" that is homosexuality. The question is when reading the scripture, should I equate the prostitutes, the drug addicts, the tax collectors with being gay? I know in some sense that one point of the story is that Jesus befriended those on the fringe of society, and thus it makes sense. But I keep getting stuck at the part about praying for drug addicts and they miraculously give up their addiction and repent and prostitutes finding the Lord and changing their lives ... what about the gay person? The traditional reading (and practice) of the church is to love this sinner as well and hope they repent and give up their unnatural lifestyle and follow Jesus and become straight! So help me out if you would :) I know that I need Jesus in my life more than ever, but I have to be able to answer these questions to truly open my heart to His presence.

I realized in the writing of this book seven years later, with Katie's help, that I had completely misunderstood what she was asking. Tom and I were still inhabiting evangelicalism's concepts of sin and moral responsibility. My first out loud question about queerness four years prior had been, "Do you think that homosexual sex is sin?" which was where I assumed everyone began their queer-Christian wrestling. So to reassure Katie, I responded:

Hi Katie,

We DO NOT think of being gay as sin!!!! I in no way intended to communicate that. Just the opposite. So, I'm sorry to have confused you. I will happily talk scripture and the different ways people interpret. Does this help? No bait and switch. We just love you. I will, if you like, share my own journey with this issue with you. Thank you for asking me about this right away. My point was that all of us are sinners. I never intended in anyway to communicate being gay as sin. I mentioned gay only to help normalize it to our congregation. My hope was to communicate the opposite.

To which Katie quickly responded:

Adey,

Hey, thanks for the prompt response. It was more my interpretation as opposed to your preaching. I know how you feel and all of the pastors for that matter. I just want to be able to make sense of it for myself. I want to feel like I am reading the passages and not looking through rose colored glasses to make it fit my world, but to genuinely feel really really good and comfortable about it. I know how you feel and that you do not think being gay is a sin. I know it was not your intent and I don't think that it was implied at all. It is more of my really trying to delve into it and come out on the other side feeling secure. Be in touch soon.

Katie:

As I read this again, I think what Adey missed, as she notes, is that I was not at all questioning if being gay was a sin. My wrestling was instead that Jesus had turned my life around and welcomed me into this awesome church, and thus I really had this profound reason to believe. But on the other hand, if the only interpretation I could make sense of from the Bible told me that being gay was a sin, then I could never really be all in for Jesus. It was a deal breaker for me. If I couldn't have made sense of it, I would have checked out. The option was never to stop being gay if the Bible said it was a sin; the only option then was to give up on Christianity because the whole thing must be bogus and Jesus wasn't it. I honestly don't think I ever doubted who I was or that a divine power out there was working for good in my life and loved me. I was just trying to determine if it was in fact Jesus.

And whatever my misgivings about Adey's message, I finished by telling her how much I loved experiencing myself being lovingly represented in her messages:

> And let me be clear that hearing a sermon inclusive of all people and actually hearing the pastor use the words and the stories of gay people NEEDS to be done. I agree that it normalizes it for the congregation, but it also validates the lives of those gay folks sitting in the seats too. It is like finally seeing yourself or someone like you on television or in the movies—it creates this sense that you are not alone and there is a larger community out there. I couldn't get enough of Queer as Folk, Will and Grace, The L Word, and now Glee and just about every other hit show thankfully which includes at least the token gay :) Seeing your stories, struggles, and angst play out on TV or hearing them on Sunday morning just makes it real. And that is important in a

community that has been forced to be silent about who they really are, especially in the church.

But She Still Loves Us

Adey:

Two months later—so less than five months after the meeting in my office—Katie and Paula formally became members during a church service on January 13, 2013. I sent them an email to set up a celebration dinner, to which Katie responded:

> We are both so thankful to you and Tom and the rest of the staff and the church. Our good friend from out of town was in last night and we talked about church and she mentioned how she thought she had found a place that felt good to her until there was a sermon about the sin of interpreting the bible to fit your lifestyle, including "unnatural sexual lifestyles." She walked out of church with tears streaming down her face before the service was over and hasn't really been back since. It is so amazing to have found a place that I can call home and can continue to break down the resistance that I had put up in an attempt to protect myself.

A week later, I wrote to Katie and Paula:

> Hi friends,
>
> I am teaching next week on "Can Church Help?" so, I thought I'd ask you the question: has church helped you in any way? If so, would you be so kind as to take a moment and write a few sentences as to how. If I am able to use your responses I will keep them anonymous!

To which they responded:

> PAULA:
>
> YES!!

- Church has given me support by listening, understanding, accepting and praying with me
- Church has given me options to get involved with fun small groups and volunteering
- Church has given me things to look forward to (Sunday mornings and mission trips)
- Church has given me a community of people I connect with and look forward to becoming friends with

KATIE:

If you already wrote your teaching I am sorry this is late :)

I keep looking at this question and thinking that it is rhetorical because yes of course church has helped! Church—actually being at church and worshipping and listening and praying and taking communion—fills me with great hope. I think it gives my wife hope too because she is always extra nice to me on sundays :) I told paula yesterday that for our sakes I wish we had church everyday. She agreed :)

But really though, THIS church is where it all began for me. I was definitely in the, "I believe in God, but not organized religion" crowd, because I associated organized religion with judgement and pain and exclusion. It was actually getting in the door and doing church that made me realize what I was missing when I thought I could do it all on my own before.

It couldn't possibly get better, right? Sentiments that I, as a pastor, would fantasize to hear—*church gives me hope … gives me friends … things to look forward to*—and completely uncoached! If we'd been doing church only for Katie and Paula and Will and Parker, it would have been totally worth it.

Emerson Thinks Adey is the Bomb

The Sunday Katie and Paula became members, Emerson came to church. He'd sent me an email just a short time previously asking if I would meet with *him* (Emerson's chosen pronoun). He said he was 17 years old, had just come out to his family, and had immediately been asked to step down from worship-leading in his church. Then someone had told him about the nice accepting pastor lady an hour away in Iowa City.

Emerson told me about himself over a coffee date. He attributed some of his "confusion" to rather bizarre behavior he experienced growing up in his alcoholic home, but I also felt his sense of the inadequacy of environment as an explanation. He said it was hard for him to define his sexuality. He searched my face for judgment when he said to me, "Adey, you know when you go to the doctor and you fill out your forms and you are given one box that says 'M' for male and one that says 'F' for female, and you have to check one? I am the air outside the boxes."

I was confused by what he meant (it took Katie to help: "Adey, Emerson might exist somewhere under the trans umbrella."), but something in my heart was forever changed. While Emerson stretched my notions of gender and sexuality towards a different realm of non-categoricalness, he himself was just a sweet 17-year-old who I immediately loved. The moment he came out, he was cast out. But sitting in front of me, Emerson was not a number or statistic; he was a wonderful young person, with a story, and hopes and dreams, and an identity, trying to make his way in a hostile world.

I invited him to church, and he came the Sunday Katie and Paula were welcomed as members. I was busy afterwards, and so he wrote to me:

> Hi Adey,
>
> Just wanted to let you know that this past Sunday service was fantastic, and I look forward to seeing you all again! You are the bomb! I went to go say hi to you before I left, but you were with a group of women, and looked like you were having a moment. So I let (Tom?) know that I wanted to say hi to you.
>
> See you all again soon!
>
> Emerson

I am the bomb! Swoon.

Tom and I had Emerson over for dinner. He came for coffee with me and Katie. But an hour to and from church is a long drive, particularly if you hope for friendship. Emerson said as much in an email somewhere around June of that year, and we have not seen or heard from him since. But whatever we did for him, Emerson had awakened me to yet one more expression of sexuality and gender. I found myself praying for every trans person in our vicinity who was hungering for a Jesus connection to find their way to us.

13

Tracy and Luke

Tracy and Luke came to Iowa City straight out of college from downstate Illinois in the early 2000s so that Luke could be our youth pastor. Luke's dad was a successful pastor of a large Vineyard church, and Tracy and Luke had both been longtime attenders of a Vineyard in Illinois and had envisioned ministry in their futures. They were an easy fit for our church because they were younger versions of Tom and me.

But things over the years had not flowed straight. Luke had found after a couple years on staff that pastoring wasn't for him, and so he'd jumped over to education and was now a beloved teacher at our local high school. Tracy, meanwhile, had begun to go after becoming a physician assistant. All well and good. But when in 2005 the Vineyard national director and board formally stated their support for women as leaders, seventy churches, including Tracy and Luke's Illinois Vineyard church, left the movement. And then our church began to lean towards inclusion …

⇝

Tracy: I was nervous all the time.

Adey: Which is saying something, because you're the most consistently happy person I know!

Tracy: Yes, but this was right before *The Meeting*, and I had just had a looonnng conversation with my very best friend from high school—who told me he was gay. And then I saw him soon after at our high school reunion, the winter of 2009. He was there with his partner. I loved him, but I was so freaked out. We had no diversity in my hometown, at all. A "racial" couple moved into town once, and racial slurs were pretty quickly everywhere—on the walls, in the air. And it worked—the racial couple moved out.

Tom: We must have grown up in the same town. For us, queerness was so suppressed that gay didn't exist.

Tracy: Yes! Oh my God, we knew it was wrong, but it was so beyond wrong that a person would never actually be gay—we couldn't even conceive of a person being it. But Jeremy was. And he had known it, all through high school. And he never told me. He had realized it by the time he was 13; it probably would have come to him sooner if it hadn't been wrong. I just felt so sad—I said to him, "I'm so sorry that you were carrying that through all our high school years, alone."

Adey: So how did that affect you?

Tracy: It threw me into crisis. The only construct I had at that time was: You need to change that to be part of the church! We are assuming that, if you start coming here, God will somehow move you from being gay to being not gay. That's what it was like in my home church, and even though here we were about to have *The Meeting*, that's what it was still like there.

Luke: *[laughing]* Oh man, I remember *The Meeting*, with afterwards you, Tom, saying, "We're never doing that again!"

Tracy: Oh, it was awful! Jeremy had tried Living Waters, and it didn't work. So I started reading *Love is an Orientation* by Andrew Marin. He was really helpful. He was super nice, and safe, and still—at least then—conservative. And his experiences in the book were just like mine: friend after friend, *Oh no—not you too!!*

Adey: I remember reading him too. Back then we thought he was radical by being friendly and welcoming—but not affirming! We weren't ready for that yet. Just having open interactions was radical.

Luke: I didn't have friends who were gay, so as our church here started asking questions, I began worrying about things like: If we say this is okay, then what is sin? Is sin even important anymore? Are we just sliding into moral relativism? Just trying to be good people, but nothing about truth matters? I needed to know what was right and what was wrong, because then I would know I was right. I needed everyone to come to Jesus the way I did, because that's how I felt good about myself, with all the boundaries and the in versus out. Being right was comforting, and so living in the gray area was awful. And I had worked so hard to get to Jesus!

[*becoming tearful*] I felt assurance because of all the work I'd done, because I did it the right way. And I'd think, was all that I've done for naught? If gay people have it so easy, if they're just welcomed, what did all my hard work mean? I had had all these fears pounded into my head—do XYZ for Jesus! I had so many belief structures in place. It was hard to be gracious. It felt threatening. They didn't deserve to have it so easy. I prayed a lot! How could God be so generous with them when I've worked so hard? I deserved it!

[*sighing*] I know now that all of that is not true—I knew it then, but I *KNOW* it now—that grace is real, and it's not my effort, and they had been shut out while I had been let in. But I resented their ease—and probably my effort. I hated the parable of the workers in the field.

Tracy: And so I came into *The Meeting* super raw and activated about Jeremy. His mom was panicking—maybe her husband had been gay!—and he had no one, no one to talk to, nowhere to go for help. So when we went around the circle to share where we were at with LGBTQ individuals, and welcoming and inclusion, and it got to me, I told his story. When I was done, it was quiet. Then someone in the circle said, in front of everyone, "I think God wants us to deal with our sexuality. He wants to transform us." I was uncomfortable with that and said, "I don't know anymore if I think God has an agenda for us like that." That's all, and I thought we were good, and the meeting went on, and I don't remember much else, though apparently it wasn't that great for Tom either—

Tom: True that.

Tracy: But I got a call later from that same person. She was upset because she felt that I had confronted her, or contradicted her, in the meeting, in front of everyone. We hung up and I was a mess, wanting in my heart to be progressive, but sad. Was I wrong for listening? For encouraging sin? Being loving? And what about Jeremy! I had no idea how to reconcile all of it theologically.

Adey: So given that we're sitting here now, friends all these years later, what was it for you both that got you through?

Luke: Being open to questions. You both, and David too, made it clear that you didn't know the right answer and weren't here to give us the right answer. You were uncertain. We didn't have to know. Like, we didn't go from one certainty to the next certainty. You know what I mean? We didn't go from being certain that homosexuality was wrong to being certain that homosexuality was right. And that was so different than anything we had experienced before in church, and so refreshing, and so freeing—it was the single biggest "thought" thing in us, feeling happy and alive and welcoming in this church.

And we got that that was the purpose of *The Meeting*. You weren't there to "hear our hearts," but then tell us the right answer. You weren't checking, like, the depth of our heresy so you could understand how much theological correction we needed. You just genuinely wanted to hear us, and to have us put our questions and uncertainty on display for each other.

Tom: Yeah, I think one of the things Adey and I had shed early on, without really even planning it, was the fear of questions. We had actually come to feel the opposite—afraid of certainty, mixed in with a hunger to live into unanswered, and perhaps unanswerable, questions. Which also meant that we'd stopped treating you as children, but instead as the adults you really were, with good and deep thoughts, who didn't want to be told what to think or do.

Tracy: When we'd find ourselves years later with those for whom certainty was still important, I'd say something like: "I'm glad you're confident about what's right. That's totally fine! But Luke and I ... well, we're just not so sure as we used to be." I thought I was being nice, trying my hardest to not be provocative, but wow!

Luke: Yeah. "What do you mean you're not sure?!?" they'd respond. "How can you not know? Scripture is clear!" But we weren't even arguing. We were just being *not sure*.

Tracy: And then there's Jeffrey. *[Jeffrey is Tracy and Luke's second child of four total. When Jeffrey was about a year old, he lost whatever speech he had developed up until then, and became less relational. He was subsequently diagnosed with an autism spectrum disorder.]*

Tracy: When Jeffrey was diagnosed we and both of our families began praying for a miracle. A miracle for Jeffrey. Complete healing, for him to be "normal" like he was supposed to be. We prayed, we fasted. We knew that God wanted him to be better, to be "fixed," to be healed. My parents, Luke's parents, us—that's how we understood God to work and to be, and what we knew we were supposed to do.

Luke: But then after, like, two years of this—and I mean my family was a praying miracle-believing family—so two years of daily praying from lots of Christians, the miracle happened. But the miracle was in *us*, in me and Tracy. Jeffrey didn't need to change—the miracle was God changing the perspective of our hearts. The miracle was God making us the parents we needed to be for Jeffrey. The work I have to do is to work on me. I'm the problem, and I've always been the problem. It's not what I can do for God, it's what God can do for me. God reveals to me the crap in the way I perceive the world wrongly. The daily work is Jesus revealing myself to me. "I'm going to do all the work," he says, "all you have to do is say yes!"

Tracy: So with LGBTQ, we had been praying for "them" to become straight, to be healed, but the miracle God wanted to do was in us. To change us. The conversation was always coming back to us, and what God was doing in us. We needed to change, we needed to be healed. We needed to re-understand concepts of identity and Jesus and belonging. God revealed so much of what was wrong with how we saw people.

Luke: And so we made friends. Not needing to be right made it so that we could just be friends with people. Get to know them. Go out to dinner. See them with their kids, and have them see us with ours. Seeing Jesus being kind to them, loving them, being fruitful through them. Knowing people who were gay and coming to church, and hearing them say, "Jesus is making my life better." Knowing the other makes them not the other anymore.

〜

Tom:

Tracy and Luke continue to be our dearly beloved friends and parishioners. And to state it clearly, their story of Jeffrey is yet another place where a group stands in for LGBTQ individuals not because both groups have problems, but because both groups are stigmatized by power which has the purview to declare normalcy. The conversation is not actually at all about flaws, like that both groups have flaws and so our attitudes about one group are applied to the other—we ought to be kind to *this* group with its flaws, because we're kind to *that* group which also has flaws. Rather, the path to goodness comes when we "normal" ones realize, through one group that we have diminished, that stigmatizing and excluding is a wrongness in us that needs to be universally repented of, and that celebration and inclusion for all are the only godly options towards all stigmatized groups.

14

Mim Is Going to Hell

Adey:

Mim has been a dear friend of our family for decades. She was given up at birth into the foster care system. As a young girl, Mim was adopted into a "Christian" family with a conservative Christian minister as father, who so spiritually and religiously abused her that she, as an adult, formally severed ties with them. Tom and I met her adoptive family just once, when they were visiting from out of town, and within seconds their toxic religiousness had pushed Tom closer to apoplexy than I'd ever seen in him. Mim was, many years later, adopted into a wonderful and loving evangelical family.

In her 20s, Mim had become a nurse and moved to the north side of Chicago. She attended a few churches over the years, eventually finding her way to the Vineyard church that Tom and I had joined in Evanston. She and I met there and we became friends for life.

Mim moved out to Iowa City in the early 2000s to help us grow our young church, and so has been with Sanctuary from nearly the beginning. She married a man from within our church when we were still a Vineyard, who we all loved and thought was great. But within a short time, it became apparent to Mim and me and Tom and others that he was not ready for marriage to a degree that made it unsafe for Mim to continue to be in a relationship with him, so she divorced him. We talked one evening through how Mim's personal religious journey connected with that of our church's toward inclusion ...

⌒

Mim: My initial reaction to thinking about inclusion was fear. I was afraid that we might be doing something bad, something contrary to scripture, and ultimately something against God.

Adey: Oh Mim, fear doesn't come close to what this whole thing has meant for you. Say again what church was like for you growing up.

Mim: Well, my first memory of church is of me standing like a statue, grabbing onto the church pew in front of me, white-knuckled. I was paralyzed with fear. I had just heard a sermon about *HELL!!!!* and I was pretty sure I was about to drop into an intense and painful fire, but I was too frightened to go up front for the altar call. I knew I was a sinner, unclean, undesirable, an "other," one of them instead of one of us. And I had just heard Bible verses shouted at me to whip me into shape and get me to run forward, but I was scared and I couldn't move! I was 6 years old.

Adey: So church for you was not a happy place?

Mim: No, it was not. My growing up years in the church were guilt, fear, and anxiety. I was petrified I would be shut out by the very people who told me how to live. I never felt safe and I rarely thought about Jesus. I was only conscious of rules from the Bible. My rule for life was to obey scripture—in my child's mind this equaled "love." The logic was something like: Sin equals rejection from my family, then from the church, and finally from God, which results in eternal damnation to hell.

Tom: That's a sad logic of love. Say more what you mean by "other."

Mim: Well, twice on Sundays, and every Wednesday evening, I heard how God hates sinners. We were taught from the pulpit which people were sinners, so that we could not be them and could keep away from them. It was like if we came into contact with them, we'd become dirty. They were easy to recognize—non-churchgoers, smokers, those who wore red nail polish, anyone who drank alcohol, went to movies, or wore immodest clothing. But the most horrible sin of all was having sex before marriage.

Adey: What about homosexuality? That had to have been worse.

Mim: Well, "sex before marriage" was in reference to heterosexual sex because homosexuality was so horrific that it didn't really exist. And so homosexual marriage wasn't even a consideration. But then when I moved away from home I slowly started to realize that my impressions of God,

Jesus, and scripture were askew. I was challenged to learn about mercy, love, forgiveness, context, acceptance … Jesus. I learned to feel safe in church, even vulnerable. I began to wear slacks to church, and eventually denim jeans. I went to movies, wore colored nail polish, drank alcoholic beverages, and was still a Christian. I was moving away from rules, toward relationships.

Tom: But Levi's and Sephora are still a long way from welcoming and inclusive!

Mim: Yes, absolutely! I still knew that some behaviors were wrong. So people could still be an "other" versus an "us" due to their actions. To me that was Truth, reinforced by scripture—a reality, not a judgment. My rules list had become kinder and gentler, but it still existed.

Adey: Then you came to Iowa City, which I think began to affect you in the same way that it did me and Tom, right?

Mim: Oh my gosh, yes! My first Iowa City neighbors were a lesbian couple. On the first day I moved in, they came over and offered me lawn tools. "Buying a home is expensive—feel free to use our stuff!" they said. Their loving, long-term relationship was an inspiration to me. I was single and saw something in them that I hoped to have one day. But I still felt guilty respecting and appreciating their relationship, because I knew it was not God-ordained. After all, scripture was clear about homosexuality. It was sin.

Adey: So what did you do? Did church help?

Mim: Not at first. Homosexuality hadn't yet touched me in church, so I left it in my non-church world. I ignored my questions, and had only a superficial relationship with my neighbors.

Tom: So if our church wasn't of much help, what happened?

Mim: Well, real life kept intruding and making a mess of my nice, neat, good-me bad-them categories.

Adey: Are you talking about your marriage?

Mim: Yes. Well, no. I'm talking about my divorce. As I grew more and more afraid of him [husband], I realized that I was probably going to become a divorced woman, which was a type of person that my entire Christian upbringing had told me to judge. But what most showed me that something was messed up with my Christianity was when I began to wish that my husband would be unfaithful to me in order to make getting a divorce scripturally justified!

And then, around the same time, I learned that a close friend of mine was a closeted homosexual. Her life was sad and stressful as she lived in two different worlds, wanting to follow Jesus, but feeling doomed to celibacy for life. I really began to wonder, how did the rules of God fit into these questions and real-life circumstances? I felt like life and friends and the craziness of what my faith had become loosened me up to be able to consider something different. I was ready to hear what the two of you and David had begun to talk about.

Tom: So what stands out as having helped you most in making the turn to where you are now?

Mim: The first thing, and probably the biggest, was just the freedom that we always had in Sanctuary to ask questions. You taught us to not be afraid of questions, even to like them! And our church made safe spaces for them, like in small groups. My small group was all about questions and conversation and discussion, without there being right answers at the end of a study. We could share ideas and thoughts, listen to podcasts from all sorts of sources, without feeling overwhelmed.

Adey: What were some of your questions?

Mim: I started with fear itself. What was I afraid of? Why was fear such a companion in my life? What was it about homosexuality that caused me to feel anxious in church? Why did I feel like homosexuality was a dark secret? Did I really believe a homosexual person could corrupt a child? Or that homosexuality could be "cured" or reversed if a person really loved Jesus? Voicing my fears out loud helped me realize their strangeness. And because I was doing it with people, I wasn't alone. I could voice my doubts and it would be okay. I didn't have to be "right."

And then leaving Vineyard was really huge for me.

Adey: Oh, I didn't know! Why was that so big?

Mim: It's kind of the same thing as with being able to ask questions. When we eventually left Vineyard—which had been my source of truth for most of my adult life—it was in part because of a difference in belief about welcoming and inclusion, but it was also about centered-set versus bounded-set and openness versus certainty. The concept that belonging is moving towards God, instead of being safely inside our rigid walls, was a new idea for me and it helped erase learned boundaries.

Don't get me wrong—it was still frightening! I remember being at a conference in a small group that Dave Schmelzer [the leader at that time of the

Blue Ocean group of churches] was leading, and I asked, "How can you live without the fear of rules, or without clearly defined boundaries?" The concept was so other. Could I really just trust Jesus to lead people? That did not seem very wise. What if they heard him wrong? What if I heard him wrong? And that's where your Sunday morning teachings did help.

Tom: Oh—do tell!

Mim: Tom was talking all the time about context for scripture stories, that you needed to understand the people and places of the stories to get the meaning, that you couldn't just pull out a verse to prove a point or claim a promise, and that there was very little in there that was universal, or one size fits all. And then you, Adey, talked so much about justice, and how church people had used the Bible to condone slavery and exclude divorced people, and you had your own story about how hard it was to be accepted in the church as a woman leader.

And all of it just seemed to come together in friendships. I became friends with a lesbian married woman who'd started coming to church, and who told me her story of how the church had hurt her. The moment she came out was one and the same with the moment she was no longer welcome in church. Her marriage was not a church marriage. I knew what it was like to be afraid in church and feel unwelcomed. That didn't seem like the Jesus in the scripture, and it wasn't how he treated me. So I let go of my anxiety, and I said I don't know all the answers, but I'm willing to learn.

15

Friend of "Sinners"

Tom:

Here's Jesus party #2. We again reconnect two linked stories that are typically separated, in which, again, religionists become angry while reviled persons are heroized. We witness here again scandalous interactions of Jesus with the sinfulness of sinners, through which he dissolves and reconstitutes the meanings of those terms so thoroughly that "sinner" rather than "righteous" is what in the end we all wanna be.

⤿

Luke 5:17

Large crowds were gathering together to hear Jesus and to be cured of their illnesses. When he returned to Capernaum after some days, word got out that he was at home. On one of those days, while he was teaching, there were pastors and priests and theologians in attendance (who had come from every village of Galilee and Judea and from Jerusalem). So many of them

gathered around that there was no longer room for anyone else,
not even in front of the door; and Jesus was speaking the word
to everyone. Just then some men came, carrying a paralyzed
friend on a stretcher. They were trying to lay him before Jesus,
but they found no way to bring him in because of the crowd ...

Well, damn. A sold-out show. We four of the proletariat have carried our
impoverished friend, because his crummy insurance didn't cover medical
transportation, all this way. But now that we're here we can't get close to
The Man because the visiting elite have commandeered all the good seats!
There's even my hometown priest, dressed to impress, front and center, with
his Grand Poobah to the left. But they don't need Jesus like we do! What to
do ... what to do ...

So they went up onto the roof, and having dug through it, they
let down their friend with his bed through the tiles into the
midst of the crowd in front of Jesus.

Okay—that's a novel approach. I try to imagine the thoughts associated
with the flip from a mopey departure to an activated assault on the literal
and metaphoric religious structures. As the friends are turning to leave, one
of them notices the earthen roof overhead, maybe sagging a bit, pregnant
with possibility. He nods upwards to the others—and it's beautiful. Roof
stuff flying as four men scrabble down through dirt and clay and sticks and
straw—not carefully—with all that crap pelting down onto the heads of
the pastors and priests below, who scatter as a stretcher carrying a paralytic,
followed by four breathless sweaty dusty men, plops down into the suddenly
vacated space in front of Jesus.

And as the dust settles, Jesus perceives something: "Jesus saw their faith."
Now I've since forever understood faith as a spiritual concept. Faith as a
belief that Jesus can do supernatural things, faith as an awareness that he's
kind and that he'll reward sincere efforts to seek his help. But faith in this
moment actually seems to be a bit more ... physical?

The palanquin bearers and their charge trust that Jesus will welcome them
even if (or because?) they demolish the religious structure of power as a necessary step in getting themselves close to him. They trust that Jesus will bless
them even though—or because—they assertively supplant the pastors and
priests and theologians in proximity to him. So their act of faith is, in the
end, a physical sacking of an actual house that symbolizes a spiritual sacking of a religious house, perhaps even providing Jesus himself with a whiff

of inspiration for a remodeling that he will soon visit upon the Jerusalem temple courtyard.

But right now Jesus, in this room, follows their lead, perpetrating his own form of mayhem:

> When Jesus saw their faith, he said to the paralyzed man, "Courage, son! Your sins are forgiven."

Woohoo! shouts the paralytic, just what I came for! And his jubilant friends hoist him up on his stretcher and carry him back home …

It's a legitimate question, right? Would the paralytic—and his weary friends—have been satisfied if the primary outcome of their effortful encounter with Jesus was him being carried away still paralyzed but with his sins apparently having been forgiven? Jesus seems to think they should be good to go, as he turns back to resume his lecture. The only reason the story plays out as it does is that Jesus detects negative thought vibes, though not from the still paralyzed man:

> Some pastors were sitting there, thinking to themselves, "Why does this fellow talk like that? He's blaspheming! Who can forgive sins but God alone?"

The religious leaders inwardly decry Jesus for having the hubris to wrest away from God control of human sinfulness. Though in truth, of course, Jesus is displacing not God, but them. God, after all, was not going to show up in person to adjudicate the absolution of the paralytic, nor of anyone. Fixing the big bad problem wrought by sin and sinfulness happened instead through God-rituals in God-places overseen by God-men. And this God-system was complicated. What counted as sin? How were sins categorized? What, in each instance, was sufficient recompense? And when did you get to use the smoky incense? The most powerful male intellects in the land devoted their entire lives to learning the intricacies of the God-sin-system, and then administering it.

But here was Jesus poofing all that away! No penance, no robes, no temple; no fear, no trembling, no smoke; and nothing notable about the man either. I remember studying this passage, and the many others like it, with my friends to try to identify what about this lucky man qualified him for this kindness from Jesus so that we could be sure to get it, too. Was it a marker of identity in him, or some admirable quality in his attitude or actions? But we could never find anything … because there was nothing to find—the

man remains completely unknown to the reader *and to Jesus*. He is not inter-
rogated by Jesus in any way, and he himself has not done anything—he
literally could not have done anything—to bring himself to this moment, to
qualify himself for the "generosity" of Jesus. The action of the story is Jesus
sending a complete stranger skipping away guilt-free after a brief and very
unorthodox encounter with him. And skipping only because of a well-if-
I-have-to miracle through which Jesus validates his sin-system dominance:

> "But so that you may know that the Son of Man has authority
> on earth to forgive sins"—Jesus said to the one who was
> paralyzed—"I say to you, stand up and take your bed and go to
> your home." Immediately he stood up before them, took what
> he had been lying on, and went to his home, glorifying God.

How authority in the physical domain validated it in the spiritual is not
made clear by Jesus, but who was going to argue? Jesus did whatever he
needed to do to commandeer his religion's sin-system so that he could liberally free people from it.

We readers tend to focus on the spectacle of the singular miracle, particularly us in the Vineyard with our Pentecostal bent. We marveled at the
rare and irreproducible physical event that benefited the one man, while
ignoring Jesus' seismic religious alteration that benefited all humans. But the
point of the story is not that this man was uniquely fortunate, nor that Jesus
was compassionately generous *toward this one man*. Instead this interaction
presents to the world how Jesus felt about the whole construct of sin and
forgiveness at the center of his religion, and what he was going to do about
that. The story is telling us that the healing was genuinely secondary, with
the main point to Jesus and to the religious establishment being Jesus's sup-
planting of their sin construct with his.

And so story #1 ends:

> Amazement seized all of them, and they glorified God and were
> filled with awe, saying, "We have seen strange things today."

Get ready for stranger …

Jesus exits the house, which is now demolition-prepped for *Extreme Makeover: Messiah Edition*, en fuego. What super-crazy thing will he do next? Strolling out into the sunlight of the Capernaum village square, he …

saw a publican by the name of Levi sitting at his tax booth.

Publican … *eww*. Capernaum appears to have been at this time home to both Jesus and Levi (aka Matthew). The town back then was, according to Christian scholars,

"located on the Northern shore of the Sea of Galilee."

"a town of approximately 1,000–1,500, though of some significance."

"a major trade and economic center in the North Galilean region."

I note the complete lack of irony in "of some significance" and "major trade and economic center." The Sea of Galilee sits in the rural northern hill country of Israel. Capernaum is on the north side of that sea. So North Galilee is like North Iowa or North Nevada or North North Dakota— empty, dry, the other side of nowhere. Is *though of some significance* stated because Jesus once lived there and so we Christians can't permit it to have been inconsequential? Because it's a pretty universal truism across human history that there are no towns of 1,000–1,500 "of some significance" unless someone important has left them.

The real significance for our story is familiarity. Everyone living in a town the size of Capernaum would have known everyone else living in that town *well*. My dad grew up in Hamilton, Michigan, a by-comparison megalopolis of 3,100. When I go back to visit, everyone there still remembers the Wassink boys (seven) and girl (one) roaming up and down the Rabbit River with their pellet guns, camping out on the banks, working at the Farm Bureau, populating the school, going to the (singular) church. Everyone saw everyone else almost every day.

So it seems not a stretch to imagine that Jesus and Levi knew each other. And while Jesus, on career day in high school a few years prior, because *Savior of the World* wasn't an option, chose "Whatever it Is My Dad Does," Levi had taken the path less traveled: "I think I'll become a publican." Publican is usually translated "tax collector," but that does not do its willful perfidy justice. A publican,

> was essentially a local public contractor hired by the Roman government to do a variety of services on their behalf. These services included the overseeing of public building projects; providing supplies to the military; and collecting all sorts of taxes from the people, which eventually became that most common function of a publican. During the time of Jesus, publicans were "outsourced" by legitimate tax collectors to do their work on their behalf. In return, the publican will add a kick-back that usually ranged from five to twelve percent additional to the actual legal tax.[2]

So Levi had become Judas before Judas was Judas. He was Benedict Arnold and Mata Hari; he was Roger Clemens to Red Sox fans. He extracted money from his compatriot God-fearing Judeans and gave it to the unclean oppressor gentile Romans, adding to the take however much he wanted to keep for himself. Because of which betrayal he is officially categorized in Judean society as a *them*: "Tax collectors and sinners." One who, because of his reprehensibility, is deemed irredeemably contaminated, banished from community, permitted contact only with other similarly castigated sinners.

So Jesus sees Levi sitting at his tax collection booth and pauses. Is this the moment of comeuppance? Jesus, sizzling with power, calling out Levi for his tormenting oppression of the locals—*Pack your bags and leave my town, traitorous dog!* with the crowd cheering him on. I mean, if Jesus wants to tear down systems of oppression, what better starting place than the acquisitive arm of Rome reaching through a Jewish man into rural Israel's pocketbooks? But instead,

> "Follow me," Jesus said to him, and Levi got up, left everything and followed him.

Well, that's ... weird.

The first thing "Follow me" tells us is that Jesus was continually on the lookout for more disciples. He had not yet filled the cabinet posts for his new religion, and so a standing agenda item on his internal task list was to scan all those he encountered for suitability. The second thing this "Follow

---

2 http://dumaguetemetropost.com/levi-the-publican-p3290-326.htm

me" tells us is that Jesus did not find any suitable candidates in the room he had just left that was packed with the best and brightest of his day's religionists. The third thing we learn is that Jesus did find a suitable candidate sitting alone in a solitary tax booth.

We as readers tend to accept people in the way that they are presented to us: a sinner is a sinner, a prostitute a prostitute, and a tax collector a tax collector. But Jesus is suspicious of labels, particularly labels of villainy, particularly labels of villainy affixed by a crowd. He distrusts terms of disparagement pinned onto one by the many. So maybe Levi was just genuinely greedy from the womb, but I wonder if Jesus knew of … *something*. A blemish, a mark of ignominy on Levi's person or in his family, or a bad occurrence that produced lasting shame—illegitimacy, deformity, poverty, social awkwardness. Something that marked him from early on as an Other, as someone useful to his peers for ostracism. Perhaps in response to which Levi goes all in: *If I'm going to be the villain, I might as well get paid for it.*

Whatever Levi's origin story, Jesus favoring his identity is not an outlier event. For both Levi and Zaccheus—a compatriot tax collector to whose home Jesus invites himself for dinner—lots of watching non-villains would have given their eye teeth for such communing. And in parables where Jesus directly contrasts pastors and tax collectors—which are unusually frequent— the tax collectors are always more godly and have better outcomes. And would for sure throw better parties.

A Reason to Party

Because like Jesus, Levi asks no questions as he mulls over the invitation. He engages in no deliberations, and doesn't consult his friends or count the cost. He instead instantly drops his entire life to go all in:

> Then Levi held a huge party for Jesus at his house, and a large
> crowd of tax collectors and others were eating with them. But
> the pastors and theologians complained to his disciples, "Why
> do you eat and drink with tax collectors and sinners?"

So Jesus is again the honored guest in the middle of a packed home, but this time there's little room for those with power because at Levi's party, the religionists are the ones marginalized by the crowd. Could it be that this ignominy, this slight, this unfamiliar narcissistic wound, was the sufficient reason for their protest? The proximate cause for their scowling? Not high-minded worries about blasphemy or heresy or the contagion of sinfulness, but simple offense at exclusion? Or maybe it was the raucousness of the party—too many motorcycles, lots of wine, carousing late into the night, the neighbors calling 911, the sheriff circling—because Levi was letting loose.

Flip back to the first house party. The story tells us that prominent clergy were coming to hear Jesus from as far away as Jerusalem, which was ninety-five miles to the south. Jesus had to have been preaching for multiple days, or perhaps weeks, for word of him to have reached Jerusalem. And he must have been sensational for the elite in Jerusalem to bother with a trip to a tiny town in the hill country to check out the preaching of an uneducated Galilean peasant. So what happened—or didn't happen—for Jesus inside that first house packed with religion? What did he experience, or not experience? "Whatever I'm looking for," Jesus apparently thinks to himself, "I'm not finding it here." And upon leaving, Jesus goes straight to its opposite, to the anti-religious house, the house of sin and darkness where all that is reprehensible resides in one flimsy reviled booth.

Levi watches as Jesus leaves a gathering which he could never in a million years hope to attend, turn, walk up to him, and say, "Follow me." And given (Levi thinks) that Jesus knows both them and me, he apparently really wants *ME*. Specifically Me. Me me me. Not them, but ME. Me as the anti-them. My thoughts, my feelings, my history, my expertise, and my credentials. My identity. My life. And not whoever my me might become one distant day when I'm all repented and cleaned up, but the me that is ME right now!

It's seems eminently plausible, in fact, that Levi's experience of vilification is why Jesus recruited him. Because if a central mission of Jesus is to undo the social mechanism of ostracism, who better to help found your faith community than one who has experienced it firsthand? Who better to symbolically communicate to all other social and religious villains that they are the heroes here? The typical evangelical reaction to the inclusion of Levi is, "Well isn't that nice—Jesus is kind to sinners too!" akin to the white savior mentality toward people of African descent, or to how evangelicals like having token queer people in their gatherings toward whom they can be condescendingly gracious.

But the "Follow me" of Jesus to Levi is, as far as we can tell, an unqualified and immediate invitation into the inner circle. Levi instantly becomes a disciple, one of a select few who will live, eat, and minister with Jesus every day and to whom Jesus, when he departs, will entrust the future of the enterprise. Levi is not vetted, not given a period of probation, not started with an unpaid internship and forced to work his way up. Neither is he told to repent, nor to verbalize a cognitive understanding of the core beliefs of the organization, nor to sign a commitment to refrain from collecting taxes. And Levi would have immediately understood, like with the paralytic, that this kindness of Jesus towards him was not because he was unique or special. The kindness of Jesus reached beyond him to all who were like him. My fellow outcast friends are centered with me in this new God-enterprise. Woohoo—*PARTY AT MY HOUSE!!!!!*

A last thought before actually joining the party: The commitment of the gospel writers to this ethic of the Jesus faith movement is remarkable. We might, after all, wonder about the factual accuracy of the stories. They were written decades after the events themselves, derived from oral accounts, and circulated through many small faith communities before being shaped into the text that we have today. And Jesus had nothing to do with the writing himself. He did not author anything, nor commission the writing of anything, nor vet the writing of anything. So we are dependent on the recollection and conceptualization of the essentials from the writers—we do not have Christianity without their gospels—and they were free to include, or not, whatever they wanted. So that they included, as inner circle partici-pants themselves, multiple stories in which sinners supplant religious power at the center, including this one in which the blazing message is that Jesus selects as a pillar of his faith movement an untrained excluded tax collector while spurning the best candidates from a room packed full of eager religious experts and acolytes is stunning.

Sick Sinners

So Jesus is at Levi's party and the disciples have happily followed him in—*religion can be fun, who knew?* But the concerned, or angry, pastors have a few questions for them:

> The pastors and theologians complained to his disciples, "Why do you eat and drink with tax collectors and sinners?"
>
> Jesus answered them, "It is not the healthy who need a doctor, but the sick. I have not come to call the righteous, but sinners to repentance."

> They said to him, "John's students often fast and pray, and so do the students of the pastors, but yours go on eating and drinking."
>
> Jesus answered, "Can you make the friends of the groom fast while he is with them? But the time will come when the groom will be taken from them; in those days they will fast."

So both questions are about eating practices: "Are you sure you should be eating with sinners?" followed by: "Are you sure you should be eating at all?" The first question is directed to the disciples, who are perhaps easier to confuse than Jesus. Guilt by contamination was religiously codified back then, and so "Why do you eat and drink with them?" was meant to activate in the disciples the awareness that by sitting at table with unclean people, they themselves would become unclean, putting their good God-standing at risk. So they ought to flee the premises, and when the dust settles, Jesus will find himself all alone with his band of outcasts.

And the question would also strike chagrin into the hearts of the sinners themselves. Damn, they'd be thinking, we knew this was too good to be true! We're used to priests hating our parties, but this party has been different because Jesus—one of Them—has been with us, here, in our house, with us. Liking us, smiling and laughing with us as Us, and bringing God with him into our house, into our party. God with us. So so good! But then Levi and friends would have heard the pastors questioning it all. There's no way, they'd say to themselves, that he'll stay. Those are, after all, his people, and he'll go back to them. And deep down they'd think, And they're probably right. We are, after all, "sinners." But … damn.

But with his disquieting attunement, Jesus detects the intrusion and, as a good leader, takes the conflict unto himself:

> Jesus answered them, "It is not the healthy who need a doctor, but the sick. I have not come to call the righteous, but sinners to repentance."

So channeling my inner sinner, I'd think:

> Wait—what did he just say? The religious party crashers are "the healthy righteous," we're "sick sinners," and he's a doctor— of course. But in his strange new world, the healthy righteous are dismissed, the doctor stays here with us, and the Sick Sinner

party is where God wants to be. I don't quite get it—but I think
God just stood up for us! We're the Sick Sinners—yeahh!

Jesus unravels the practice of labeling that is employed as a tool of power.
The term "sinner" in these gospel stories is affixed by power to an ever-ex-
panding group comprising those whom the religious leaders don't like. The
term is neither theological nor moral; it is instead functional. The religious
leaders identify an individual or group whom they revile, then affix to them
the label "sinner," and then are justified in expelling them. Which is why all
these Jesus stories about sinners are *absolutely* relevant to Christian LGBTQ
inclusion. They are not telling us that Jesus welcomes defective people, and
so he'll welcome queer people too. Nor are they telling us that Jesus welcomes those who are unclean, and so he'll welcome queer people too. Nor
are they telling us that Jesus welcomes people who misbehave, and so he'll
welcome queer people too. Rather, Jesus is calling foul on religion's branding
of people with the label "sinner" to justify their exclusion. And as a remedy,
he is explicitly centering those who, because of the moral and theological
subterfuge of those with religious power, have been wrongly and condemn-
ingly labeled as sinner and sent into exile.

Likewise, our Sanctuary Community Church story of inclusion is not
that we realized we got it wrong with calling queerness sinful, and so we had
to recant of that. Our story is that we constructed and propagated a system
in which sinfulness was an organizing principle that we used to label people
so that we could suppress them. Our repentance was not to admit that we
were in error on one particular assessment, but rather that we had to demolish our nefarious system and build up a new one in which the construct and
consequentiality of sinfulness had nothing in common with what we had
practiced previously.

New Wine

But the pastors at the party have one last question. *Our disciples*, they say
to Jesus—now addressing him directly—*and even those of your good friend
John, fast, while yours at this party eat and drink: what's the deal?* Maybe they're
just mad about religion being fun, but the substance of their challenge is: *If
you're not going to flee these "sinners," at least make them behave religiously like
us!* To which Jesus responds: "You can't make the groomsmen fast while the
groom is here," thereby linking this party of sinners and tax collectors to the

grand eschatological heavenly wedding banquets of God foretold in the Old Testament, which would again suggest a radically different guest list than anyone would have anticipated. But before the experts have time to puzzle that out, Jesus offers one final subversion:

> He told them this parable: "No one tears a piece out of a new garment to patch an old one. Otherwise, they will have torn the new garment, and the patch from the new will not match the old. And no one pours new wine into old wineskins. Otherwise, the new wine will burst the skins; the wine will run out and the wineskins will be ruined. No, new wine must be poured into new wineskins. And no one after drinking old wine wants the new, for they say, 'The old is better.'"

To paraphrase, Jesus is saying to the Religionists:

> I have invited this man Levi to have a cabinet-level position in my new God-connection enterprise. As such, he will have a lot of influence on our thought, practices, and policies. He's pretty excited about this, and so he invited me, through this party, into his world that he inhabits with his friends. I accepted that invitation, and I must say it's pretty fun here.

> But just to warn you, while I will be at the center of this enterprise, its structure will arise from their world—their practices, perspectives, identities and outlooks. Which—going out on a limb—might not work for you. In fact, them trying to do faith in your structure or you in theirs would probably produce disaster! Both structures stretched to bursting, blown to bits, with all of you spilled out on the ground and spiritually homeless.

The patch metaphor of Jesus is particularly apt to LGBTQ inclusion. We can't just "patch" the defects of conservative religion with inclusion because the two entities are made from two distinct and unblendable materials. We can't just add "welcoming" onto the conservative Christian container and hope that it will hold. The container for these new followers needs to be completely remade from one new unified substance. Which is driven home by a last remark from Jesus, "And no one after drinking old wine wants the new." To finish the paraphrase of Jesus' warning to the pastors:

It may be that some sort of yearning draws you towards this party. You may be personally intrigued, or you may feel that you should be here to help us lost souls. My advice to you—and I say this with all sincerity—is to seriously consider just staying where you are. Given the faith structure that you've happily inhabited all these years, the likelihood that you would come to be happy here is pretty low. I'm not saying it's impossible, but you would have to come as a learner, without an agenda, knowing your place, honoring this space and all who inhabit it. To quote a wise sage, you would have to be "born again," and you might in the end wistfully long for what you left behind.

Our practice of the Christian religion has established two classes of human beings: The Righteous and The Sinners. Jesus says, I'm happy to use those labels and categories. It's just that in my organization they have different functional consequences. "Sinners" can access the help that I bring, while the "righteous" cannot. So to get my help—access, for example, to my God-connection—you must be classified as a "sinner." Which shouldn't worry those of you reluctant to be labeled "sinner" because you, as you've indicated, don't need my help.

So while in the religious community, "sinner" marks a person for exclusion, in the Jesus community, "sinner" is the necessary mark for inclusion. Which sounds all revolutionary and cool, except what then qualifies Jesus himself for admission to this group? And if LGBTQ individuals are conservative Christianity's "sinners" of today, what do those of us who are *not* queer do to belong? How do we enter this privileged space of favor?

The labels arising from the religious leaders again provide the clue. Jesus is called many things by many people: teacher, Lord, prophet; Elijah, Messiah, Beelzebub. But the religious leaders, in describing the way he relates to "sinners," use the word *philos*, which means "friend." "Here is a glutton and a drunkard," they say of Jesus, "a *philos* of tax collectors and sinners." Not *Lord* of the sinners nor *King* of the sinners, nor even *Rabbi* of the sinners. He's not Master or Emperor or Guru of sinners. He's not Pastor or Reverend or Priest of sinners. The people who derided Jesus recognized something more personal, less hierarchical, less *other* than any of those terms in the way he related to religiously marginalized people. Something appallingly friendly. Sitting at table, drinking wine together, laughing, walking, talking, helping, loving, liking, fond of, intimate, mutual … friendly. A strength and type of friend connection that qualified Jesus, in their eyes, to be labeled as one of them, as a "sinner."

So as we stumble home buzzing from the strangeness of it all, even if we do not meet the objective religious criteria of our day for "sinner," hope is not lost! *Philos* gives us a way in. *Philos* of "sinners." Feasting together at the table of that first Last Supper and hearing Jesus say to all of us, as he said to his disciples, "I no longer call you slaves, but *philos*."

16

Our Movement Entrenches

But while our church was bumping clumsily toward inclusion, our movement was not. Even before Katie and Paula came to us, and for sure continuing forward, we increasingly experienced our leaders entrenching our denomination's restrictive LGBTQ policies and practices. The suppression of us and of our queer friends, and how we responded to that resistance—or didn't—epitomizes so many stories of inhabitants trying to restructure their culture of origin …

⤳

None of Us Left the Room

Tom:

In 2009, Vineyard had launched the Society of Vineyard Scholars (SVS), a group that leaned academic, existing "to foster and sustain a community of theological discourse in the Vineyard movement." SVS was the first place where, from within our movement, we heard real questioning of many of our dearly held evangelical beliefs. On the first evening of an SVS conference that we attended in Minneapolis in April 2012, a young woman from a

Midwest Vineyard church gave a presentation that Adey described to friends back home in an email:

> young lesbian woman presented paper. people were super great. i think svs attracts a certain demographic. folks more like us. also, freedom with papers. they don't represent anyone but the paper writer. she openly stated that she believes God told her that it was fine or good for her to find a woman partner. she is totally working it out in community with folks who support her, but some on both sides of issue. i didn't have time to talk with her, but folks were pouring at her with love and compassion.

The next night, a successful Vineyard pastor and national board member—arguably the Most Powerful Man in Vineyard (MPMiV)—functioning as the last of four respondents in an onstage discussion of a book of interest, tempered that love. The session speakers were discussing *Scripture and the Authority of God*, a book by N.T. Wright, a favorite conservative scholar of Vineyardites. Wright had recently written about inclusion that …

> … someone, sooner or later, needs to spell out further (wearisome though it will be) the difference between (a) the "human dignity and civil liberty" of those with homosexual and similar instincts and (b) their "rights", as practising, let alone ordained, Christians, to give physical expression to those instincts. As the Pope has pointed out, the language of "human rights" has now been downgraded in public discourse to the special pleading of every interest-group.

But the MPMiV lets us know, when his turn to comment comes, that he's not in fact going to say anything about N.T. Wright. He's instead going to instruct us all in how to do Bible exposition using human sexuality as a topic to demonstrate his method because, it's clear, our errant Bible exposit-ing is threatening to loosen things up for homosexuality. I remember feeling panicked. *What's happening?* I twisted around, crying out wordlessly to a yet-to-materialize person of authority—the conference bouncer or the reli-gious police—to storm the stage and take control. As part of this writing, I found a video recording of the session,[3] and the instant I see again the MPMiV start talking at thirty minutes and forty-seven seconds in, I realize *it was all true* and I feel just as short of breath now as I did back then.

---

3 https://vimeo.com/42696875

The MPMiV begins by disparaging all Bible exposition but his own, and follows that by disparaging many different categories of people, with every one of us in the room fitting into at least one. He launches at 43:52 into his exposition, which begins in Genesis. As I listen, I realize I'm not going to be able to resubject myself to it all more than this once, so I type scattershot notes as quickly as I can:

> As I teach about sex in the bible • sex and sexuality are pointers to God in the bible • sex points to the Trinity • sacrificial love complementarity permanent christ paul • ephesians = genesis • jesus exclusive • new testament • purpose distorted • creation upside down • men were meant to rule over creation but instead of us ruling over animals they rule over us • birds sex turned upside down which leads to us finding sexual completion not in the complementarity of the other but in someone just like us • so how do we as pastors help those who fall short of god's ideal? who struggle with something less? • marriage alcoholism fidelity • total fidelity within a lifelong heterosexual marriage or complete abstinence • here's where the story offers healing for our sexual lives we do what paul does • love never fails • cs lewis asked how do you love someone whose behavior you find unacceptable? or actions you find revolting? that person is me! you love yourself you forgive yourself so we have practice loving someone who disgusts us, we can still function we still love ourselves without approving of everything we ourselves do • christianity is designed for moral failures • it's designed for flawed people • and then we're back to the beginning with a catalogue of flawed bible people: abraham and a bunch of others • then a third story that we offer is the church offering community • then it's back to the garden one more time to the not good of being alone with marriage only one way to be not alone which is exalted inappropriately • then there's the hope for change just two more • wesley breaking the power of cancelled sin in his hymn with blood that can make the foulest clean • lastly the church speaks a call to self denial to every human being on earth • the abundant life now • no matter what our sexual orientation or marital status • i'm developing a warm friendship with a transgendered person at a coffee shop that i go to and we've had wonderful conversations about

sex and jesus and i say to him "did you know that jesus never practiced genital sex?" the entire coffee shop turning to listen and yet jesus was the most self-actualized person ever • and we're all called to this high call of jesus to deny ourselves to live the abundant life that christ offers • all right • that's it for me

At 52:49 he finishes ... and the room applauds. Even though in just under ten minutes he has referred to LGBTQ+ individuals as: disgusting, revolting, moral failures, flawed, fallen short, something less, distorted, disapproved, upside down, unacceptable, sinful, foulest, *less than animals*. And we envelop him with denial and minimizing and approval. I could watch the video a thousand thousand times and none of us, including me, will have left the room.

A few of us did declaim in our hotel rooms that night. But while our subsequent email communications are filled with glowing recountings of the brave lesbian woman who spoke the day before, none of us write anything to each other about the MPMiV drubbing us into LGBTQ submission, even though I remember that with more vividness than anything else from that whole week. That's how trauma works—you remember best the very thing you can't talk about. But these beliefs, given to us here in one inchoate rapid-fire exposition, were what we were contending with, and would be expunging out from within ourselves, for years to come.

The Teller of Tales

In 2013, we attended the annual SVS meeting in California. A plenary speaker who had been, for the previous four decades, one of the most influential evangelical leaders in the country, and who had now attained official emeritus status, gave an evening talk. Emeritus does not specifically name homosexuality ... but everything at those meetings was about homosexuality.

The first forty or so minutes of his talk are nicely informal—a few missionary stories, some winsome anecdotes, infused with grandfatherly cultural reflections. But then at 43:15 (so yes, this talk is also on video), Emeritus starts talking about "the Inklings crowd." I become strangely alert. J.R.R. Tolkien, he says, wrote an essay on fairy tales that C.S. Lewis subsequently applied to Christianity. Tolkien, according to Emeritus, describes the fairy tale as a unique genre of literature that has a consistent structure that Tolkien calls the "eucatastrophe." Everyone in a fairy tale experiences a good catastrophe, a catastrophe that is flipped on its head to turn out well. So in the fairy tale, Emeritus says, there is always something that goes terribly wrong, a curse or a spell, an ogre or a witch, a wicked stepmother. And the situation is virtually hopeless. Emeritus gives the example of the handsome prince who is turned into a frog. The prince is stuck in a frog's body, and transformation is hopeless. *Well*, Emeritus continues, *I guess though there is one outside possibility; it's so absurd that it really shouldn't even be mentioned. What if—no, well—what if, on the outside possibility, a beautiful princess were to actually see the frog—this is just wild, inconceivable—and would just happen to kiss the frog. And turn it into a prince. The marvelous thing about the fairy tale is that the princess does just that, kisses the frog.* (It would seem that Jesus, in this analogy, is the princess.)

Emeritus then moves on to Snow White who, in his telling—which we listeners presume is from Tolkien—has been placed at the top of a tall tower that's surrounded by thickets and thorns. *She might as well be dead*, Emeritus tells us. *The only outside possibility of a rescue is that a prince would come through and, for some stupid reason, would see the tower and then, for some stupid reason, cut through the thicket, and then—this gets even more absurd—that he would climb the tower and go in there and then see the dead body, decide to kiss the dead body. She might as well be dead. It's hopeless. But a prince does come and for some stupid reason decides to cut through the thicket. For some stupid reason decides to climb the tower. And then—this gets even more absurd—he kisses the dead body—gets more weird—and it works. Prince Charming dislodges the apple that was stuck in her mouth, and they live happily ever after.*

And then Emeritus says that Tolkien, "after doing that kind of analysis of the structure of the fairy tale," says that the structure of the Christian gospel is like that of these fairy tales. But, Emeritus says, there's one thing that's different: this gospel fairy tale is true. The gospel of Jesus Christ is the true fairy tale. Emeritus concludes:

> You're going to forgive me for being a Calvinist *[uh oh]*. There really is a curse. It really is virtually hopeless. We've rebelled against the Living God. There's nothing we can do that can initiate or in any meaningful way contribute to the rescue that we desperately need as lost sinners. It's hopeless—well, not completely hopeless. There's this weird thing hardly worth mentioning because it's so unthinkable. That the Sovereign Ruler of the universe would send his Only Son to earth, and he would die on the cross, shed his blood on behalf of the

very people who have rebelled against him, who have denied
his rule over their lives. And the wonderful thing about the
gospel is that's exactly what happens. So to discern that for
Tolkien, the gospel has that kind of structure. To think that
the way the gospel speaks of good news is in so many of the
kinds of stories we tell. These are the stories that as little kids
thrilled our souls. And that embedded in that is a narrative plot,
a narrative structure, that in the gospels turns out to be true.
That's a wonderful thing.

I remember thinking as he finished, *This is why evangelicalism must die.*
Because far from "a wonderful thing," what I had just experienced was,
more accurately, a *travesty*: "a false, absurd, or distorted representation of
something." Emeritus had presented, as a particularly influential evangelical—someone more positioned to shape evangelical thought than almost
anyone else during his lifetime—a capriciously dispassionate and unaware
divine being who is *the exact inverse* of what the Judeo-Christian God is
actually like—the one described in the text and experienced by me as being
driven inexorably and implacably, with full awareness all the time of everything and everyone, toward the lonely victim, by love.

Which God I myself had only just come into contact with! Emeritus
was a genuinely well-intentioned man practicing love as he understood it.
Much of my activation toward him, and probably towards the MPMiV the
year prior, was, I think, because I was on the cusp of seeing God differently
and coming to terms with how much harm the evangelical conception had
caused me and my new queer friends. Both Emeritus and the MPMiV were
the voices of evangelicalism to me and to many. We had knighted them lords
of this realm, and they had accepted that identity. So while he was not personally culpable for my activation, he was also inseparable from it. Hearing
the conservative conception of God articulated so clearly and lovingly by
evangelicalism *in the way that I would have done it yesterday* activated my
panic to free myself, and all those in the room, and all those on the planet,
from it.

Including freeing Tolkien …

In *On Fairy Stories*, Tolkien's essay to which Emeritus says he is referring,
Tolkien is commenting on an expansive collection of fairy stories assembled
from many traditions and cultures by the Scottish writer Andrew Lang. But
Lang's collection does not include *Snow White and the Seven Dwarves*. It does
include the completely different story *Snow White and Rose Red*, but Tolkien

never mentions either of these Snows in his essay on Lang, and neither Snow bears any resemblance to the one described by Emeritus. Instead, in the Grimm Brothers' *Snow White and the Seven Dwarves*—what Emeritus was most likely referring to—after Snow White bites the queen's poisoned apple and falls as if dead, she is not secreted to the top of a hidden tower behind thorns and thickets. Instead, her dwarf friends "had a transparent glass coffin made, so she could be seen from all sides," with her name engraved on it in golden letters, which was placed on a mountain with one of the dwarves present there at all times, and animals daily coming by to visit and mourn. And a prince passes by who sees the glass coffin *with the beautiful Snow White clearly displayed inside*, and far from being repulsed, he begs the dwarves, "Give it to me, for I cannot live without being able to see Snow White. I will honor her and respect her as my most cherished one." They acquiesce, and as the prince's servants are carrying away the coffin, one of them stumbles and the apple is dislodged from her mouth and Snow White wakes up and she and the prince fall in love and are married. (At which wedding, the wicked queen must wear molten metal shoes that compel her to dance until she dies.)

Emeritus's evangelical telling of the frog and princess story similarly gets the details and their meaning exactly upside-down. Here's Tolkien:

> The frog shape was and is preserved in the fairy-story precisely because it was so queer and the marriage absurd, indeed abominable. Though, of course, there is in fact no wedding between a princess and a frog: the frog was an enchanted prince. And the point of the story lies not in thinking frogs possible mates, but in the necessity of keeping promises (even those with intolerable consequences) that runs through all Fairyland.

According to the governing rules of the realm of Faerie, that the kiss would happen was never in doubt! This, as spelled out by Tolkien, is the seminal point, the thing to pay attention to, just as it is one of the preeminent points in Christianity: the certitude of God keeping God's promises, such as the promise of God taken up centrally by Jesus of searching for and restoring those who others had tried to expunge (Luke 19:10). Because to God, none of us have never been lost or not in view. Our location, to God, has never been mysterious, and neither has God had to overcome reluctance or disgust to draw close to us. God has always been pursuing and shouting and calling and singing and showing and demonstrating. God has been sending to us

Moses and Ezekiel and Jeremiah and Isaiah and Hosea and Zecharaiah and donkeys and angels and the Spirit and tongues and flames and Jesus and book after book and story after story and signs and wonders and healings and moving stars and magi and Gabriel and the Heavenly Host and clouds and fire and thunder and manna and quails and water and rain ...

The travesty is that evangelicalism had come to believe in, and promulgate to the world, a being so completely opposite *as God*. A being who just chances upon us, unaware of our plight, who finds us objectionable, who probably won't pay attention, probably won't in the end deign to help. Whoever this self-absorbed deity might be, it's not YWHW of the burning bush, nor Elohim, nor Immanuel-God-with-us nor the Son of Man nor the Son of God nor a Good Shepherd searching for lost sheep nor the lamb nor Abba nor the woman searching for a lost coin nor the gardener who says "Mary" as she stumbles around bewildered outside an empty tomb. Isn't the most consistently exercised superpower of Jesus that he's perceptively and lovingly paying attention to all of us all the time? *I saw you underneath the fig tree ... have you caught any fish? ... go call your husband ... what were you talking about on the road? ... touch my hands ... ask me for anything ... do you love me?*

Part of me wants to say, or feels I should say, *oh lighten up*. So an obscure essay of Tolkien is misconstrued as part of an evangelical talk given to eighty-five friendly listeners of an evening on the outskirts of LA ten years ago. But I'm not sure Tolkien would have felt so sanguine, and to the point of our inclusion experience, what Emeritus did is representative of how evangelicalism appropriates unto itself the privilege of storytelling, claiming proprietary rights particularly to the God/Jesus narrative. There is a blithe hubris to how Emeritus patches fragments of Tolkien onto evangelicalism's pre-existing fiction and then calls that the gospel. Which fiction is particularly suited to LGBTQ exclusion because, as much as we conservative Christians attempt to equalize the disdain of God toward all humans, we know that queerness is particularly deplorable, banished to the toppest darkest remotest cell in the tower. The Emeriti and powerful men and theologians of Christendom can say, *we are also lowly and not worthy of God's love*, but it's not a convincing performance. They don't really believe it, and neither do any of the rest of us. All of us who've inhabited the evangelical world know that exuberant gay sex is the apotheosis of Rebellion, and that homosexuals are nonpareil as both objects and representations of God's curse.

So while this memorable moment was not explicitly about LGBTQ people, it was perhaps more elemental, containing the foundational thought constructs of judgment, condemnation, and violence, and the appropriation of storytelling, that are essential for undergirding a system that practices exclusion. The explicit came to us the next night.

Adey:

I was, at the time of the 2013 SVS meeting, still a member of the group's steering committee. Tom and I were at dinner with the committee members at a pastor's home the evening after the conference had ended. The conversation at one end of the table turned to LGBTQ issues. Inclusion disquietude was in the air, and so a steering committee member who was a beloved theologian related a story in which she concluded: "… and so I asked him, 'But how do you envision yourself when you come to be with God in heaven? What will your sexual nature then be?'" "Him" was a gay man, and the obviously correct answer toward which she had lovingly guided him was, we all knew, and he knew, "I picture myself as a straight, virile, heterosexual male. Which helps me understand who I am supposed to be now."

17

Why For So Long?

Adey and Tom:

So why did we stay in for so long? By 2012–13 we had become pretty committed to becoming inclusive, but we didn't formally leave Vineyard until our leaders published their eighty-page no-to-queer-sex position paper nearly three years later. With Katie and Paula being great, and Gusty trying, and core church members advocating, and the Cult of Man imperious, why didn't we get out sooner? *Why doesn't everyone get out sooner?!*

Especially because we were now provoking! Secular culture, in advance of our conversion, had flipped in favor of queer freedom, and we had followed. So we were now contributing to the public questioning with which our leaders increasingly had to contend. Our leaders had come to resent both queerness and being forced to say so. They would have been relieved to see us go, as they communicated clearly a couple years hence.

But it's hard to leave …

Love and History

Adey:

Tom and I had come to life spiritually in Vineyard. We had found Jesus there and received benefit and developed long-term friendships and collaborative relationships. Our Senior Pastor, who just a few years hence would become rageful in his anti-queer vitriol, had spiritually parented us, presided at both of our adult baptisms, and officiated our wedding and our ordinations. We'd cared for the children of our pastoring friends, and they ours. And we had all together developed a common conception of God that we once upon a time cherished.

And I also had come to love, in Vineyard, my two Forever Friends (FFs). I had met them in the early 1980s when I first started coming to our pre-Vineyard Chicago church. Their husbands had started the church—the Senior who didn't and then did ordain me, and the Executive who for decades was my boss—but my FFs lived way beyond the archetypal constraints of pastors' wives. FF1 was a crazy smart therapist and FF2 was the kindest person I'd ever met.

And we became forever friends. When I had a miscarriage, they wept with me and prayed. For the birth of our third child, Joe, FF1 spent the delivery night at my bedside with Tom, comforting me when contraction pain broke through my morphine fog and then resuming spiritual chatter with Tom when my haze re-descended. I still remember the day a few years later when I got home after taking Joe to the doctor. Our housemate told me that while we'd been out, FF2 had called to ask her how Joe was doing. Our housemate had wondered what might be confidential and so had answered vaguely, to which FF2 responded, "It's okay to tell me because I'm one of Adey's best friends." When years later in Iowa City Tom had surgery to remove a tumor from under his brain (benign), FF2 came to distract me, and when that failed, she hugged me and we cried.

Our closeness was built on a scaffolding of shared church endeavors, one of which, for FF1 and me, was advancing the cause of emotional and relational health into our little corner of counseling averse Christendom. We loved and believed in therapy. We worked, with a third counseling partner, to integrate into therapy our Vineyard experience of the Holy Spirit. We launched a counseling service as a ministry of our church. FF1 was the director, which produced some fraughtness of our relating, but we navigated, and were (most of the time) invigorated and thrilled. And we brought an appreciation of open and vulnerable communication and of the heart into the heady world of male-centric pastoring. With Tom as a budding psychiatrist sometimes joining our conversations, what could be better?

When in 1996 Tom and I moved to Iowa, our friendship didn't miss a beat. We found the Country Inn and Suites in Rock Falls, Illinois, right off I-88's exit 41, midway between Iowa City and Chicago. We'd converge in the midst of the stunningly flat cornfields at 11:30 on a Thursday morning three or four times a year. We'd take turns catching ourselves up with each other—kids, husbands, churches; families of origin, failures, delights. We'd walk through Centennial Park in the afternoon, scheming and dreaming, and arrive back in time for dinner at the Candlelight Inn Restaurant—*Delighting our Guests Since 1967*. Saturday morning we'd have breakfast followed by one last talk/pray session, and then, filled up with love and healing, we'd head in opposite directions on I-88 for home. No mythologizing here—it really was that good.

So we *together* became leaders on our regional and national task forces seeking to advance the standing of women in our movement. We hosted an annual national Vineyard Womens' Conference that was, time and time again, magical. And I felt always the power of our synergy, our little unity of the trinity. We each brought something different to the table, and shared openly with the Vineyard women why that was important and how it all fit together. And through it all, the three of us came back again and again to our cocoon of recuperation and re-envisioning at the Rock Falls Country Inn and Suites.

So lots of us-ness *that kept me in*. We'd had to overcome so much across the decades to stay together. We'd spoken out loud to each other our insecurities, squashed down our competitiveness, yelled out our hurts and wounds and insults, and brought healing to each other. All of it now keeping me tethered to them in Vineyard, even as the threat of inclusion slowly began to loom—our friendship and victories and love surely bigger—*for I am convinced that nothing can separate us*. I couldn't bear the thought of losing our us-ness, couldn't even conceive of such a thing.

The Blue Ocean as Oasis

Tom:

Conservative entities often have spaces in which progressive thought safely occurs. Think tanks, the R&D wing, the denominationally affiliated undergrad college in a picturesque town with pretty fall colors and a scrappy basketball team—there must be containers for questioners and polemicists. So with Vineyard: Society of Vineyard Scholars (SVS) and Blue Ocean Faith (BOF) were two groups within Vineyard where thought unconstrained by prior commitments was meant to occur. SVS you've met—a conversation group for academics and theologians—while BOF was devoted to pastors doing the practicals of Vineyard style church in progressive settings.

I had been at home when Adey emailed me from a 2007 Midwest Vineyard Leaders' meeting: "I think we've found a friend!" Dave Schmelzer was the pastor at that time of a Vineyard church in Cambridge, Massachusetts. Dave and his crew, like their fellow Cambridgites, were suspicious of religion, but had found their way into an expression of Jesus that was welcoming and provocative, and that satisfied the longings of their secular neighborhood friends for connection and spiritual meaning. And they had operationalized this expression of Jesus into thought structures and practices that Adey could immediately tell we would love.

So a year later we attended together the first meeting of what would become the Blue Ocean Church Network. About twenty of us drew up folding chairs to rickety tables in the dingy basement of the Cambridge church, which felt deliciously subversive. "Hi," Adey said when her introduction turn came. "I'm Adey. I'm here with my husband, Tom, and we pastor a church together in Iowa City, Iowa. What? Oh, no, not Ohio—*Iowa*. No sorry, no potatoes, *Iowa*—the flyover state in the middle, with the Field of Dreams, where Captain Kirk will come from one day, or so Tom tells me." The others in the room were all from big cosmopolitan cities like Atlantis and Dubai and Gotham. But Iowa City is a haven for all things progressive, so we belonged.

The core of Blue Ocean thought was to turn away from fishing for congregants in the overfished (and typically conservative) waters of those-who-go-to-church and dive instead into the expansive but neglected secular liberal Blue Ocean. So there in Cambridge we shared with each other how our concepts of God had been shaped by the cultural waters in which we now swam. We talked across the hours about the relevance of Jesus for our secular but spiritually interested friends. We strategized about translating our grand ideas into real-life practices.

That week Blue Ocean within Vineyard became for us at that table a home within a home. We launched a yearly meeting in the Cambridge basement. We shared books and emails, and occasionally our pulpits. We sought each other out at the bigger Vineyard conferences. We together developed Blue Ocean values and distinctives that we still love. Blue Ocean provided time and friends with whom to expand our question-asking about topics that would become important as the threat of *No!* to LGBTQ inclusion descended—what is the Bible and how does it work in a faith community? What is the nature of authority in a Christian setting? How do we want church to interact with culture? By the time Blue Ocean had come along, Adey and I had begun to feel uncomfortably different from mainstream Vineyard, but I remember us saying out loud to each other, "Oh, I think we can stay now."

And ... Vineyard loved us! For a day. Blue Ocean was all good ... until it wasn't—which ultimately had to do with LGBTQ people and inclusion—but for a while it was kind of the *It* group. Dave asked to speak at regional and national Vineyard meetings. Blue Ocean materials gobbled up by pastors everywhere. There was probably some cache, some allure, however wrong-headed, just from our academic intellectualism, which I'm sure those of us in Blue Ocean did little to dispel—*Yeah, we're cool because we do church in cool hip college towns, and so, it turns out, does Jesus. Who knew?* But it was genuinely fresh and contemporary, and while it thrived within Vineyard, it proffered the hope that maybe Blue Ocean Faith would be the mustard seed of freedom that would transform Vineyard into a home of welcome for our LGBTQ friends. And so our little enclave of hope kept us in.

The postscript is that neither of these groups survived. At least not as originally constituted, and certainly not as what we had counted on them for. To SVS, a new national director and leadership team said explicitly, "Thou shalt not discuss the LGBTQ issue in thine conferences and forums!" and our progressive think tank complied. So while SVS continued to exist, the thought constraints imposed by the movement undid what had made it safe and life-giving for us. Likewise Blue Ocean was never declarative about Christian freedom for queer people during its entire tenure within Vineyard. Not stating a position was felt to be truer to an ethic of non-coercion, and was itself a provocation to the institution, but the protracted absence of anything committal was dispiriting. When Blue Ocean did eventually depart Vineyard, it/we immediately declared "Freedom for queer people!" But only about six Vineyards came with us. Lots of Vineyard pastor friends said, "We so wish this wasn't happening," and "You're so brave!" as they waved us goodbye. We had hoped for more, expected more, but Blue Ocean as a church network never advanced beyond a loose affiliation of pastors united by being inclusive and by having been expelled from the same denomination.

The Cult of Man

Tom:

One conceiving of history, or at least of our story, is of being complicit captives in the cult of men. The Israelites, in order to emulate their enemies, demanded of God, "Give us a king!" Which wish, once fulfilled, produced unremitting disastrous dysfunction. So it's not a new problem, but in Vineyard we produced a particularly potent instantiation of the inspired man as unassailable hero. John Wimber, Wayne Grudem, John Piper, William Webb; every (almost) national board member ever; the next national director, the next next, the next next next, and whoever will be the next next next next; Evanston's Senior, Evanston's Executive; our Blue Ocean national director; Moses, Abraham, David, Solomon; Peter, Paul, ~~Mary~~ ... and all of us, women and men, who colluded in creating the system that produced their exaltation—*Give us a king!* What a mess.

Way back in the 1980s, when Adey and I first started attending our-church-that-would-become-Vineyard, we parishioners were distributed on Sunday mornings, for the sake of community, into smaller groups called districts, which meant that leadership was also distributed. They still were all men, and the system was not without flaws, but at some point we installed the man who became Senior as the leader of it all. We needed, we felt, centralized leading. We affirmed His calling, His visionariness, His *Authority*. Our mantra that we all took pride in living out was *When Senior says* "Jump!", *we say,* "How high?" *Give us a king.*

I remember our admiration of John Wimber. He would actually sometimes try to downplay his awesomeness—*I play golf to get ready for a teaching*—but whatever was going on for him, we needed a king, we needed him to be kingly. I remember all the men who rose up to be pastors of large churches, and successful worship leaders, and regional overseers, all exalted onto the stage, speakers for all the plenary sessions at all the national conferences. I remember the "prophets" we were brought to over the years, all men, all speaking to us with the God Voice, and toward whom we were explicitly instructed, *do not harbor doubt.* Our denomination's governmental structures—a visionary male executive director surrounded by his chosen team. We imputed to them expertise on everything—unassailable, prophetic, apostolic. God's anointed. You do not mess with God's anointed ... *give us a king give us a king give us a king.* They gave us answers to all our questions from their vast seas of unknowing.

And their unassailability kept us in.

The Possibility of Power

Adey:

I've already told about how, while Tom was still in training in Iowa City, I had packed our bags to go be a pastor at a Vineyard church in Indianapolis, but Tom wanted to stay in Iowa City, so he and I retorted lasagna and telephones at each other, and then God retorted *Stay!* The point of which is that right from the start I was longing to remain in Vineyard in a way that would have prevented our turn towards queerness before it had even been conceived.

Advance to 2011. The national director who had led Vineyard for nearly ten years was stepping down. The candidate who seemed most likely to replace him was my former Senior from Evanston. Senior had invited me, anticipating his ascent, to join his national leadership team with the task of advancing the cause of women in the movement. I and Tom were excited for a million reasons, but we immediately knew that however much he supported women, our nascent interest in the cause of LGBTQ individuals would have to be tabled because it was of Iowa City and Satan and was not shared in any way by our Senior or our movement. But he was defeated, and we were devastated.

Nearer the end of our time in Vineyard, we began to be courted by longtime Vineyard pastoring friends to become leaders in the world mission effort of the denomination. Whatever one thinks of such Christian efforts, we had not been involved as leaders in any way, across our more than twenty-five years of Vineyard, in what we were being invited into. Yet we said yes to attending dinners where we were presented with the vision, and went to missions conferences, and had long discussions with our friends about the delight of riding out the rest of our ministry days doing this stuff together. We even talked with our church board about whether we would be able to free up some of our pastoral time for this opportunity. But it was also corrupting to Tom and me because, whatever the intent of our organization toward us, we again knew that saying yes to this invitation would include us abandoning our LGBTQ aspirations.

There's a moment for Jesus where the crowd clamors to "take him and make him king by force!" but Jesus slips away because he knows they would be enthroning their conception of a king—to which he would have to conform—rather than his. We, until that last go round, would have let ourselves be enthroned as king and queen but for disruptions from circumstances beyond our control. We would have chosen such enthronement for the sake of friendship and power at the cost of freedom for queerness. And however much our institution wanted us to leave, it would have served them better for us to have stayed on their terms.

Leaving is Hard ...

Adey and Tom: There's just so much that makes leaving hard ...

Tom: I was nervous about becoming an independent local nondenominational church. The lack of structure and camaraderie, and of a national meeting to attend, and of people to take responsibility for organizational things—I felt nervous about being alone. I also had long-standing critiques of unaffiliated churches. They were small and idiosyncratic and maybe couldn't get along well with others. Is that what we were becoming? How would we convince people to even visit us if we didn't have the marketing cache of an institution?

Adey: And I had seen the implosions. Well intended but hasty comings out—*the Holy Spirit came to me in a dream last night!*—usually ended in collapse. And our church was the culmination of my life's work! I loved loved loved all the friends, *including all the ones who would not come with us.* I wanted my church to make it as a family ...

Tom: And as long as we were in, we did not know the cost of our staying to those who were *not* in. We could not perceive the cost to the queer people who were not coming *because they were not coming.* And we could not perceive the cost to ourselves of them not coming until we were out. We really only began to perceive the goodness of being queer after being out.

Adey: But the movement we were leaving was where we had first, both of us, come into real contact with God, where we had first met and learned how to interact with Jesus. Where we had come into a new Truth about ourselves and people and God's heart for the world—and all of that had stayed alive for years!

Tom: As I look back, I think my "I should have left then!" moment was at the 2012 SVS meeting when the MPMiV drubbed me into LGBTQ submission, because I consciously felt the wrongness and abusiveness of what he was doing, and that his was the course our movement would follow, but I did not stand up and leave.

Adey: And I think mine was way earlier, before inclusion was even an aspiration. Remember back in the early 2000s when our Midwest regional director took away the position he had given me to lead women in our region because the male pastors were angry about that [*a story for another book*]? That whole Cult of Man thing—it was so real, and I stayed in it.

Tom: But I was in it too! I was in that room with you when he did that, and I did not stand up for you or get you out. We were both still so new to faith, and hopeful for this movement. And we didn't yet understand power or systems, and the Cult of Man was the water in which we swam, and there was still the possibility of us contributing to this awesome mission for women …

Adey: Awww honey, you're way nicer to 1990s-Adey than I am 😊. Yes, to face that what we had invested in and believed in *deeply* had become insufficient or even harmful was undoing. It's not just that we had to perceive the flaws in our system, it's that we had to perceive the flaws in ourselves that caused us to not perceive the flaws in our system—"seeing but not perceiving." It's one of my most recurrent therapy topics—*how could I not have seen?* I think it's why many who leave the conservative church, while still believing in a good God, never find their way back to any sort of Christianity. It's unnerving to trust religion again, but it's even more troubling to trust your own ability to evaluate religion again.

Tom: Yup, that's how trauma works. It's hard to leave, but even harder to come back. And then too there's my Catholic guilt.

Adey: Honey, you're Calvinist, not Catholic.

Tom: Yes, but I mean guilt for despoiling the Holy Catholic Church, meaning the one unified church. Catholic dissenters are known for protesting from within as an expression of some sort of ethical integrity, with leaving being seen as both weak and as producing a fracture that tarnishes the witness of the church's unity to the big wide world. And that thought nagged at me, and made me reluctant to go.

Adey: Wow, you have some weird ones. I did not know that was ever in you until this very moment. How much time do you think that delayed our departure?

Tom: Oh, maybe six to eight weeks.

Adey: Sheesh.

18

Twenty-Two Words

On April 31, 2013, so less than a month after the 2013 Anaheim SVS meeting, the Vineyard national director sends out a letter to all Vineyard pastors. He begins by taking us with him through lively meetings filled with young leaders who are hatching grand plans, telling us that, "the Vineyard movement is flourishing all over the world." But not all is lovely:

> Over time, engaging in the mission of the Kingdom means addressing pastoral and leadership issues that arise, whether from inside churches, or from the surrounding culture.

Which issue is confirmed to be queerness:

> One of the most common questions I get asked in gathering after gathering is how the Vineyard will address the many questions surrounding the issue of homosexuality. What is our stance on gay marriage? Can a Vineyard church ordain gay clergy? Can gay people lead in our churches? Because of the level of cultural intensity surrounding this subject, there is often quite a bit of emotion and anxiety related to these issues.

The "issue," with its attendant impositions of emotion and anxiety, will apparently not stop intruding, and so we are now going to be presented for the first time with a declarative statement from the executive team about homosexuality in our movement. The Vineyard position is developed through four points, which are at their cores:

1. We must be committed to both mission and holiness.

2. The Bible promotes, celebrates and affirms marriage as a covenantal union between a man and a woman.

3. We are all sinful, and it is profoundly unbiblical to pick out one sin that is stigmatized above others. In the history of the church, homosexual persons experienced such sinful stigmatization. We repent and renounce this sort of sinful treatment.

4. We believe that outside of the boundaries of marriage, the Bible calls for abstinence.

Points one and three are packaging. "Holiness" is the evangelical antidote specifically to queer sex ("purity," for example, being the specific vaccination for premarital sex), while point three is a boilerplate evangelical repentance for uniquely stigmatizing homosexuality, which is what an evangelical must say in order to uniquely stigmatize homosexuality. Points two and four convey the message:

> Marriage is a covenantal union between a man and a woman.
>
> Outside of the boundaries of marriage, the Bible calls for abstinence.

Point four continued:

> We know that in our culture, premarital sex, along with many other forms of non-marital sex, has become normative. We want to lovingly help people of any sexual orientation to live up to this standard [abstinence]. We recognize that it can be a difficult journey, and there must be grace along the way. The powerful, beautiful gift of human sexuality must be stewarded with seriousness and compassion within our movement.

It's kind of chilling. Our movement's leadership is pressing adherence with the intimation of coercion: "calling people to high standards ... We want to lovingly help ... human sexuality must be stewarded *with seriousness*." But a steward (noun) is a person who looks after something that belongs to someone else, while to steward (verb) means to manage or look after another's property. So am I stewarding my own sexuality as if it is a thing that is detached from myself? Or does Vineyard become the steward of my sexuality? As if all our sexualities are a collective possession of the denomination to be administrated by the National Board?

How we as Vineyard pastors were to interact with the content was further obscured by the personal disengagement of the author. The national director writes glowingly in the first paragraph, "I can tell you from firsthand experience" about a lot of Vineyard things that are making him personally happy. He is witnessing these uplifting things himself, emphasizing his physical presence, "I have seen ... I have seen ... I have seen." But as we shift to LGBTQ people, any sense of his personal presence, affectedness, agency, or responsibility from him vanishes. For the director, his only encounter with LGBTQ people is from culture or from the anxious questions asked of him by intrusive parishioners at meetings.

And just as the LGBTQ problem originates from the emotion and anxiety of unembodied "culture" against which we must be "resolved," the solution, it turns out, will also not be in any way emerging from the souls of us as Vineyard human beings, but rather from disembodied entities: "the mission of the Kingdom ... the message of the Kingdom ... the Bible promotes ... the Bible calls for ... the church must respond." All of which conspired to produce an often baffling inability to interact with them or it. The "gay issue" is abstracted into systems and kingdoms and messages and texts and cultures that are all devoid of people—of bodies—of physical and emotional flesh and soul human selves. The people who speak as overseers practice selective detachment, emptying themselves of humanness, of those things that are essential to human relating, when LGBTQ tension intrudes. When the director is describing happy travels, he is there. When it comes to queer inclusion, poof! He's gone, replaced by impersonal constructs. You feel yourself channeled toward the data and the content and the issues instead of having human conversations with other human beings about human concerns.

So ... a letter. Ink on paper. Delivered in an envelope. Signed. Something in writing. The content a bit vague and allusive, some hemming and hawing, all of it communicating our evangelical anxiety about engaging with this "issue" at all. But the twenty-two words of content from points two and four were Vineyard's way of launching us down their slippery slope toward excluding from which there was no braking to clamber back up. It's like sifting through hay to get to the needles which, once they prick you, there they are. Which made the letter sadful (sadly helpful). Sad because we could no longer hope for something different, some last-minute turn toward inclusion from powerful executive team allies uncloaking themselves in the eleventh hour as champions of the gays! But helpful, because we could no longer hope for something different, some last-minute turn toward inclusion from powerful executive team allies uncloaking themselves in the eleventh hour as champions of the gays.

Sniff

Adey:

After receiving the letter, I wrote to my Blue Ocean friends:

> I suppose it gets a little messy for me because of my many good friends in the Vineyard, the task forces I am a part of, and our mission's involvement. In other words, our years of sowing in the movement. But not only has Jesus brought us queer folks who have come to faith and had their lives turned around, but now their hetero families are coming. Their gay friends are coming. They perceive us as a faith community where they can encounter God and there is momentum. This is super exciting for me. A small revival. Folks who have little or no prior relationship with Jesus looking our way. At this moment I am calm and grateful. On the day I received the letter I cried a lot. I am grateful for you all.

Tom was unusually emotional, ranting in his reply-all:

> I'm angry about LGBT betrayal, but perhaps under the anger is hurt. I feel that something beautiful, My Movement, the movement that gave me spiritual life and introduced me to the possibility of a God I could relate to, is being stolen from me. I want to say, "What gives you the right? What gives you the right to do this to My Movement?" And then I want to cry.

But it was Leah who left first. Leah was a next-gen me—not the Jewish part, and she can sing well—but a through and through secularist who came into connection with God through our Evanston Vineyard church, and who then came to aspire to be a Senior (Woman) Pastor. In 2008, she and her husband and their three children had uprooted themselves from Evanston

to Iowa City for her to be a pastor with me and our church. She was the
worship leader on stage who, with purple hair and a rock vibe, helped Katie
feel safe on the first Sunday that she and Paula and their kids visited.

Leah's goal became to return to California where she was from and to
start a Vineyard church in Berkeley. She had come into faith 100% inclusive,
was schooled out of that by evangelicalism, but had now been converted
back through Gusty and Katie and Blue Ocean, and her own friends and
family. Her church would definitely be fully inclusive, so Leah had begun
asking national leaders, *What does the Vineyard position on LGBTQ mean for
me?* Responses were hedgingly noncommittal until one person of power at
last said: *Why would you want to be in a movement whose leaders disagree with
you so strongly on this issue?* So Leah began saying goodbye. A letter sent by
her to the Evanston church pastors in October of 2013 concluded thus:

> Leaving the Vineyard is in many ways a grievous event to me,
> and I think that is in large part because of my respect for you …
> I'm not asking you to agree with my ethic on homosexuality.
> I am asking you to receive my gratitude and supreme respect
> for each of you. I am who I am in no small part because of
> your influence, your character, and your belief in me. That will
> always be the case, and I will always be profoundly grateful for
> the Kingdom riches you have given me. I pray I could steward
> them well, and give them away as generously to those Jesus
> puts in my path to lead as you do.
>
> With sincere gratitude,
>
> Leah

Tom:

I would definitely have expressed different sentiments in my farewell
letter, but Leah is a more evolved human being than me. All her fare-thee-
well notes were like this—truthful, kind, grateful. But what also caught my
attention was how she had introduced this particular one to Adey, David,
and me when she forwarded it to us for vetting before she sent it to Evanston:

> Ugh, this is an emotional one. I've been crying at my computer
> writing it. So I'm sending it to you before I send to them. You
> think this is ok?
>
> Sniff.

A task for me in this whole remembering endeavor was to sift through our past communications, identify those that I deemed to be of interest, and then select bits from them for inclusion in the book. Mostly I selected bits with momentous thoughts, or interpretations of events, or insightful premonitions. And while I had not failed to notice that many communications from Adey to her ministry friends, or from them to her, mentioned crying—*i was crying last night ... sobbing as i write this to you ... tearful when i think about what you're going through ... your kindness makes me cry*—these bits were diminished in my INTP mind as emotional packaging for the substantive content. But this time as I wrestled with what from amongst Leah's words to include, I paused:

> Ugh, this is an emotional one. I've been crying at my computer writing it. So I'm sending it to you before I send to them. You think this is ok? Sniff.

We were all trying, as we wrote this book, to understand what had helped us successfully transform *together* from conservative evangelical to inclusive, and so I wondered, was that "Sniff" it? We've said that our church came into being within the Cult of Man, and that part of our escape has been fleeing that. But we have not fled into a vacuum. We are led by Adey, and with and through her we have had, and continue to have, women leading at all levels of our organization. Two consequences of this were highlighted in Leah's email: We know and regularly express our feelings; and we are not shy about having our thoughts, words, and plans seen by each other. I recognize that engendering these practices leads into the fraught realm of stereotypes, but neither David nor I would ever have prefaced an email to our team with *I'm crying as I write this*, nor with *You think this is okay?* nor with *Sniff.*

But because of Adey's commitment to her own and our emotional health, we pastors at Sanctuary value crying, and talking about crying. And being angry, and talking about being angry. And being joyful, and talking about being joyful. We regularly say to each other *I love you.* We work to maintain healthy emotional connections with each other so that we all actually continue to like each other. We constantly make sure that we're all safe for each other.

And then when Leah writes an important communication, she seeks help illuminating her unawareness. She's aware of the obvious factors shaping her content—audience, desired outcome, potential repercussions. What she needs help with is: What triggered or broken or anxious part of me is communicating through me unbeknownst to myself? Am I raging against my brother? Protecting my mother? Fearing abandonment? These unperceived motivations and reactivities are the most common causes of post-send regret, but because it's almost impossible for us to perceive them from within ourselves on our own, the only way we can produce the kinds of communications we desire is to have someone else read what we've written and tell us what of our messed-upness has snuck itself in.

For Adey and Leah, this was strangely okay, even—dare I say—enjoyable. I, by contrast, bristled: *I don't need such help! I'll say whatever I want! And you all can clean up my messes!* But none of us were competent to independently navigate the emotional and relational fraughtness of the separating that we were doing. Being excluded or evicted, or just plain leaving, is bewildering and triggering. So by us crying and sharing, we encountered fewer surprises, fewer unanticipated consequences. We could talk with and pray for each other. We didn't get stuck in depression or anxiety or bitterness. We were less likely to be rash and impulsive. And we never came to be alone.

Sniff.

More Goodbyes

Adey:

In the spring of 2014, I went to my final National Women's Conference, where I taught and interacted much with wonderful young female church leaders. Here's what I wrote to my Blue Ocean friends afterwards:

> The "last supper" was bitter sweet. The celebration/debrief convo … oh, I love those young women! We ate at a great restaurant on the beach in Newport and had some drinks. We did what you do when you have bright, talented young people with you. We laughed and talked about everything. I think they weren't used to the kind of space we made for them and they wanted to talk forever about all of life. It was so sweet and fun and engaging at all levels, but my own inner turmoil kicked in. These women wanted to know me! When can we talk again, Adey? We love you, Adey … blah blah blah …
>
> This would be nice if it weren't for the fact that I am leaving their beloved movement.

So I told them. I framed it as potentially leaving. But they got it. They got pale. One said, I feel like I just got shot. Oh man! It was intense. The whole next day I got the "I love you, Adey!" emails. "Bless you on your 'potential transition!'" Ugh.

My heart broke in many ways, but I also felt a little help getting on with my transitional process, now that people outside my church know.

Then that May, we went to a Blue Ocean conference in Ann Arbor, Michigan. Phyllis Tickle was the plenary speaker, wonderfully spiritual and wise and with a deep historical perspective on the meaningfulness of our turn toward LGBTQ inclusion occurring now. I led a packed room of people through a prayer practice that facilitated perceiving and interacting with Jesus. And Tom presented to an attentive audience his take on Darwin and Jesus, leaning into his sense of the irreconcilably divergent principles underlying Christianity and evolution without needing resolution. Tom resisted the rush to easy answers, had fun, and spawned animated and happy conversations. So later that day, walking with fellow Blue Ocean pastors down Liberty Street toward the Jolly Pumpkin to get some Ann Arbor sour ale, Tom began skipping, which is prohibited amongst the Dutch. "I'm free!" he shouted.

He explained between skips his epiphany, that for the past two decades he had lived under the suspicion of his denomination toward his science. Evolution, genetics, the scientific method, even the intellect were all perceived as threatening, and so anxiety-provoking, by the form of Christianity that we had, until essentially this moment, inhabited. But that morning Tom had felt for the first time in his adult Christian life that his whole self was welcomed and celebrated by his new faith community and the God they worshiped. Which was exactly what we were hoping to produce for our queer friends! While he as a scientist had not suffered anything close to the degree of vilification endured by LGBTQ individuals, his experience of constraint was of a kind. So this, for Tom, was a foretaste of the joy of welcoming. "I'm never going back," he said. "I'd rather do this with ten people than whatever it was we were doing before with a million!"

In early June of 2014, we sent a "Something's Coming" letter to our church members, letting them know that our departure from Vineyard and entry into Blue Ocean would likely occur within the next year. It was a long letter, replete with history and values and process, and also describing our movement's increasingly public anti-inclusion stance, combined with their more assertive approach to enforcement. We addressed the anxiety of change, while also expressing excitement about, "walking through a spiritual door into the next stage of life and mission for our church." Upon rereading, what we wrote was pretty good. All the sentiments held up well . . . except for our remarkably naïve answer to our self-posed question, "How will this shift affect your experience of church?"

> As best as we can tell, not much. Sunday services would be no different, teaching content would not change, and our church values and priorities would continue to be what they are now ... We will in a sense be acknowledging who we already are, and the influences that shape our thought and practice will remain essentially unchanged.

Sheesh! We were anxious about unsettling our parishioners through departure, and so were reassuring. We probably also believed that we had pretty much arrived thought-wise. But everything changed! You cannot know from within a system how much it constrains you. Once free, we would examine the culture and belief structures that enabled us to exclude, and be horrified with what we found. Our values would be turned upside-down. We would come to perceive twenty other practices shaped by our ethic of exclusion that we needed to repent of. But it was nonetheless joyful to anticipate journeying into queerness with our church.

Goodbye Forever Friends

This heading works punctuationally as either "Goodbye, Forever Friends" or "Goodbye Forever, Friends." My FFs and I had tiptoed around the coming apocalypse, denying its portent for us, and affirming our foreverness. But such blitheness felt increasingly untenable. My FFs, I could tell, still held out hope that I might yet land at mostly the same place as them regarding queerness and Christianity, so I had written to them in late 2013 to clarify how my views had shifted: "I don't think the current system is working ... at all ... for the vast majority of gay people," and then I declared myself:

> I don't know all the theology. I just think that I'm willing to risk (not eternal hell-fire, just being wrong). I think scripture is clear that women should not lead. It is only our hermeneutic

that allows it. That is the reason Wayne Grudem was so afraid. Perhaps rightly so! But, we've convinced ourselves that women can lead, that slavery is wrong, etc. Each time we were absolutely convinced the forerunners were wrong. Truthfully, I just want to welcome folks to our church and I don't think the current system is working well.

So it would be ok for you two to be sad about your wayward friend together. Not because I have everything figured out ... just because I may be landing in a different place. I know you will be sad having read this. I will talk about anything at all or give you space. Whatever you need.

Gulp, gulp, gulp ... I guess I've shifted ...

Love,

Adey

Oh God, I could breathe. Of course I had shifted! Anyone close to me knew I had shifted, knew that I had long been giddily hurtling pell-mell down Grudem's slippery slope hoping to land *plop!* with Katie and Paula and all their queer friends in a big ole pile o' sin at the bottom! But I had never said *I have shifted* to my FFs, to my spiritual birth church, to my former boss, to my former Senior, to my movement, to evangelicalism, to Grudem, to Piper, to Webb, to the MPMiV, to the Cult of Man, to Father God, in a way that they and I could all together hear. *I guess I've shifted!* Oh God, YESYESYESYESYESYESYES!!!!! A thousand times, Yes! *I guess I've shifted.* A million times ... *I guess I've shifted.*

The three of us did go for one more trip to Rock Falls in January of 2014. We were still in love, fighting for our togetherness, walking long walks, eating tuna salad for lunch, with dinner at the Candlelight Inn. I had just completed my doctoral work at Fuller, and my FFs brought champagne and a sweet card to celebrate my graduation. But that weekend I also shared again my struggle staying in Vineyard. There were tears, and a thickness in the air. After sending out our letter to our church about departing Vineyard, I wrote to them, "we will likely leave the vineyard in the next months."

Our final conversation happened in a video call late in the morning of July 9th, 2014. I had a teary conversation the day before with one FF who couldn't imagine us ever not being friends no matter what, but in that last half day it had somehow become clear to them, and thus to me, that this was farewell. There would be no miracle-beyond-miracle, no 11th hour intervention, and so no forever. My anxiety was high, but I also remember anticipating relief—like even if I was totally hurt, I wouldn't have to keep having these awful conversations! My stomach had become constantly tight.

And the conversation was terrible. I don't have a transcript … but it was terrible. Nothing could have prepared me to hear them say, "Likely we will never talk again." I remember crying and saying, "I love you guys. I will always love you." They said the same thing back. I also, true to form, apologized: "I am so sorry. I am the one who changed. You guys didn't change. I am so sorry."

My FFs and I have not talked since.

Later that day I wrote to a friend:

> Had official break up conversation. We three Skyped. Everyone cried. There was actually a ton of sweetness to the whole thing. God answered my prayer. I think I was tender and honoring of 30+ years while at the same time in no way capitulating. There was no loaded(ness) and I did what I tend to do in these contexts. I felt good about me when we hung up.
>
> Hardest thing is that I can't touch their faces again. I love them a lot and we have been through so much. I sort of wanted to touch them.
>
> Hung up and sobbed. Will sob, I imagine for a long time, but feeling close to Jesus …

Five days later I wrote to a friend:

> Mostly I'm ok. But excruciating pain is right there. I hoped I could get by without feeling it. But it's waiting to be felt.
>
> A friend helped me be angry for a bit. That helped. How long will I hurt, o God? :)

One month later I let them know that my son had gotten engaged, writing, "It would be easier if you didn't write back. It still hurts a bit!" Two months later I let them know that Tom's father had passed. Five months later I wrote to a friend,

> Once again prayed about [forever friends]. Sobbed for sooooo long! Must be healing. Jesus was there.

I described careening, in my hour of praying, from anger to longing to ranting to love, ending with:

> … bless them, lord.
>
> In reality I'm sobbing the whole time and only finding out what's in my heart as it comes out my mouth! It was exhausting. I don't know if I felt better. I know it needed to happen.

Eight months later, in February of 2015, I read an article by philosopher/theologian David Gushee on the moral conflict that Christians experience related to LGBTQ inclusion[4] and wrote to my Blue Ocean friends:

> I don't think Vineyard is a cult, but, for [FFs] to say permanent goodbye … I think at first I was just hurt. But over time I can see clearly the posture that "evangelicalism" invites. Really sad in these situations.

One year and four weeks later, when a group of people were leaving our church because of our going yet deeper into inclusion, I wrote to Tom and David about how my longing for my FFs was showing up in my dreams:

> I want to apologize that my anxiety got the best of me at staff meeting last night. I'm sure it's the looping around to potential repeat of losing FFs that is messing with me. I know this is my mission in this season, but, I'm a little dreading it. I had a dream a week ago that I was at a banquet and [FFs] were there. I was going to walk up and say something kind. But one of them grabbed me and collapsed in my arms. I hoped she'd say, "I'm sorry. We love you so much!" But what she said was, "we didn't get to hug enough!" I woke up sad.
>
> I have prayer with a friend this morning. Hopefully being with Jesus will help me get to a better space. If I need to talk with someone beyond that I will! :)

Two years and six weeks later I was writing to someone about a time of prayer with Tom and a friend in which Tom named how my movement had scapegoated LGBTQ persons and, with them, me. Tom described the pressure in a scapegoating system for everyone, including the scapegoat (me), to blame the scapegoat (me) for harming the system:

4 https://www.baptistnews.com/article/the-painful-inevitability-of-moral-conflict/

i went nuts. i was so mad, i was going ballistic, hitting the couch ... but jesus was wonderful!!! 😊 by the end of our praying i saw nothing but light. holy cow. light filled my whole view for minutes on end. that's all i could see. getting there, on the other hand, was hell!!! i'm so grateful to Jesus

I sometimes picture doing the call again. This time I'm quiet. FFs tell me how distraught they are for us having to say farewell to each other. I listen, and when they seem to be done, I say, "Is there anything else?" And when they say, "No, there's nothing else, Adey," I say, "Then I think we're done." And I hang up. And I cry for days and weeks and years. And my husband and my friends help me. And I pray and Jesus finds me. But I do not ever say, "Sorry that I changed." I do not say sorry at all.

19

The Big Goodbye

Tom:

Adey was on the SVS advisory board through 2014, so in April of that year we went to Columbus, Ohio to attend what would be our last meeting. On the final evening, the MPMiV, joined onstage now by our movement's MPTiV (Most Powerful Theologian in Vineyard), described to us how a position paper (PP) they had written would soon be published. The PP and additional material would be taught to us pastors by the MPMiV and MPTiV and one or two others in multiple regional webinar sessions. There would be no discussion with us about the topic, as there had been with equality for women, because: "This current process is not about arriving at a different policy, or debating the policy." Rather, "We certainly have to find a way to equip our pastors in the increasingly difficult task of pastoring both 'straight' and LGBT people, and we have to determine how we react to those in our midst who have already deviated from the Talking Points, even if this is a microscopic constituency."

Why "straight" was in "quotation marks", I'm not sure. Certainly not as a liberal nod to the nonexistence of the gender binary; more likely as a veiled reference to the nonexistence of anything other than straight, and so to the nonsense of the whole conversation, particularly given the apparent near nonexistence of us LGBT persons and allies. And "pastoring" in our Christian denomination no longer means *kindly guiding willing parishioners into helpful connections with the divine*, but has instead become assertive instruction with enforced adherence, with the objects of our pastoring having become quite expansive. Beyond "straight" and LGBT people, we learned that we will also have to "pastor" LGBT couples who come into church with a "blessing" in place, and persons with sexual orientation difficulties, and professionals in the social sciences, and Christians in public life (lawmakers and local government officials and etc.).

F---.

Pastoring LGBT Persons was published electronically on August 29, 2014. Though we had been expecting the document, we were nonetheless surprised, and a bit cowed, by its anti-homosexuality heft and venom. After an intro paragraph with the obligatory nod toward kindness, the PP plowed through why homosexuality is an abomination that impels us helplessly towards the abyss. It's a carrying forward of the MPMiV's ten-minute SVS diatribe, but exploded out into eighty pages. Along the way the authors disparage psychology, and psychiatry, and all of science, and liberalism, and feminism, and Ken Wilson, and knowledge, and …

A few of us tried to mount responses. I wrote what I called a rant. Dave Schmelzer wrote something more thoughtful that he put on the Blue Ocean website. But nobody was listening to us, and we were all still experiencing the traumas of our expulsions while struggling into what we were becoming. I don't think any of us actually made it all the way through the document; we instead just left.

So coming back to the PP all these years later is strange. I read through the document all the way, twice, with the experience being disturbingly generative. For this book, I drafted two full chapters, and *three* appendices, of response. That was subsequently reduced to one chapter and two appendices. Which is now this subsection of this chapter, for which diminishment you can thank my wife and our editor.

The PP, make no mistake, is a vile, vile document, gleefully unhinged in its anti-LGBT invective. The "Christian community" and the "LGBT community" continue to be definitionally non-overlapping, no LGBT voice speaks to either the authors or to readers from anywhere within the eighty-plus pages, and the authors trumpet their resentment at culture for forcing them to waste time addressing this trivial issue. The content is rambling and disjointed, with the same kind of appropriative travesties perpetrated against science that Emeritus perpetrated against Tolkien. We are presented with myriad controversies surrounding sex and sexuality and God, all of which are complicated, and tenuously interconnected, and disputed by other MPMs. Which is perhaps somewhat understandable given the task the conservative church has set for itself: to show that God, through *all* the stories and statements contained in the Bible, uniquely abhors and prohibits non-heterosexual sex, that violating this prohibition will be catastrophic, and that the whole thing is a manifestation of love.

But the outcome for at least this reader, instead of enlightenment, was to feel soiled. As we come to the end of the document, we're caused to think neither: *Oh, I get it now,* nor: *I could have done that, too,* but rather: *I'm a busy pastor and this is obviously way beyond my pay grade, so whether you MPMs are very good at this or not, I'll just let you do my thinking for me.* Which we, of course, did not. The PP instead helped ensure that we'd leave soon. What Vineyard itself at this point thinks of the PP is unclear. They have not formally recanted of it, but while other earlier PPs are readily available on the Vineyard's national website, this one is nowhere to be found.

We'll close our internment of the PP using a metaphorical image that the MPMs present early in the paper:

> In communicating to our culture about sex, we must remember that a Christian understanding of sex and the morality of certain sexual practices is deeply embedded in a comprehensive understanding of a Christian understanding of God ... In other words, a Christian view of sex cannot be outside of an appreciation of a Christian worldview.
>
> Perhaps an illustration would help. Imagine an old Gothic cathedral with stained glass windows. Outside the cathedral, the windows look gray and cloudy. The picture in the window is incomprehensible. But when one steps inside the cathedral, the picture in the window comes to life. One says, "Ah, there is Jesus teaching from a boat in the Sea of Galilee, or there is a portrait of the Risen Christ." Only inside of a Christian worldview do statements by Christians about sex and sexual morality make sense. Thus, it is wise for a Christian to never offer "sound bites" about same-sex relationships. They are almost certainly going to be misunderstood outside the cathedral.

But ... if from the outside the windows are dark, that means there's no light within. Which means that the only way to perceive the beauty of the windows when you're inside is if they are brightly illumined from a source of light outside. Like queerness. Or Iowa City.

Adey:

On October 24, 2014, I emailed the following letter on our church letterhead to the National Director of the Association of Vineyard Churches:

> Dear [National Director] and Vineyard USA Executive Leadership Team
>
> This letter is to inform you of our intention to disaffiliate from Vineyard USA. We are grateful for our many years doing church within Vineyard. As you may know, the Vineyard was our first church home where we fell in love with Jesus, the ministry of the Holy Spirit, and the value of "everyone gets to play." The Vineyard has blessed us in countless other ways: dear friends, stories of God's healing, and many years of fruitful partnerships in the kingdom of God.
>
> But now the time has come, for a variety of reasons, for us to move in a new direction. We plan to formally change our name within the next three months. We do wish all the best for Vineyard USA and pray for God's blessing on the movement and your leadership of it. May it continue to bear much fruit!
>
> Please let us know if there are any additional actions that we need to take in order to formalize our disaffiliation.
>
> Warmly,
>
> Adey Wassink
>
> Senior Pastor
>
> Vineyard Community Church

To which the National Director responded later that evening:

> Dear Adey,
>
> Thank you for sending this letter defining your intentions.
>
> Please know, we wish you and the church the very best in what the Lord has for you in the future.
>
> I will pass this on to the Executive Team.
>
> Blessings,
>
> [National Director]

And that was that.

20

Kevo

Tom:

Kevo first visited our church in late fall of 2014. I noticed him from the stage while I was preaching one Sunday and went straight to him after the service. His first sentence after "Hi, I'm Kevo," was, "Are gay people fully welcomed here?" We were in the midst of our transition, meaning on the way but not there yet. We had just left Vineyard, didn't yet have our new name, and *Coming Out!* was still more than a year away, so ... "Yes!" I said. "Absolutely! Gay people are fully welcomed here with no restrictions of any kind on participation!"

It was probably a bit aspirational, but with Kevo it worked, and we just didn't know how to do the in-between time differently. He became a regular onstage member of our Sunday morning worship team, led and attended tons of groups, was at the nexus of every after-church social gathering, and marched every year in drag at the head of Sanctuary's Iowa City Pride Parade contingent. He was with us from 2014–2023.

Kevo:

When I was young, I was nerdy and a little bit picked on. By the time I was in junior high school, I knew I was attracted to boys. But I stayed closeted, not sharing my true self, and just worked extra hard to be awesome. I sang in show choir, was in student government, did really well in classes. I started attending church when I was 12. I loved it because the social hierarchy I found everywhere else just didn't exist there. I hung out with peers—it was a real community for me. But the culture of that community included negative views about homosexuality, so I became very involved and worked super-hard at being an upstanding Christian to prove to them that I was worthy despite my sexuality. Which meant that the validity of my relationship with God had to go through other people. It felt like there was always something in the way between me and God. *My* salvation had to get a stamp of approval from other Christians. But straight Christians didn't have to do that. And so I had constant rage, most of which was self-directed. I was praying ceaselessly that I would change to become straight, and it just wasn't happening, so I must have been doing something wrong. I was mad at myself for not doing Christianity right.

But by the time I got to college, I was no longer trying to pray away the gay, and I was also not willing to hide my identity on Sunday mornings anymore, which meant that I mostly wasn't going to church. And then I came to Iowa. In August 2014, I drove a cute little Nissan Cube from Los Angeles to Iowa City to move here to start medical school. For the first few days of being an Iowa Citian, I had one thought running through my mind: "Oh God, what have I done?" I'd had only two prior experiences in Iowa: In summer of 2009, I rode in the passenger seat of my sister's car as we were doing a cross-country road trip along I-80, and all I remember of Iowa was that every time I looked up from my Nintendo DS, I saw cornfields and … really it was just cornfields. The second time was for my med school interview. I was staying with a friend's friend who asked me "What do you want to see while you're here?" and I said, eagerly, "Can you show me what kind of food Iowa has to offer?" and he took me to Culver's.

So I already had an impression of Iowa coming here, and based on that impression I had pre-fabricated a narrative for myself, which was that during the FOUR years I was going to be in Iowa, I would just focus on my studies and not interact with or invest myself into the community. I visited Sanctuary, nee Vineyard, and my MO by then had become to talk directly to the pastor about LGBTQ inclusion immediately after the service. I remember being convinced that the church was inclusive because Tom's answer was so unhesitating.

But my prevailing personal narrative—the story of restriction that I was telling myself about myself—still had a lot of influence over me and really limited my experience during those first few years. I wasn't here to have a good time, I said to myself, and so I didn't. But then when I realized that I was going to be in Iowa City for a bit longer, I also realized that I needed to change my attitude and the way I understood this season of my life. And so I changed how I described Iowa, and its people, and the things it has to offer, and I changed how I described my experience of all these things around me. And life became so much better. And I felt so much freer to enjoy and love my time and myself in this place.

In some of my work as a psychiatrist, I emphasize with my patients this idea that when we limit ourselves to a single story, the story can become a trap. But when I reflect on my NINE years in Iowa, one of the most obvious truths that sticks out to me is how much Sanctuary helped me re-author my Iowa story into one characterized primarily by belonging, joy, support, growth, and home. And it's not even just that. Sanctuary gave me the freedom to rewrite the narratives I've had about faith and God the Father, sure. But now also God our Mother, and God our Queen. When I say the word "church" now it feels different in my mouth and in my chest compared to before. It's not as heavy, it's less guilt-ridden. The new script I have about church and its relationship with women, social justice, other faiths, Pride parades—it's just so much better than the old script.

I am the same person I was in 2014, but I'm also not. The narrative I have for myself is vastly different. Back then I viewed myself as somewhat of an outcast, I thought I was unoriginal, I felt like an imposter in medicine. I thought of myself as a man, but one who just couldn't do masculinity right. I identified back then as gay, but not really as a member of the "queer community." But then I started asking new questions: What if I challenged all the rigid, fixed, singular thoughts I had about myself? What if I started claiming, rather than doubting, my belonging in Iowa, in medicine, in church? What if I started believing that I had a perspective to bring to the table, a voice to lead? What if I freed myself from this box of gender and sexuality that I was trying so hard to fit into? What if I opened myself up to more possibility? To being multifaceted? To fluidity? What happens then?

What happens, I learned, is that we get a taste of freedom. A liberation in identity that I think God wants for us. Throughout scripture we see God's invitation for people to take up a new story for themselves all the time. Sarai, who doubted her ability to bear children, became Sarah, mother of nations. Simon, after becoming known by Jesus, becomes Rock. Doubters become doers. The meek become inheritors of the earth. These aren't transformations. These are affirmations of truth that were just waiting to be recognized.

As I've grown and discovered new truths about myself, I've been really fortunate to have had people—friends, colleagues, strangers—earnestly thank me "for being me, and for doing what I do" in this community. Which was always so nice to hear, but honestly still kind of astonishes me. Because as I reflect on my time at Sanctuary, I see myself less as an agent of change, and more as the evidence of it. I can't really put into words why I feel it's so important to show people that you can love God wearing both a mustache and high heels, but I can tell you that if I had seen someone else doing it when I was growing up, church would have felt like a much safer place. And we're also having fun! Being a gay Christian, you're always hearing about how you have to bear your burden, carry your cross, learn and learn and learn … But we like having fun! Once you feel safe, the whole thing becomes joyful!

21

Hello, Sanctuary!

Kevo had arrived as we were saying good-bye to Vineyard Community Church of Iowa City, and hello to . . . If you could name yourself—what a privilege! To generate your own moniker not from a wisp of possibility, an inchoate bundle of the unknown wrapped in swaddling cloths, but from your own developed identity. It's kind of frightening—what if you get it wrong? To boil your complexity down like a slow-simmered reduction to one fragrance, one word.

But name ourselves we must, which we did—as is our wont—through a party. After so much angst and heaviness and *goodbye goodbye goodbye*, we were doing something *AWESOME!* And if our community participated in the name production, none of us could blame-shift if it turned out crummy. So we invited the whole church to our naming party, provided child care and treats, and had an expert in branding lead us in naming games. From that mid-September 2014 event we generated over three hundred possibilities, including:

> Far Side Church for the Gifted • All Saints and Skeptics • Open Table • The Well • God's Rodeo of Life • Sanctuary • The Way • New Way • Light Way • Naked Way • Muddy Creek Community Church (Muddy Creek runs below our property) • Fecundity Church • The Fountain • Thrive • Abundance

Hills also featured prominently in many names—rolling, prairie, grassy, Grant Wood—along with religious themes and friendliness. The kids contributed some possibilities, replete with crayoned pictures:

> The Christ Community • One of God • The Loving Church • Community Church • Christ the Lord • The Beautiful Church • The Best Church • Jesus Church Community • Jesus the Church • The Cross Kingdom • Twinkler • Loving Community • Jesus Kingdom Community Church • Jesus is the Lord • Jesus • Wrecking Ball Church

A branding team of eight of our parishioners winnowed down the possibilities to Story, Thrive, and Abundance, then some folks argued compellingly for including Sanctuary. Thrive and Sanctuary were the finalists. One last hurdle was not offending a favorite local pub, Sanctuary, so Tom wrote to the owner asking whether he'd mind having a church nearby called Sanctuary, to which the owner responded:

> Tom,
>
> We would have no objection. We do hold the Sanctuary trademark for restaurant and bar operations, so as long as you offer no more than communion wine there is no problem (just kidding). Good luck with your changes and if someone comes in looking for good beer you know where to send them.
>
> Sanctuary Pub

So Sanctuary Community Church was good to go! And a few years out we're nothing but grateful as "Sanctuary" has served so well to describe the space of welcome and safety that we endeavor to provide.

22

More Queer Friends Come to Church

Chris

Adey:

Chris started attending our church more than a year after *Coming Out!* A gay African American son of a baptist pastor, dance professor, with a doctorate in queer theology from a prestigious U.K. institute of higher learning, he at first came warily, a couple of times. Then he saw two married men, worshipping with their two children in the row ahead of him one Sunday. He said to me and Tom later that day, "For the first time in my life I saw the possibility of all of who I am being present, integrated, in one space. It was magical!" Chris now preaches from the pulpit 3-4 times per year, and I am presiding at his wedding to his husband next summer.

Jeremy

Tom:

One Sunday as I was preaching I saw someone I didn't recognize and so made a beeline to him after the service. "Yes, this is my first time here," he said. He looked about my age, but with more gray and less tummy. "Can we talk out in the foyer?"

We moved out there, a little off to the side, and he started crying. "I meant to wait to have this conversation, but … my son is gay. He hasn't come to church for years, and I don't know if he ever will again. I've been going to [conservative church in town], and I just can't do it anymore. My wife stopped going years ago because she can't stand the exclusion, but I've kept going. I need church. But these last few months—I just can't do it anymore. I can't keep going to a church where my son, even though he might never come, wouldn't be welcome. Would my son be welcome here?"

"Yes!" I said, channeling my Kevo confidence with unwavering eye contact, "Your son, should he ever choose to visit, would be absolutely and completely welcomed here."

Jeremy's wife, Angela, came with him the next week, and they've been with us ever since.

23

Why Not Just Go For It?

Adey:

Our old denomination had declared its *No!* to inclusion, and we had left. I had bid farewell to my Forever Friends and welcomed in new queer ones. Our church had a new name. Nothing now stood in the way of us finally, and formally, and celebrationally, *COMING OUT!!*

Except for me. While I had guided us to the verge of being welcoming and inclusive in all the ways described in this book, with all of our thoughtfulness and measuredness and meetings and conversations, I, at the precipice, wavered. Still, I loved the people who would not come with us. I still had in my head the implosions that happened to churches at this moment. And it would still be years before I would truly dispel from within my soul the haranguing voice of the God of evangelical rectitude.

So thank God for Steve. Steve Watson is a good friend who is now the pastor of the Reservoir Church in Cambridge, Massacheusetts, in whose basement we had hunkered down conspiratorially so many years ago. Steve and I were talking regularly about everything—excitements, struggles, vision, anxieties. He heard me say, "I'm there in my heart! Our newer folks assume we are fully inclusive. Our gay attenders declare our welcomingness as their reason for joining the church, and I don't correct them ..."

I hesitated, and Steve said, "I'm detecting a 'but.'"

"Yes ... 'But'—I just haven't done it. I haven't yet made the leap."

"So, if you are actually 'there,'" said Steve, "why not just go for it?"

And that was that.

I don't know what magic Steve used, but it was a troubling mystery to Tom and David when at our next staff meeting I announced to them my readiness. "Really?" they said. "Well yay!! But what happened?" I related my conversation with Steve, and after processing with them a bit why they did not seem to have the degree of influence with me that a remote pastor friend did, we spent the next three months getting the church ready.

Three months of one more time talking to everyone we could in the church in restaurants, coffee shops, homes. Three months of anxiety wondering how each conversation would go. Three months of listening, not being defensive, saying, "Tell me more!" Some folks responding, "Oh—okay. Thanks for letting us know!" Some: "What?! We've been attending a non-welcoming church?" Some weeping happy tears, some sobs of frustration and loss.

We set January 17, 2016, the Sunday of the weekend of Martin Luther King Junior Day, as the date for our *Coming Out!* service. I was excerrified (excited and terrified), with the baseline anxiety of preaching multiplied by eight thousand. This is what I wrote to friends on December 13:

> We are doing well. Today we had our all time biggest service with the exception of Easter! It was super fun except there was standing room only! :) But that was kind of fun, too!
>
> We have told lots of people we are moving to put a public statement on our web page and make an announcement that we are fully inclusive … marriage and ordination. This will be January 17 and I will give a teaching.
>
> I thought we'd lose a lot but again we are gaining people so I'm not sure. I've had tons of sweet conversations and a few harder. But, way better than I anticipated. There is a distance, I learned, between welcoming and fully inclusive.
>
> Our LGBT community is growing; currently between 16 and 20 people, I believe.
>
> As much as I miss my former Evanston friends :(I have never felt freer and more in love with Jesus and our church. This is worth a lot!
>
> Love to you all

On January 13, four days before *Coming Out!* we sent this email to the church:

> This letter is to communicate an important development in the life of our church:
>
> Sanctuary Community Church will now be fully welcoming and inclusive of individuals who are lesbian, gay, bi-sexual, transgender, or queer (LGBTQ). We currently have LGBTQ individuals participating as members and leaders, and we are removing any remaining limitations on full inclusion in our faith community.
>
> Sanctuary was born as a church in a denomination that placed limits on LGBTQ participation, but about five years ago we began to question whether this practice was consistent with what we had come to know of the heart of Jesus. Our questioning was driven by our encounter with Jesus in the scripture and by our friendships with LGBTQ individuals who wanted to know God through a faith community just as we did.
>
> We began reading extensively, talking with other church leaders, and having conversations with leaders and members of our church about LGBTQ inclusion. We also began having LGBTQ individuals attend our church, enjoy the party that God seemed to be stirring up here, and join in the conversations.
>
> Through this process, we have come to embrace full inclusion for LGBTQ persons in Sanctuary Community Church. We believe this approach reflects the heart of God for LGBTQ persons and for our faith community, and that it represents a faithful reading of scripture.
>
> This inclusion has particular implications for two church-related matters: marriage and ordination. Sanctuary has already been welcoming LGBTQ individuals as members and leaders, and henceforth we will perform weddings of same gender people in the same way that we do with opposite gender couples, and, should God's affirmation of a person become apparent, we will ordain LGBTQ individuals as pastors in our church.
>
> At the same time, consistent with our approach to most matters of belief, we will neither assess nor require agreement with

this stance from those who attend Sanctuary. The practice of the church will be welcoming and inclusive. Members and attenders are free to maintain beliefs that are consistent or inconsistent with this practice and to keep those beliefs private or discuss them with others, knowing that such discussions will be met with the same respect and openness those in our church community treat all discussions of belief.

This coming Sunday, January 17, our Senior Pastor, Adey Wassink, will be preaching on this topic and what it means for Sanctuary. Pastoral staff is available to talk about anything related to this move with anyone in our faith community. We are thrilled to continue journeying forward together, receiving all the good things Jesus has for our church!

Sanctuary Pastoral Staff

Sanctuary Board

The next day we had only three requests for removal from our email list. 😖

Evangelicalism Says Goodbye to Us

A couple months before *Coming Out!* Tom had said to Mark and Anna, our leading voices of evangelical dissent, "Let's have breakfast." They had increasingly been questioning Tom about his perceived diminishing commitment to their central concern, the authority of the Bible. Over breakfast, Tom had affirmed that their perceptions of him were accurate: while he loved the Bible more than ever, he no longer adhered to their evangelical conception of scripture, with the disparity between their views and his probably only going to increase with time.

We went to their house one evening in the week before *Coming Out!* While they served us tea and dessert, they told us that we were being too hasty, and that we were making our decision without input from them and other like-minded church members with whom they had been talking. They felt we were ignoring important biblical principles of marriage and gender. They described their years of investment and connection to a church that had become home to them, but that they would no longer be able to attend. It was a heavy and raw evening. When Tom and I left their home, we drove to David and Ali's to have them pat us on the shoulder and say, "There, there, everything's going to be okay."

Mark and Anna soon wrote a letter to the pastoral staff and to many in the church describing their decision to leave, which included:

> We seem to differ in how we understand the interplay of biblical text, ancient culture, and current culture.
>
> We agree with the principles articulated in Webb's *Slaves, Women, and Homosexuals.*
>
> We don't agree that LGBTQ sexual activity is consistent with the Scripture's overall teaching about human sexuality and marriage.
>
> The good news of Jesus also includes aspects seldom unpacked on Sunday mornings (e.g., the good news of his atoning sacrifice, his triumph over evil and sin, his enthronement as Lord over all, his return as judge, etc.).

They concluded with a heartfelt affirmation of love and blessing toward the church and its leaders. It was, I think, a fair letter. Mostly accurate perceptions of us, and a pretty good summary of what I think evangelicalism's critique of who we had become would have been. Mark and Anna were connected to a group of friends in the church who were going to leave with them, perhaps four families beyond theirs which, including kids, totaled about fifteen people. Their last Sundays at Sanctuary came within a month or two of each other. We never tried to control what those considering departure could or couldn't say, or to whom. Some notified church friends of the last Sunday they'd be in attendance, others didn't. Some had tearful gatherings with friends in the foyer, others just became not there anymore.

On January 15th, 2016, *two* days before *Coming Out!*, Anna and I met one last time. She made the case again that she and those she represented felt unheard, and she continued her critique of Tom. I wrote to my Blue Ocean friends that evening:

> Thank you all for your unending support. I like my *Coming Out!* teaching. I think it will be good. A vast majority are with us. I recovered after only an hour today. Vast improvement!!!! :)
>
> So, here we go!
>
> Love to you all,
>
> Adey

Tom wrote a little while later:

> I think, for the most part, I'm feeling fine. I've got weaknesses and proclivities, but I basically feel good about how I represent Jesus to our little corner of the world through the bible. I actually feel vindicated being the villain ...
>
> Bleh.
>
> Thanks for all of you being in this with us,
>
> Tom

Then on January 16th, 2016, one day before *Coming Out!* ... nothing happened.

24

David and Ali

David, remember, grew up in Indiana, studied philosophy at the University of Iowa, then worked for an evangelical college ministry for a few years. He then pursued and obtained a master's of divinity at North Park Theological Seminary, the denominational seminary of the Evangelical Covenant Church. We welcomed him as a pastoral intern, and urged him to stay on with us, which he did. Ali is a young adult novelist and high school literature teacher. While she was in college, she also was a leader in one of the first Christian student groups in the U.S. to be shut down by their college because of non-inclusion.

Ali and David came over to our house one evening, and while their son watched game five of the 2017 NBA Eastern Conference Finals between Cleveland and Boston in our living room, the four of us sat out on our porch under a quietly darkening Iowa sky. We talked through the narrative arc of their conservative religious background, their coming to us, and them becoming all in with *Coming Out!*

꒰꒱

Adey: David, when we first began having conversations about LGBTQ inclusion, you were totally in the *No!* camp. What do you remember being most afraid of?

David: Nothing—because even framing the conversation around "afraid," around fear, denies my narrative from back then—what, seven years ago? I wasn't afraid, I just knew the truth. The whole conversation was about Truth. But our story makes more sense if you start with Ali because the whole issue came to her in a big way, long before it did for me.

Adey: Oh, okay. Ali?

Ali: *[pauses]* For me, the story starts a lot earlier—like when I was a young girl—followed by what happened in college. My earliest romantic/sexual experiences were with girls. I would today describe myself as a bisexual person. But in seventh grade I converted into a conservative Bible church, so I quickly dismissed the sexual stuff as experimentation. I shut that down—"Turn it off, like a light switch!"

Tom: So your inner proclivities were toward freedom, but the church taught you otherwise …

Ali: Totally. And it was the same with gender roles, and women being leaders. I read a Bible passage—Acts 2—to my pastor in which the gender-specific language had been corrected, and he corrected me! He later preached a sermon about how gender was rigidly fixed. And while I personally made some progress with leadership issues, I never felt comfortable reclaiming my own sexuality. So I arrived in the fall of 1995 as a Christian freshman to my tiny militantly liberal private college in the middle of the Iowa corn fields.

Our guiding ethics were freedom, equality, and self-governance, and that fall we were in the middle of being really activated about LGBTQ acceptance, the kind that says, *There is a problem!!* The campus was vibrating like a taut string around inclusion, and when it came to the Christian scene, many churches had joined in, displaying rainbow flags out front. I had come from my conservative church and walked into a production on campus of the Jesus Seminar by Marcus Borg who said that all claims of the supernatural about Jesus were bogus. I went to chapel and freaked out when they prayed to Mother/Father God. *Where's Jesus?!* This was my first Sunday—we hadn't had any classes yet. I left chapel weeping and headed to my dorm room across the quad through wafting bong smoke to call my parents to come get me.

Tom: But you graduated from there, right?

Ali: Yes. I was saved by two white T-shirts. As I got to my dorm, two boys coming towards me were wearing T-shirts with crosses. *Thank God,* I thought, *my people!* They were from InterVarsity Christian Fellowship. My pastor knew and had told me about their staff worker. "Take me to your Anna!" I said. They did, and I went. They were thrilled that there was a freshman who wanted to come—not a good sign—but I had found people who knew the Jesus I knew.

Adey: They knew the "True" Jesus?

Ali: Yes! They now seem to me cult-like. I remember, when later describing them to a friend, starting out, "It wasn't a cult …" which was probably telling. But they helped me make it through my freshman year. Then, in the fall of my sophomore year, the explosion happened.

Adey: That sounds ominous.

Ali: Yes, *[takes a deep breath]* through one of our student members, we had invited a pastor from nearby to come in and lead an evangelistic event. For us, it was a huge deal—lots of prep, posters all over, energy and excitement, and a big room reserved. And of note, the advertising posters had pictures of our faces on them above the caption, *Come Hear the Truth I Stake My Life On!*

Adey: Oh my.

Ali: Leading up to this, one of our student leaders had come to the leadership team after studying one of Paul's letters, saying, "I don't see the Bible anymore in the same way you do." Her issue was with LGBTQ exclusion. She had written us a letter about her concerns, offering to step down from leadership, and we had said, "Let's wait to talk about this till after the event." There was also a young man in our Bible study who was gay and celibate, and therefore to us a hero. We all felt, what other alternative is there for a gay Christian?

Anyway, the big event came and … the quality was not good. Not a good event. But quality turned out to be way secondary. Our real undoing was the press coverage. The school paper had gotten hold of the letter of concerns from our female leader, and had heard about our celibate gay leader, and had published a scathing article about the event with the headline ***Campus Christian Group Refuses to Welcome LGBT Students Into Leadership!***

Our pictures had been on the ads, so everyone knew exactly who we were. So *all* the students in my sophomore class—except for me and one other— and *all* the new students in the freshman class, left our Christian group, like, that day. They were enraged. They didn't want to be aligned with non-inclusive people. Within a week, the dean called us in and revoked our student group status. Freaking out, we went to our fellowship's regional director, asking, *What do we do?* The RD told us point blank, "Our Fellowship will disavow you."

Tom: Wait—"disavow"? Like in *Mission Impossible*?

Ali: Yup. Our regional people said that if we didn't have official status on campus, the national organization wouldn't send us help. "You are dead to us," they were saying, "unless you fight this." We were the first—or maybe the second—chapter of our national group in the whole nation that this happened to. In the end, we got reinstated for reasons of due process, but the group was left in ruins.

Adey: And what about you? What happened to you?

Ali: It was devastating, horrible. Our group claimed to have the corner on Jesus Christ in this place, but I had no friends. The only people who would talk to me were the few still in our chapter. Everyone else in the entire student body disconnected from me, shunned me, like some Amish punishment. Professors in class would refuse to call on me, acting like I wasn't in the room. Students in the quad would turn away, or spit at my feet. A columnist with the *Des Moines Register* got wind of what happened, tried to reach us, ended up talking only to me, and then derided me in print: "I hope one day she has the humanity to see …"

And with us now having been reinstated as a student group, our staff worker just doubled down on our "theological truth." We were reading conservative stalwarts like Leanne Payne, Mario Bergner, and lots of others. I remember a meeting with student leaders where a staff worker mapped out thirteen arguments against homosexuality.

Adey: Did it ever get better?

Ali: *[sighing]* Yes. Junior year, a friend of mine from the group and I chose to live together in a dorm with a lot of LGBTQ students. We went in telling ourselves, *We're not going to evangelize, and we're not going to try to start a Bible study. We're just going to make friends and love people.* And it was great! We all hung out together, baked brownies together, and the whole floor really bonded, became close. I think my own sexual identity got reawakened because I kind of fell in love with one of the women. I still believed it was wrong …

David and Ali Come to Sanctuary

We took a break, got some food, checked email, shook out our *shpilkes* (yiddish for nervous energy that makes you need to run around the house three times). David and Tom checked on the game. Cleveland was ahead 75-57 at halftime which made Ben happy because he thinks Lebron is awesome. We settled back onto the porch, with wine for Adey and Ali, beer for Tom and David. The sun was low, winking through the leaves, with tree frogs and cicadas screeing in the background.

Adey: So, Ali, I know you're in a totally different place now. How did you get there? How did your conservative theology and college trauma affect you when our church here began to wonder about inclusion?

Ali: Oh, it just continued to be a jumble. At the point that the church began the LGBTQ conversation, neither David nor I had changed that much theologically. We still believed it was wrong. But bigger than that, as soon as I heard that you and Tom were beginning to question the church's LGBTQ stance, I was triggered—*Oh no, not again! I can't do this again.*

David: We'd started coming to what is now Sanctuary in 2003. We had just gotten married and wanted to choose a church that was new to both of us so that we could make it ours together. And back then, it was the home church for a ton of our InterVarsity friends and staff workers.

Tom: Yeah, the Vineyard movement, and our Vineyard church, had been just right back then for modestly progressive conservatives—contemporary worship music, safe and occasional contact with the Holy Spirit, an aspiration to social justice, but all of it still safely ensconced in the Authority of Scripture.

David: Right. So after I'd become an intern, I'd come home and tell Ali about our staff meetings. I remember when I first started, Gusty had been coming to the church for a while. You both were really messed up by the restrictions she experienced—by how trapped she was. I'd come home and tell Ali, "Tom and Adey may be more liberal than you and me on this issue."

Ali: I remember! We were in the bathroom getting ready for bed. "If this thing happens again," I said to David, "we're leaving!"

David: And I was with her. The whole thing was still very academic for me. I had a theological commitment to heterosexual sex, so I said back to Ali,

"Yup—if it goes any further, we're leaving." We still had all this evangelical teaching in our heads—being gay wasn't a thing you could actually be because it reflected a wrong understanding or corruption of the concept of identity. We'd been educated about homosexuality and the politics of truth.

Ali: And about how clever liberals had developed deceptive "plausibility structures" that created space for homosexuality as an acceptable thing.

Tom: I remember "plausibility structures"! Just the term—*plausibility structure*—sounded smart, and implied the deep systematic deceptiveness of pro-LGBTQ thought.

David: But as much as we tried not to be, we were increasingly conflicted. A number of things had happened to produce chinks in our evangelical armor.

Ali: Like becoming a parent! We adopted Josh in 2007. I remember rushing to the hospital when he was born and holding his little self for the first time. I thought, "If he's gay and I have to choose between him and Jesus, *I choose him!*" Then I thought, "Whoa, where'd that come from??" I was totally surprised by how fiercely I loved him. And then for David, a class he took on the cultural construct of disability was really important.

David: Yeah, for the first time, I was asked to consider a way of understanding disability that was not centered around deficit or lack or something that needed to be fixed. That individuals with disabilities were not flawed or less, but were fully human and complete, and actually often had much to teach us about perceiving and loving.

Adey: That's exactly what Luke and Tracy came into with Jeffrey!

David: I remember talking to them. And I wondered, does this connect at all with how I'm thinking about inclusion? How much do I think about gay people as if they were flawed or impaired or less? What if my thinking about them has been all wrong?

So I was all over the place. The division between desire and behavior, or identity and behavior, was still important to me. I needed categories, with tidy clear-cut boundaries. *We don't know why they're gay—and we love them— but they cannot act on it!* At the same time, my theological commitments were breaking down when I tried to bring those commitments into the world of real people who I loved.

Tom: So there were more real world things?

David: Oh yeah. Front and center were Alden and Adan.

Ali: It was another bathroom "conversation"—meaning "argument." All conversations of moment for us happen in the bathroom. David was saying to me, "I haven't changed theologically, but what am I supposed to do pastorally? Tell them to divorce and lose their children?" And I was like, "Of course not—that would be awful!"

My reaction was exactly the same as with Josh—immediate and certain. This was no longer theoretical but pastoral, and it was the first time that David named it to me. *Oh, thank you,* I thought. *That gives me language for what we've been stumbling toward.*

David: Alden and Adan weren't with us for long, but it was enough to give human form to what had been for us until then imaginary. They stirred in us *pastoring*—caring for real people—that took the place of asking theoretical questions about constructs of people.

Ali: And somewhere in there, David and I had a really meaningful conversation with friends who were visiting us from out of town. One of them was African, from Ethiopia, and we were describing the church's questionings about LGBTQ inclusion to him, that we were maybe leaning towards being more open, specifically wondering if marriage was a gift to everyone. And I remember him suddenly declaring:

"I say, Let them marry! Let them marry! Let them marry!"

I was totally shocked, maybe because he was from a more conservative part of the world, but also just the surprise, the way his statement leapt out of him, like a biblical pronouncement. And I thought, *If he says it's good, it must be good!*

Tom: I keep waiting for the Sanctuary Community Church moment— but that's probably not going to come, right? Where one of our awesome teachings lifts your blinders, or you have a prayer experience in the church in which the unveiled Jesus intones at you with outstretched finger, "You shall henceforth *include!*"

David: Yeah, sorry. Many of the church's supposedly seminal moments were kind of lost on us, like your teaching from 2008 about the woman caught in adultery, or our leaders' conversation at The Meeting. Even though our theology back then still leaned conservative, we had both wanted something more.

Ali: It felt like in *The Meeting* and in the adulterous woman teaching, people were saying nice things, but there wasn't much substance. It was mostly sentimental and emotional—*let's all be kind*—but I couldn't tell back then if anything useful came from those things.

Tom: If I may venture an obviously self-serving wondering: It seems that most of your remembered shaping experiences happened either outside the church or, if inside, they were unplanned. Maybe we at least provided a safe space in which we were working out the same stuff, and so in which it was possible for your experiences to produce influence in the direction of inclusion?

David: Yes, totally. And however it all worked, by the time we left the Vineyard in 2014, and then came out as fully inclusive of LGBTQ individuals in 2016, Ali and I were all in.

Ali: By the time it happened, I felt great about our church's coming out. The process was great. We did talk a lot. We talked and talked … and talked. Which was good, or it wouldn't have gone as peacefully as it did. And so once it happened, we were ready. It was so celebratory!

David: And I attribute my own transformation a lot to you guys. After about a year on staff with you, I realized that my primary commitment had shifted away from my principles—a commitment to Truth, or to the Bible—and toward our community. I had come to trust the two of you and had come to feel that my primary loyalty was now to this church and to you both as leaders.

The way you live your lives is an invitation into the bigger, more profound issues that are occurring. You taught me to think about relationships, and power dynamics, and fear. I would never, for example, have been able to frame this whole conversation in terms of fear—*what is the anxiety that is driving exclusion?* You worked hard to make clear what the goals of the process, and of all the individual pieces of the process, were. You led with wisdom. You focused on fruit and fruitfulness as a primary guide for what to do.

The Sun Sets

Tom:

The Iowa sun had set. Our faces floated in darkness, illumined with a soft yellow glow from a dim overhead porch light. David went inside to check on Ben: "Lebron's on his way to the finals!"

And I wondered, *How did Ali keep coming to church?* The question burned in my brain. She helps launch a celebration of Jesus that lurches horribly awry; she's recognized and called out—"you're one of them!"—jeered, vilified, brought before the authorities, abandoned by her friends, expelled. It all sounds strangely Christlike, but topsy-turvy because she was back then on the wrong side! She was against the ones who we and she have now come to be for. She nonetheless keeps going to church, but just when she thinks it's safe, David says, "Tom and Adey may be more liberal than we thought."

How does she back away from "We're leaving!"? How does she turn the corner with us? And to the point of this book, what of Ali's story speaks to how to do church? I was also, once upon a time (1981) a freshman in a conservative Christian campus group while attending a liberal-leaning college. The group gave me ready-made friends and a familiar structure that tethered me to the God of *No!* in a strange new world. I dove deeply into the same evangelical know-the-answers save-sinners way of life. Then I apparate ahead 35 years, and I'm an activated liberal progressive railing back at my conservative college self.

Is it possible for every iteration of our time-stretched beings to inhabit one faith community? For the same faith community to contain all that we have been and all that we will become? Can we create a sacred space for the freshpeople Alis in our midsts to wend their way into inclusion, while simultaneously fully welcoming those whom Ali herself had tried to exclude, including Ali's true self? What if our guiding ethic is: *We are beings who are becoming!* Flux is our state of being. No one has arrived, and so no one has finished, and so no one can be judged or assessed, at least not in the usual way, like by administering objective cross-sectional tests or questionnaires. And belonging comes not from having safely entered into The Good Place, but instead from accepting the reality of always being en route.

෴

David: Can I tell one last bathroom story?

Adey: I must have a prayer time in your bathroom. It is to you what Newport Road is to Tom and me.

David: I was brushing my teeth one evening after we had made the turn and were heading towards *Coming Out!*, and I asked myself, *What's the problem??* Why would God withhold from anyone that which produces good in the world? I couldn't name one good reason for saying no to welcoming and inclusion, because the fruit was so good. That moment, I felt released from my academic quandary. There is no command against love.

25

A Cold Rainbow Sunday Morning

On January 17ᵗʰ, 2016, the temperature in Iowa City at 10 a.m. was -7°F with winds out of the northwest at 17 mph for a wind chill of -30°F. But cancel church we would not! Our daughter had come down from Evanston, IL to be with us for this service. Katie had lesbian friends who would be attending for the first time. Katie and Paula would lead us in communion. All our Blue Ocean friends were cheering us on. Total attendance turned out to be 221, which was pretty good for doing church on a holiday weekend (MLK Day) in an industrial freezer. Attendance the same Sunday the next year, when the temp was 23°F, would be 319.

The congregation was expectantly restive, bursting, tearful from go. Cory and JJ led worship, beginning at the top of the service with *I Love to Tell the Story*:

> *I love to tell the story / Of unseen things above*
> *Of Jesus and his glory / Of Jesus and his love*
>
> *I love to tell the story / Because I know 'tis true*
> *It satisfies my longings / As nothing else can do*
>
> *I love to tell the story / 'Twill be my theme in glory*

To tell the old, old story / Of Jesus and his love

I love to tell the story / For those who know it best
Seem hungering and thirsting / To hear it like the rest

And when in scenes of glory / I sing the new, new song
'Twill be the old, old story / That I have loved so long

I love to tell the story / 'Twill be my theme in glory
To tell the old, old story / Of Jesus and his love
To tell the old, old story / Of Jesus and his love

We won't put in the lyrics for all the songs we sang that Sunday, but after everything it had taken to get us to *Coming Out!*, to linger just a bit, even now in the remembering … Next came *Be Thou My Vision* with *Spirit of the Living God* as a refrain. A bit hymn-heavy for us, yes, but overlaying this Sunday morning on Christianity writ large felt right.

David then stepped up to the podium and began announcements with a new statement of welcome, crafted from a template that Leah developed for her Berkley church, that is now the first thing people see printed on the wall as they come into Sanctuary's foyer and that we read every Sunday morning:

We are a community that makes space
for every race, ethnicity, age, orientation, and gender identity.
We welcome belief and doubt, devotion and exploration,
while hoping to connect with God, one another, and our world
as we do life together.

Then announcements—an upcoming women's retreat, welcome back students, *blah blah blah*. David stepped down and I took the stage. Carrying twenty-five double-spaced rustling pages containing 3,197 words. My hair done the day before; don't remember what outfit I wore. Fidgeting with the stupid cordless mic. Sighing and looking out, making eye contact with a few, pausing an extra beat, smiling beatifically, tearing up:

Welcome everyone. This morning is unusual because we are marking a specific occurrence in the life of Sanctuary.

This morning I am publicly sharing the decision by the church staff and board that Sanctuary Community Church will be fully inclusive of LGBTQ people. This means that we will place no restrictions on any church participation or practices based on sexual identity.

[cheering and applause]

For some of you, you may be confused thinking, "Hasn't the church always been this way?" Not exactly. That's what today's story is about.

I began by talking some about my experience growing up Jewish, with my people the object of pervasive and multi-layered stigmatization. However much we Jews had banded together to oppose the many historical attempts of humankind to eliminate us, and to decry the many daily exclusions perpetrated against us by dominant gentile culture, nonetheless:

Like many children who grow up being discriminated against, I internalized our collective shame ... It is a terrible thing to live in a community and yet be denied the accepted rights of that community.

Christianity, I was aware, had not helped us:

There are four verses in the Gospel and Paul's writing that were used as a rationale to persecute Jewish people. Many people don't know that Martin Luther who led the Reformation also led the burning of synagogues. As a result of the antisemitism I experienced, I became sensitized to any type of exclusionary practice.

I talked about Jesus inviting the woman Mary into the role of disciple; Paul's vision of Jesus as one who tears down, rather than builds up, walls; the history of exclusion and harm perpetrated against LGBTQ individuals by the church; and the goodness for both *us* and *them* of having LGBTQ individuals worshiping freely in Sanctuary; ultimately asserting that:

Jesus rejects the whole project of exclusion—the whole mindset that underlies it.

I made a plea for those who thought differently to stay with us, and then said:

> As our views on gender have changed, friends would say to me, "Adey, you've changed." Yes. I hope I/we are changing all the time. Change is not a bad thing. It is not something we fear. God is continually opening our eyes to see differently in all domains of life. And it is never a neat process when it happens. Everyone doesn't see at once. Everyone doesn't see the same things. Change is often messy. People get hurt. I don't say that lightly—it's real.
>
> Over the last few years, something happened to me. It is something I can neither boast about nor apologize for. It is just the truth. I can no longer in good conscience lead a community that is not fully inclusive. Some people may say that this is an emotional decision, that because I have many wonderful LGBT friends I'm being led by my emotions. Well, let me just confirm that. I am an emotional being as well as an intellectual and spiritual being, and this decision comes from all of me. In my heart of hearts I am convinced that this is the right decision for our community. God forbid we disconnect our heart from our theology.
>
> Ultimately we wish every single one of you all of God's blessing. Paul says of the divisions in his day: *There is neither Jew nor Gentile, neither slave nor free, nor is there male and female, for you are all one in Christ Jesus. If you belong to Christ, then you are Abraham's seed, and heirs according to the promise.* The good news of celebrating full inclusion is that no one is excluded, and if any one is excluded, then we're all in jeopardy.
>
> Let me be clear: This isn't a moment for straight people to pat ourselves on the back. It's not as though straight people are the gatekeepers. Jesus himself is the gatekeeper *and* the gate. He has thrown wide open the welcome into God's presence. So this is the moment when we're celebrating Jesus including us all. The divine work of Jesus is that he brings every person from a place of exclusion to a place of profound belonging, inclusion, and welcoming.

We all need this. This is why Sanctuary exists! This is why we do everything we do. And we hope that as we continue to follow Jesus' lead in this area and every other area of church life, we will experience the abundant life and joy that Jesus offers.

From this moment on Sanctuary community church will welcome all people into full participation in every aspect of community life!

I am quite sure that this was met with applause and cheering. But the best was yet to come. Here's what we did next, per my Sunday morning script:

Adey: For communion this morning, I'd like to invite Paula Boback and Katie Imborek to come forward to help serve.

[Katie and Paula come up on stage. Tom and David come up also.]

Adey continues: Katie and Paula and their two children have been members of our church community for several years, and they have been an integral part of our process and they are beloved friends. Katie will first read the Scripture from 1 Corinthians, after which Paula will serve our pastoral staff—Tom, David, and me—the communion elements.

Katie reads: Paul wrote in 1 Corinthians: "The Lord Jesus on the night when he was betrayed took a loaf of bread, and when he had given thanks, he broke it and said, 'This is my body that is for you. Do this in remembrance of me.' In the same way he took the cup also, after supper, saying, 'This cup is the new covenant in my blood. Do this, as often as you drink it, in remembrance of me.' For as often as you eat this bread and drink the cup, you proclaim the Lord's death until he comes."

Paula speaks as she serves: "This is the body and blood of Christ, broken and shed for you."

[David, Tom, Adey receive the elements.]

Adey: The worship band can come forward now as we continue with communion. If you wish to be fed by Jesus, you're welcome to participate in communion. There are stations in the front and back, and you're welcome to come individually or in groups, serving yourselves or one another.

You can also take this opportunity to receive prayer. There are church members available to pray with you in the foyer for (specific item related to teaching) or anything that you'd like prayer for.

But now, I'd like to lead us in prayer—please stand as you're able. [pray]

[Katie, Paula, and staff exit stage. Music starts.]

Then four songs for our worship set, and we were *OUT!!!*

A Happy Rainbow Sunday Evening

At 6:33 p.m. that evening, I wrote to Leah Martens and Emily Swan:

Well, we did it!

We had around 220 people which isn't bad considering it was -7 degrees and a three-day weekend and we knew some conservative folks wouldn't come because, although they want to stay, they also feel funny celebrating.

My talk was really well received. I saw lots of people crying throughout the room. I had amazing conversations. Progressives, crying with joy. Conservative folks saying they love us more because they feel so welcome and respected!!! Holy cow!

Worship was amazing! Cory prayed a deep and stunning prayer.

Katie and Paula served the pastoral staff communion on stage and we all cried.

Katie and Paula brought another lesbian family that loved the service and will likely worship with us. (A fun story.) Another family brought their aunt who is lesbian and used to attend a conservative church but hasn't been in church in decades … so sweet!!! Maybe ten or so LGBT folks in the room. Super emotional. One young male doctoral student just hugged me and cried! Thank you, Jesus.

Leah, at the raucous post-party at Katie and Paula's, Katie gave a talk and honored you as a pioneer called by god to be an ally, pastor, etc. of the LGBT community.

Thanks and love

Katie:

At 10:34 p.m., I wrote to Adey:

So … I don't want this day to end because it has been amazing. Though I am really exhausted and will fall into bed. I am helping Paula plan her school lesson about MLK for tomorrow and just listened to his I Have a Dream speech and Robert Kennedy's speech on the campaign trail the night Martin Luther King was killed. I love the fact that you chose this Sunday to do this! Maybe it was totally coincidental … regardless, I love Paul's vision of the kingdom in Galatians and MLK's interpretation of it in his speech. I think today was a perfect way to honor the vision that Martin lays out for ALL of God's children— 'Black men and white men, Jews and Gentiles, Protestants and Catholics.'

It is so amazing to be part of a community where ALL truly means everyone. I am honored to have been a part of this and love you so much … and your kids. I can't believe that Cassie came in from Chicago to be there! And Joe[5] is just the cutest ever. He was so happy today.

It was awesome. It was vulnerable and real and perfect.

How is Puck??? *[our dog was sick]*

See you soon.

Love,

Katie

---

5 One of our sons.

26

Jill and Nicki

Jill and Nicki had started coming to Sanctuary in 2015, so less than a year before *Coming Out!* Adey and I hosted a conversation with them after *Coming Out!* which we wish you could see—them loving and kind and comfortable with each other, sitting in the pastor's office of the church they attend, speaking easily there the language of crush and affection and flirtation and kissing, embellished with glances, smiles, and tendernesses. It was a sacred hour.

Tom: Jill, take us back to when you were young. Were you aware of your sexual inclinations before Nicki?

Jill: Yes, I was aware of my sexuality before Nicki, but my history with my family kept me from pursuing that. My brother and I had been placed in several foster homes before coming to my aunt and uncle. Both of my biological parents were alcoholics. My dad left first, and then my mom, but my mom was so ashamed of herself at what was happening to us that she told the state of Iowa that she didn't have any living relatives. We were taken from her when I was 2 and my brother was 3. He was at that point changing my diaper, and he was going to the neighbor's house asking for food for us.

Adey: Wait—2 and 3 years old?

Jill: Yes. My 3-year-old brother was taking care of me. So we were taken away because of the concern of neighbors—they contacted Iowa's Department of Human Services. We spent one year in the foster system, going from home to home, and then a picture of us appeared in an Illinois paper, which my grandma—my mom's mom—saw.

Adey: Why was your face in the paper?

Jill: I have no idea. But my grandma saw it and called my Aunt Nancy—my mother's sister—and told her to go get us. So she did. So we lived with my aunt and her husband as foster children until we were adopted by them when I was 8 or 9 years old.

Tom: And being fostered with them was a good thing?

Jill: No, it was horrible! I struggled early on with abandonment issues—feeling angry, questioning why did my parents not love me? Why did they leave me?

Adey: And your aunt's was a church-going family, right?

Jill: Yes, but that just made everything worse. We'd go to church together every Sunday as a family. Then back at home when we were naughty, my aunt and uncle would use the Bible to help punish us. My aunt would take me to my bedroom and read a Bible passage at me related to what I'd done wrong, like if I lied, "Thou shalt not lie!" And then every time she'd include "Do not spare the rod."

But because my brother and I were in the foster system and wards of the state, they could not punish us in a way that left marks. So they would drag me by the hair from one side of the bed to the other, and then back. This was love, this was the Bible.

Tom: Wow. So, if I'm understanding right, the main thing that changed when you got formally adopted was that now they could punish you more severely.

Jill: Yes. They started actually using a rod. That's what it meant to become adopted.

Adey: Oh dear God. Keep going.

Jill: My brother and I were homeschooled until I had gone through third grade, then enrolled in a private Christian school through sixth grade, then from there were sent to a public junior high. It was a BIG transition. I went from sheltered and Christian—crazy Christian yes, but still "Christian"—to secular and diverse. And what I noticed right away was that all my classmates were extremely sexually active.

Tom: Really? Seventh grade?[6]

Jill: Yes—and I was not. I had been taught by my parents and my church that you save yourself for marriage because when you have sex with someone, you give up to them a piece of your soul. And I had crushes on girls. I knew what those were, but I didn't tell anyone. I remember in seventh grade a girl in one of my classes who I couldn't stop staring at—she was beautiful, gorgeous—I thought she was wonderful! And then the same in eighth grade—a girl who I played basketball with, a total crush—but I was terrified to talk to her. I stayed with my group of friends.

Nicki: You did the right thing—you dated a male.

Jill: Yes. I had confessed to my best eighth grade friend about my basketball crush—"I think she's really pretty."

Adey: "Confessed?"

Jill: That's what it felt like! Anyway, she horrifyingly immediately told *everyone*!

Adey: I hate our world.

Jill: So all my classmates freaked out and I shrunk back in. I made something up—"I just wanted to look like her." And then I tried to blow it off. It was mortifying, embarrassing. They all came to me—"so and so said," and I'd respond, "Don't believe it!"

Then, somewhere in ninth or tenth grade, I was sitting with my aunt—my adoptive mother—and her daughter—my cousin—at the table after dinner. And my cousin said, totally out of the blue, "What do you think Dad would do if I told him I was a lesbian?" My aunt didn't even pause—"Dad would probably disown you."

I was not expecting that or prepared for it, but it really stayed with me. I was adopted. I wasn't going to lose the only father and mother that I knew. It would take some time for me to come to understand that my cousin was bisexual, and knew it at the time, because we certainly didn't share those kinds of things with each other.

Tom: What church did your family go to back then?

Jill: One of the big popular evangelical churches right here in town. And I loved it! I went to their kids' catechism group every Wednesday night, won Bible memorization awards, went to every summer vacation Bible school—I was a church camp kid! I sang and watched, and loved God.

---

6 Okay, Tom is clueless.

And so I was terrified that coming out would be a deal breaker. These were my only parents. I needed them to want me and love me. I was still dealing with the rejection by my biological parents. My adoptive parents provided for me—clothes, activities, everything I needed—so I was dependent on them. They also spanked us with the rod when we disobeyed, or made me run laps in the backyard, or worse, run up and down the street in front of all my neighborhood friends, if I'd been "sassy." And then, when I was in seventh or eighth grade, we suddenly stopped going to church.

Adey: You didn't know why?

Jill: Nope. I still loved it, but we didn't go anymore.

Tom: So what happened after the conversation at the dinner table?

Jill: I dated guys. They always seemed nice, but then they would turn abusive. I dated one like that, before my daughter's father, that I broke off pretty quickly. Then *he* came into my life. He was always happy and fun, and telling me, "I love you, you're amazing." He did everything to make me feel special. He was cute and at the center of our group of friends. He pursued me. He was unbelievably persistent. So I married him when I was 17 and we had our daughter, Lexie. But soon after I got pregnant, he became demeaning and physically violent towards me. I kept Lexie, but left him.

Adey: Where during all of this were your sexuality questions?

Jill: The girls I was attracted to didn't know I existed. They seemed totally out of reach. A relationship like that seemed unattainable. I couldn't say it to myself, much less anyone else. So I pushed myself towards men.

Adey: So after you finally left him, how did you end up coming together with Nicki?

Jill: It was absolutely meant to be! While all this other stuff had been going on, my biological mother had stopped drinking, gotten back her degree in nursing, and was now working at a nearby nursing home. She had turned her life around and moved to be close to me and Lexie.

Adey: And so you had reconnected with her?

Jill: Yes—she had actually been asking me to come work for the same nursing home. My ex had gotten arrested sometime in there—this was fall of 2011—and so I had to work three jobs just to have enough to make ends meet. I had resisted my mom, but being a CNA paid way better than what I was earning, so after six months of her "harassing" me, I said yes! I signed up and started CNA training at the nursing home. There were only two other students—Nicki and one other woman. So I met Nicki in orientation, and there we were, taking classes together three nights a week. And the teacher was amazing. She really cared about us as people, and so drew us out with life questions.

Nicki: I'm quiet, but she drew me out.

Jill: She drew out our passions. Nicki was in love with her grandparents, taking care of them in their illnesses late in life. She would become so happy and animated when she talked about them. I couldn't stop staring at her when she was talking. She talked with her hands, and her face would light up. I became obsessed with her.

Nicki: I gave Jill my number and said maybe my nieces and her daughter could play together, but she didn't call me for a while.

Jill: My ex threw her number away! I think he knew. "Are you a lesbian?" he'd ask me. I'd make little comments about Nicki—"I met this girl in class"—little comments.

Adey: Then what?

Jill: He got arrested for domestic. The cops called me, they pressed charges even though I didn't want them to.

Nicki: The "nice" in her.

Jill: I got a no contact order. He got out of jail the next day, and right away he was calling and texting me. I called the detective. I went to Walmart to get more minutes for my phone, and my ex came out with a new phone that I think he was going to use to call me because it wasn't blocked. The cop was there to meet us and arrested him on the spot. I knew then that I had to move out.

Nicki: I helped her move.

Adey: Did you have a crush?

Nicki: Oh yeah.

Jill: That first day I thought—I met a beautiful girl … to have as my sister. We hung out, we studied together a lot. I knew I had feelings, but I didn't know how to make a move.

Nicki: I wasn't going to do that either—not first.

Jill: So one night, we went to a club with friends. We had a couple of drinks, and it loosened me up just enough—I confessed my love and planted one on her! I gave her a kiss!

Nicki: I didn't know it was coming! And it just went on from there. But it was really hard for her to tell her parents.

Jill: My mother [adoptive] found out from my sister [cousin]: "I just got off the phone with Stephanie!" My mother was worried that my ex's family would use our relationship in court to get Lexie back. She thought—or maybe hoped—it was just a phase, though I had already had Nicki over for Thanksgiving.

Nicki: As a friend I was okay.

Jill: We couldn't tell my grandparents. My parents made me say, "We're just friends."

Adey: I'm thinking with every word you say about Katie and Paula and their parents and Grandma I. I don't think either of you have heard their story, but it's exactly the same. So much worry about grandparents, and that worry used to control communication.

Nicki: I had a meeting with Jill's parents because of how hurt their feelings were. Her mother cried and quoted the Bible at me.

Adey: But Nicki, were your parents good?

Nicki: I came out to them in eighth grade.

Jill: When the two of us got engaged after one year of being together, Nicki's mom said to me, "Please be sure because I don't want you to hurt Nicki." She was worried that I was going to change my mind about being lesbian, that it was a phase or just temporary, or something.

Adey: So Nicki—your parents?

Nicki: They got there, eventually. When I first came out, my mother wanted me to talk to a minister, but I didn't want that. I knew what they'd say. I grew up Catholic, I actually now still wonder, am I really going to make it to heaven?

I never told my Grandma Rhonda—she was my best friend, but she was so deeply Catholic—and then she got dementia. Telling grandparents is hard. I couldn't disappoint them. While my friends were out partying, I was with my relatives, my grandparents. That's where I wanted to be—with them. They were the rocks of the family. They died six months apart. The family just took shifts taking care of them. We had a sign-up for scheduling our times. They never went to nursing homes because we had a rotation.

Tom: Do you think your grandpa knew?

Nicki: You can tell by looking at me—but he couldn't see! But a lady helping to take care of him in his home had seen me and Jill together and had said to him, "Nicki and her girlfriend …" So I told him, and then asked him, "Does it bother you?" This was just a couple of weeks before he died. He said, "No—this is the best news ever!" He called all the relatives, he was excited to tell everyone—it was great for me.

But I don't know about Grandma Rhonda. She was a devout Catholic, she prayed the rosary every day, she was in a Catholic women's group. I don't know if it would have changed things for her towards me, but I regret not having told her.

Jill: When I came out, my [adoptive] mom first told me, "You're going to hell!" But my dad said we're going to love her. I had one aunt who said, "If your mother would allow it, I'd slap the gay out of you!" She went to a conservative church, her kids were really sheltered—no *Harry Potter*, no *Lord of the Rings*! My mother's biggest fear when my sister/cousin went to college was that she would get a gay roommate—which is exactly what happened! They became best friends. My mom eventually came around, but only after her life had collapsed.

Adey: So how did your getting married actually happen?

Jill: I proposed to her after a year of us being together. It was so surprising—I had never seen myself proposing.

Nicki: And I never saw myself getting married. I thought of being in a relationship, but not *married*. I had no dreams of weddings or ceremonies or parties …

Jill: The timing was perfect—we got engaged right before the Supreme Court decision, so then it was all right.

Nicki: I wish we'd known about this church back then. We had a ceremony, but God wasn't in it. Her parents didn't want to walk her down the aisle; her dad didn't come.

Jill: I sent my grandfather an invitation, but never heard anything back. So I called and said, "Nicki and I are getting married and we really want you to be there." And he said, "You know I want to support you, and I love you, but we just can't jeopardize our chances of getting into heaven."

Nicki: So they didn't come.

Jill: My parents did at least show up. I talked to them a couple months after we got engaged: "We'd love for you to participate in the planning and help with the wedding." But just like my grandparents, they said no: "If we support you or give you money or walk down the aisle with you, we're jeopardizing heaven." It was heart-crushing.

So my biological mom walked me down the aisle. She loved Nicki from the start and just genuinely wanted me to be happy. She said she could see the change in me because of this relationship.

Tom: And what about church—how did you ever find your way to us?

Jill: I think I didn't go to church for so long because I was angry at the church. I grew up believing that all the church people in my life loved me and had my best interest at heart, only to hear them telling me that if I was this way and lived my life this way that God would see me as a sinner and I would not go to heaven. The rejection from church and Christianity had put me in a dark place and made me angry, made me feel icky.

I knew that God still loved me, and that who I loved didn't matter to him. But the church said that what I wanted to do wasn't okay; it was a sin. It made me feel like I had to choose between finally being happy and in a healthy relationship, and choosing God. It changed my relationship with him; it shut me off from him for a long time. I thought I was never going to be able to go to church again.

Nicki: But her friend Sheila pressed and pressed, and Jill really wanted church—more than I did. She still loved church.

Jill: I was desperate. I loved church—I just didn't think church loved me back. I anticipated judgment, and I didn't want to feel rejected by something that I had had such a positive response to growing up. I didn't want that to be taken away from me. But now that I knew who I was, I wanted back in.

I had a friend Sheila who went here. She reassured me again and again that this church was a safe place not only for me, but for my family. I was worried that the children at church would call attention to my daughter because she was different because she had two moms. She has been made fun of at school, though she handles herself very gracefully. At church, I wanted her to be able to focus on learning about Jesus and developing a healthy relationship with God.

Nicki: I knew we would stand out. It had been twelve years for me. Growing up Catholic, once I came out, it was clear because of judgment that church wasn't for me.

Jill: But Nicki said, "Let's go try it." We met Sheila here. We were expecting eyes, a little bit of whispering, and judgment—we'll just come to appease Sheila. But it was not at all what we expected. I walked in and immediately felt at home. I was with Nicki in the sanctuary for less than one full worship song, and I remember thinking, "Wow, maybe church isn't over for me." We loved everything! I felt at peace. We felt welcomed. People would come up to us and welcome us, and they genuinely wanted to get to know us. It was completely opposite of what I was expecting. You're expecting whispers, but you get shouts of welcome.

Nicki: Even my dad now comes, and he's Catholic! He doesn't take communion here, but still … The concept of God here is different. I was able to come here and worship, and be comfortable, and know there's a chance that God could love me.

In my CNA work for hospice, there was one woman I took care of for three years. Just recently, the week before she died, she was questioning her faith and her standing with God, kind of like how I've always done. She was a strong Catholic. "Don't question it now," I said to her. "You are super-kind. I know you're going to make it." That night I dreamt that she made it over, and the next day I saw she had died. "I don't know how you're going to get from here to there," I had told her, "but I know you're going to get there." I still see her husband occasionally, have a donut with him.

Jill: You [the church] have been amazing from the beginning. There's never been one hint of doubt about our welcome. But since you've become inclusive, taken open steps in that direction, and announce it boldly and bravely—it's almost like every Sunday you are saying, "Nicki and Jill, you are welcome!" It's for us, but it's also for everyone. The opening statement hits me every time, every Sunday—it makes me feel more loved.

27

A Final Liberation

Let's advance to the center of the faith community one last outcast:

John 8:1-11

At daybreak Jesus appeared again in the Temple, and all the people came to him, and sitting down he taught them. And the pastors and priests brought a woman who had been caught in adultery and, making her stand before everyone in the open, they said to him, "Teacher, this woman has been caught in the very act of committing adultery. Now in the Law, Moses commanded us to stone such a person; so what do you say?" (They said this to test him, so that they might have some accusation to bring against him.) Jesus, however, bending down, wrote upon the ground with his finger. But when they continued to question him, he stood up straight and said to them, "Let whoever among you is without sin be the first to throw a stone at her." And again, bending down, he wrote on the ground. And, hearing this, they departed one by one, beginning with the older of them, and he was left alone with the woman before him. And Jesus, standing up straight, said to her, "Madam, where are they? Does no one condemn you?" And she said, "No one, Lord." And Jesus said, "Neither do I condemn you; go, and from the now, sin no longer."

Jill confesses to ogling her eighth grade friend and is immediately outed in the open-air court of her peers—"horrifying ... mortifying!" Katie's high school and college queer peers are publicly excoriated *by her* because she had not yet accepted her own sexuality. But these traumatic outings are only pale auguries of the Big Gay Christian Judgment Day Outing to come when all gender non-conformers will be hauled before the Heavenly Supreme Court of Austerely Heterosexual Male Deities presided over by Chief Justice God with all living beings in the cosmos watching the unveilings in horrified fascination.

The Woman Caught in Adultery story is the apotheosis of the Christian sexual deviance outing. A woman is brought into the religious square, publicly, in front of her friends and family, by a group of angry religious societally-empowered men who declaim, publicly, to Jesus, "We caught this woman in the act of being lesbian. Our law (and yours) commands us to stone such women. What do you say?" So the penchant for killing is there from the start, the capstone in a string of traumas inflicted on the victim. She's been caught, arrested, dragged—powerless—humiliated, outed publicly, and threatened with a violent public execution in which all the onlookers would be required to participate. She has been, until this very moment, a friend and relation of the people in this very crowd who might in short order be tasked with killing her. So the threat, like with lynching and crucifying and burning at the stake, is not just toward her but hovers in the air over everyone. She is a harbinger of Jesus.

Under threat of which we watch Jesus cleverly negotiate a plea deal: *Wait just one minute guys,* he says to the men, and turns to confer quietly with the sinner. *If you, Oh lesbian woman, agree to not have queer sex anymore, I can probably use my celebrity status to get these angry men to back down. But,* he continues, *it'll be just this one time. Because they, according to God through the law of Moses—as I'm sure you well know—have a legitimate case against you. And I'm heading on to the next town after lunch, so I won't be here to save you if this happens again ...*

Our Bible translators—conservative men of the religious establishment—have expanded their mandate by providing headings across many Bible versions that indicate to us tender readers the story's central problem: "A Woman Caught In the Act of Lesbian" or: "The Queer Woman" or: "Mercy for a Sinful Woman" or: "A Lesbian Forgiven." Whatever else is going on, the foundational action of the story, the thing about which we are to be taught, is how God invites us all, through Jesus, to decry the commission of lesbian by a sinful woman.

Except that it's not.

The first action of the story is men dragging a caught woman to the court of God in order to bring accusations against her in front of hastily appointed Judge Jesus. Which action is perpetrated neither for the sake of the woman nor for the onlookers nor for righteousness nor for the honor of God, but simply to harm Jesus. The woman is to the men nonexistent, a nonhuman thing that they can literally manhandle in order to accomplish their nefarious aims.

And the second action of the story is:

Jesus bent down and doodled in the sand.

The content of the doodling has become for Christians a fetish—*what did Jesus write?!* we ask, pondering the mystery of his scribbles, inscribed ten-commandment-like by the finger of God, anticipating that our fascination will reveal … *something*. But all Christian fetishizing is self-serving nonsense, engaged in by us only to distract our attention away from ourselves. That we are not provided the contents tells us we don't need them.

The meaning of the doodling is what it communicates to the men about how Jesus perceives *them*. Or doesn't. The meaning of the doodling is the nonexistence to Jesus of the murderous men standing in front of him. The first Jesus-action of the story is him wordlessly "telling" the gloweringly rageful conservative men of the religious establishment, with their parishioners and the woman looking on: "You have no substance in my world, and so no voice in my court; you as currently constituted are nonexistent to me, non-presences, non-beings. So don't even bother trying to entangle me or Her in *your* system of condemnation!"

The ethics of their two systems are so completely non-overlapping that there is no possibility of meaningful communication between them. Words cannot bridge the gap. Language fails. But only Jesus perceives this, and so he responds to their words with enraging silence. Judge Jesus communicates to the prosecution not *case dismissed!* but *prosecution dismissed!* This is the first action of Jesus, the foundational thing he does, that which completely frames his post-trial debriefing with the woman.

But we contemporary glowering conservative men of the religious establishment reinsert our offended very existent selves back into the story two thousand years later, filling Jesus's silence with our words through our intruded headings—*notice "The Woman Caught in Lesbian!" we say. That's what this story's about!* We literally mutilate the text as we ourselves reembody the dissolved prosecution assemblage surrounding her and Jesus. *Lesbian!* we say. *She was caught in the act of it! It's really bad!* While we might not today physically pummel her, we'll certainly retraumatize her and any sympathetic friends back into submission while continuing to deflect attention away from our murderousness. So Jesus speaks his first and only words to us:

Let the one of you who is without sin throw the first stone …

And then he stoops back down to the sand. His spiritual pilates are themselves meaningful—squat down, straighten up, squat down. He has not yet spoken at all to the woman, choosing first to insert himself between her and us: *Let the one of you who is without sin throw the first stone.*

And we all … one by one … *publicly* … turn … and walk away …

It's breathtaking. What Jesus says works—spectacularly—*but why?* It can't be that the assembled men have all committed the exact same "sin" as her, nor even some other type of capital offense. Do they instead each realize through Jesus's injunction that whatever they've done makes them more kindred to her than different? Do they perhaps for the first time *see* themselves and her as human beings instead of chess pieces? Or at least do they realize that to validly perpetrate condemnation requires a quality of sinlessness that not only they but no human possesses? And all it would take is one! The "first" stone. Because after the first, the mob would be unleashed and the rest would fly. But whatever their inner workings, each and every one apparently detect "sin" in themselves—which realization apparently comes to each of them easily—and every single one walks away.

But in so doing, they are the ones who are outed! They are admitting to everyone watching, as they leave the public square without lifting a stone against the accused, *I have done something that would count as sin and that according to our system would mandate towards me a punishment that I am unwilling to bear.* And I have no desire for any of you to know what that sin is. My first thought, were I in that crowd watching, would be: I wonder what he did? Followed by: And what about him? … And what about him? Followed more unsettlingly by: I guess all of my pastors—each and every one—are more like her than I realized … and more like me … Do I still feel reverence for them in the same way that I did just a minute ago? … Who put them in charge anyway? … And who is that woman who's still talking with Jesus?

If this reversal of outings is the first outcome of the pastors' perp walk of shame, the dismantling of the entire legal system over which they, until that moment, had presided, quickly follows. Jesus stands up, faces the exalted woman, and says:

Is there no one left to condemn you?

to which she responds:

No one sir.

It's not just that the men have been outed; they have been completely discredited as voices of religious and moral authority while the woman has been elevated. The men are saying as they walk away, whether with awareness or not: *This system of condemnation and killing over which we have presided until this moment is defunct. It doesn't work. The system needs, apparently, good people in charge to condemn the bad ones, and since none of us qualify, the system is nonsense.* So not the woman but the system is abandoned, condemned, earmarked for demolition. The metaphor of religion as a court of law has not just been tweaked or reinterpreted by Jesus, but completely dissolved: Jesus has dismissed the plaintiffs, declined to act as judge, and refused to try the defendant. *There is no court, and so no forum for jurisprudence or judging or adjudicating sin or condemning or publicly outing anyone.*

Which takes the deconstruction of Jesus way beyond just disrobing some bad patriarchal men. The intention of the religious leaders in "making her stand before everyone in the open" is to produce unanimity of condemnation. Everyone in the courtyard, including the woman, is being coerced into agreeing that she is bad, that her badness is a threat, and so she must be expunged. Even God agrees! And Moses! And this uniting of a group through perpetrating violence against a powerless victim who has been falsely deemed a threat is effective. If the men succeed, the commitment of the group to the current power structure will be strengthened and Jesus diminished. But then Jesus doodles in the sand. He alone rejects the all-against-one accusation of threat … and the whole structure comes tumbling down. Jesus is exposing and undermining the human practice of groups in power vilifying the powerless for the sake of cohesion and stability, and it's stunning the degree of demolition that one voice of dissent can produce.

And if a new system arises to take the old one's place, guess who the founder(ess) will be? Jesus does not bend down again. He stays standing upright facing her: He has disrobed the men and clothed the woman. He has ensnared them while liberating her, humiliated them while exalting her *in front of her family and friends and religious community*. So when Jesus says to the liberated woman, "Go, and from the now, sin no more," it's **the** now, "tou" in Greek, "apo tou nyn," *from the now*. It's the same phrase used by Mary after Elizabeth confirms that God is in her womb: "Apo tou nyn all generations will call me blessed!" And by Paul when he describes what life is like after the death and resurrection of Christ: "Apo tou nyn we regard no one according to the flesh." Apo tou nyn marks an epochal shift in the nature of existence, with what came before being completely replaced by the marvelous unfamiliarity of what comes after.

So with our ennobled woman. When Jesus says to Her, "Go, and from The Now, sin no more," he is not saying: Go, but be careful henceforth because you're on probation and trouble still lurks around the corner, nor: Go, but be sure to resist, through an effort of will, the temptation that has plagued you because I might not be nearby to protect you from the just consequences of your debauchery a second time, but rather: "The system that had ensnared you in a role of disreputableness no longer exists. That system's mechanisms for perpetrating group violence against powerless victims, along with its overlords, have been dispatched, and you remain here exalted in their stead. You, of all people in this square, understand the difference between what was and what is supposed to be. So go forward into my new Now reality of liberation, free from the dominance of male-centric heterosexual sexuality, free from coerced roles of inequitable disreputableness for women. Inhabit instead my new Now in which condemnation and castigation and scapegoating and outing and even sin as you have conceived of it do not exist, with your sensibilities now at the center. Apo tou nyn!"

28

Theology *Not!*

One vacuum in our storytelling comes from this being a tale of flight. Most escape adventures—the Exodus, *Alcatraz*, *Schindler's List*, the *Barbie* movie—focus on what life was like in captivity, then the perilous journey out, and then the moment of liberation, with typically scant attention paid to afterward. Freedom as its own reward is the end of the story. So, to some degree, with ours. Our writing was prompted by observations from friends and fellow pastors and our editor/publisher: "Wow, your church emerged from evangelicalism into inclusionism, and didn't implode! You instead came out healthier and happier! Please tell us how you did that!" Which means that our narrative arc includes about 30 years of inhabiting, and then deconstructing, and then departing from evangelicalism before *Coming Out!*, followed by only a few years after. Which begs the question, *What have you reconstructed?* What are your new tenets? Your doctrines? Your catechisms? What's your take on Christology, or atonement theory, or theodicy? What is your essential new theology for those who might wish to replicate your thing?

After you coaxed us out from cowering in the back of our transept, here's why we might plead ignorance:

We have a church of 4-500 members and regular attenders (250ish on a Sunday (minus 10% for pastor estimation inflation)), led by two full- and four part-time pastors. It took us nearly a decade to write out the story of what our problem was and how we fled that, and so even if we became markedly more efficient, we'd encounter rate-limiting personal bandwidth constraints were we to contemplate putting into words the belief structure underlying what we have become.

Which is something we're still trying to figure out. It's not that we haven't supplanted our deconstructed malpractices with new understandings, but we just don't know yet how they all cohere. And even if we thought we did, the act of concretizing beliefs through a statement of faith or a doctrine of theology would violate at least two of our new core values: non-condemnation and becoming. If we don't judge interiority or identity anymore, why would we produce a theology for the purpose of ensuring unanimity or assessing adherence? It's not that we don't declare things about ourselves (e.g., "We're fully inclusive!"), but the anxiety driving the necessity of uniform correctness is gone. And anyways, if the new and central ethic of how we believe thought works is that we have never arrived but are always becoming, then the doctrine we'd produce would be out of date the instant it was published. We will, tomorrow, have read another book, suffered another trauma, prayed another prayer, or weeded out another bias that had till now cloaked our perception of God.

Our conservative theology produced deep harm to many people who we love, like Kevo and Katie and ourselves. It's taken 25% of our lived adult lives to escape from that, and we're still expunging vestiges of evangelical beliefs from our souls. We are thus not eager to jump back into any "theology." Behind which are the meta-questions, *Who is theology from and for anyway?* It may have played an important role in shaping thought across preliterate Christendom, but the foundational social structuring of theology is unavoidably patriarchal. Not just the theological thoughts themselves, but the nature of the academic, argumentative thought world from which theology is produced is prototypically alpha male.

And all theologies are contextually derived. We today declare that we are inclusive because we just were excluding. We vociferate many important "non-"s: non-scrutinizing, non-condemning, non-authoritarian; that reflect an evacuation of what we used to be. We might have the hubris to believe that "inclusion" is a timeless essential imperative of God that must be codified in our theology, but who knows what will have the same valence 20 years from now? The three of us coauthors are aware that there is a next generation of Christians who have not had to deconstruct conservatism, and for whom inclusion has been since their formative years the central pillar of their faith as given to them by church, and so for whom our central passions seem a bit dated.

All of which leads to one last new (for us) angsty question: *What is the Christian church for?* Many of our parishioners come because they were Christian already and wanted to inhabit that identity in a welcoming container. But in constructing the new container, we have turned all of evangelicalism on its head, including its personal and societal missionalness that too closely resembles colonialism. But if we're no longer mandated to bring all of humankind, along with the entire cosmos, under the lordship of Christ, then what is the good that God is trying to bring through us into the world?

29

Pulse

Adey:

On Sunday, June 12, 2016, our daughter Cassie was visiting from college, home for the weekend, hoping for a respite—sleeping in her childhood bedroom, seeing her brother, eating Dad-cooked food. Sunday morning meant worshiping in the church of her growing up—familiar songs, hugs, and cheering words from people who'd loved her her entire life, and easy connection with God. She came early with Tom and me and went to the coffee shop next door to read and sip tea while waiting for church to start.

At 9:50 a.m.—ten minutes before start time—while I was sitting in our usual seat in the second row messing with the stupid cordless mic getting ready to teach, Cassie burst into the room, running, sobbing.

"Oh my god, honey—what is it?!"

"They're dead! ... He killed fifty people!"

"Who's dead, honey??" My 21-year-old daughter is crumpled in my arms.

"A nightclub! ... gay people!"

Running to my office ... frantically reading cellphone headlines ... people walking in, cheesing their bagels, dawdling, chatting, wandering into the sanctuary. Gay friends sitting down. *Do they know? No, they look too calm.* Tom's going to give announcements. I find him.

We've sung our opening two songs. People sit and *say hello to someone near you.* Tom takes the stage. I don't know what he's saying, but he finishes his announcements and then in a shaky voice tells a room full of unsuspecting people what they'll be hearing as soon as they leave:

A shooting at a nightclub in Miami ... targeting LGBTQ individuals ... dozens wounded and dead ... pray with me ...

There was a collective gasp in the sanctuary. Folks grabbing their cellphones. People crying. It took me five minutes to stop crying once I got to the podium. Random people bringing me Kleenex. I have no idea what I talked about. We cried as a body, people in shock, unable to make meaning.

After church we were zombie huggers. We walked around in a daze, making our way to all our friends, particularly our queer folks. Kevo said to me, "Adey, I'd stopped being afraid! You know, after all the years of being frightened, I had come to a place of peace. Now I'm afraid again!" Gay friends were terrified and traumatized. Straight friends wanted to know what they could do to help—where could they give money? Was the church going to do something?

Iowa City held a candlelight vigil the next evening, June 13th, in our downtown congregating space called the PedMall. After remarks from community leaders and a reading of the names of the forty-nine slain, the event organizers opened the microphone. For the next two hours, people tried to put into words their grief, fear, and outrage. One queer woman of color took the microphone and just screamed. A college-aged straight man told of his recent realization of the multitude of privileges that he is afforded because of his heterosexuality. A 15-year-old bisexual girl told us all that she came out to her family at age 12, that she had been embraced and loved by her peers, and that she had been promised that life for those like her in her generation would be different.

And a straight woman, through tears of anger and dismay, railed against the silence of the church. She described desperately scouring the local paper and social media for any suggestion of a prayer vigil in response to the tragedy. Finding none, she petitioned the crowd, asking those who found meaning in crying out to God through prayer to meet in the far back corner of the PedMall after the event. She didn't pray over the microphone, knowing that for some the invoking of God's name in the context of sexuality and gender identity violence might trigger more trauma.

Political figures had been tweeting incessantly about praying for the victims and their families without acknowledging that this was a targeted attack on LGBTQ people. The prevailing directive out of many churches was to pray for the victims while continuing to make clear that same-sex relation-ships are against God's design—praying for others with the all-too-common asterisk attached. So it felt right to pray with this woman after the event in the back corner. LGBTQ people have been relegated to the margins by the church for so long, now in their space it was our turn.

Our Sanctuary parishioners who attended the vigil left feeling helped but still needful. Grieving with our city strengthened our resolve and diminished isolation, but what about Jesus? We were *Out!* with Jesus, so couldn't we do more? Name our terrors to each other? Experience God close and present to our sorrow? Prevent the trauma from embedding, and at least in that way not let terrorism win? Could we even flip the script and come out, for ourselves, with healing? Tom and Katie and I talked. Tom and I would host *our* vigil at our house, and Katie would lead ...

Katie:

About twenty of us drove past the sorrowful Newport Road sheep and cows to gather at Tom and Adey's house the evening of June 17th. We invited all our gay congregants and any of their LGBTQ friends. We included a handful of straight folks—allies, friends of someone in the room. They were safe, and were grieving too. They were asked in advance to let most of the sharing come from the LGBTQ people.

The tone was somber as we made small talk over delivered pizza. When our children's pastor heard that we were hosting the grief service, she said, "I can't be there, but I'll bake every dessert I know and help you set up your house and clean up afterwards. What else can I do?" So we ate and chatted and then shifted to the living room to begin, the tension of the grief sur-rounding us like an orb, held at bay only by our desire to compartmentalize and bury and ignore.

I brought out a large whiteboard on which I had scattered words tra-ditionally used by Christianity to describe gay bars and gay spaces like Pulse—wickedness, evil, sin, drunkenness, debauchery, unnatural, depravity, brokenness. It was hard to see those words, to read them, say them aloud and feel the shame.

I then shared about my first time going to a gay bar in my twenties and the empowerment and safety I felt there—how a weight was lifted off my soul when I could hold Paula's hand without worrying about people noticing. I named the bars and the dear friends I would go with, and that these bars always seemed to be dimly lit and located in alleyways. I recalled how for our first eight years in Iowa City, we would gather with friends every

December at Studio 13 and celebrate "Gay Christmas" in the most fabulous party of the year. It was the one night when each of us could be wholeheartedly our authentic self in the company of our chosen friends. I went up to our whiteboard, erased the word *evil*, and replaced it with *family*.

One woman described the feeling of love and support when she told her closest friends she was a lesbian: she replaced *unnatural* with *friend*. One man talked about finding inspiration in the kindness and creativity of drag queens, in turn giving him the confidence to explore and freely express his own gender: He erased *debauchery* and replaced it with *joy*. Another friend described for the first time feeling like he could love God and love himself without having to choose: He replaced *wickedness* with *welcome*. Others shared stories of coming out, finding community, and finding themselves in these gay bars, nightclubs, parties, and safe spaces.

The shooting was so shattering because it had been perpetrated in a place that served as our sanctuary in the midst of a world that was too often, towards us, excluding and violent. We reclaimed these oft-shamed spaces as we one-by-one erased the words of religious derision and replaced them with words like *acceptance, celebration, safety, whole in Christ,* and *love.* As we leaned into these testimonies, the grief washed over all of us and made space for healing to begin.

Maggie stood up and approached the quite-changed whiteboard. She was in her 50s and was at our grief service because her nephew had been attending Sanctuary for a while and suggested she come. Maggie didn't know anyone in the room. Resisting crying, she said, "I haven't been in church for decades because of how church treats gay people. And I've never ever self-identified as a lesbian because of my religious upbringing." She told a little of her story—her love for God and all things Bible, her clear inclination toward being lesbian since her earliest memories, but her inability to even call herself gay because she had been taught it was so deeply sinful. She had never set foot in a gay bar, but she had managed to find a safe community of close friends over the years. She lived in two distinct non-overlapping worlds—that of Jesus and religion and that of a community of welcoming friends. So being in our living room this night and seeing the intersection of folks embracing their sexuality and proclaiming their love for Jesus was groundbreaking for her. We could feel her consider the possibility of reconciling her identity and faith as she quietly walked up to the board, erased *sin* and replaced it with *freedom.*

Cory was there, our resident poet, and to bring our vigil to a close she led us in writing our own psalms of lament. As traumatized believers have done for ages, we cried out to God in fury, despair, and dismay, declaiming against God and yet longing for the assurance of her presence:

> *Why have you let them brutalize our stories, force our lives into darkness, break the surface of our skin with their bullets?*
>
> *How can we bear this burden on top of the hate that we have received in your name?*
>
> *Why in this safe place? To these beautiful people? Black and brown and white, queens and kings, princes, princesses and those in between.*

We sought reason to hope, pleading for a glimpse of God's kingdom breaking in here with us.

> *Jesus you reside in our safe places. You have made them, the walls, the colors, the light, the darkness. The whole earth, filled with your glory, will be a safe place once again.*
>
> *We have confidence in your unfailing, unflagging love, in your capacity to make safety flow down like rivers carrying us into tomorrow.*
>
> *God, show up for us.*

As we finished praying Maggie said, "I wish my family could have been here. I wish they could have seen this, seen you all."

Our air, afterwards, felt as if it had been perceptibly cleansed. Together, in the presence of God, straight friends stood with queer friends and proclaimed the truth that the Spirit has been whispering in the ear of the church since the beginning—that this God, who knitted us together in our mothers' wombs, made us whole. This God leads us to safety, to quiet waters and green pastures and gay bars and bright nightclubs. And sometimes this God even leads us to a community of Jesus followers that show wholehearted love and acceptance.

If any of us had questioned our decision to become fully inclusive for LGBTQ people, it was quieted after this night. We experienced a taste of what the church is meant to be for its people—a sanctuary. The evening concluded with a last prayer beseeching God on behalf of the victims of the Orlando nightclub shooting and all those close to them, and all those who, like us, had been terrorized. We cried out to God on behalf of a wounded community that has existed on the margins of our society, and we cried out to God on behalf of the church we love with all of our blind spots and imperfections. We cried, Come Jesus, Come.

Connect With Us

Thanks for making it to the end of our story! Though this end is, for us, as we've said, just a beginning, or perhaps a middle, as our story—and our community—continues to evolve. So if you'd like to join in or check us out, whether online or through visiting, please do! Here's our church website: sanctuaryic.org

If you're on Facebook, you can follow us at facebook.com/sanctuaryic

We're on Instagram at: instagram.com/sanctuarycommunitychurch

Our services are streamed live, and everyone is welcome to visit on a Sunday. If you're coming with a group of any size, please let us know in advance so we can increase our Sunday morning bagel order. :)

If you enjoyed this book, and think that others would find it helpful, please consider leaving a review on the retail platform where you purchased it, or at Goodreads.com. To contact the authors about anything related to the book, or for requests you might have of them, reach out to Tom, Adey, or Katie using their Sanctuary Church email addresses:

adey@sanctuaryic.org

tom@sanctuaryic.org

katie@sanctuaryic.org

About
Read the Spirit Books

Read The Spirit Books is an imprint of Front Edge Publishing, LLC. Since 2007, Read The Spirit Books has been publishing books that celebrate inclusive, cross-cultural, interfaith books to build healthy communities. Our writers explore these themes each week in our online magazine which can be read and subscribed to at ReadTheSpirit.com.

Read The Spirit is published every Monday by noon ET—each issue consisting of a new front-page lineup of stories. At 1 p.m. ET Mondays, our free newsletters and other social-media outreach efforts distribute that new issue to our readers worldwide. Our team has never missed a Monday morning deadline in more than 15 years, which means in 2024 we will have published more than 800 weekly issues, amounting to thousands of inspiring and helpful columns.

All of our books are available on Amazon.com, BarnesandNoble.com, and other retailers in multiple formats, including ebooks.

Related Books

Changing Our Mind, Third Definitive Edition

Dr. David P. Gushee

Changing Our Mind has helped thousands of families and congregations carefully and compassionately rethink traditional religious teachings about full LGBTQ+ inclusion.

As much as ever, many people still experience deep condemnation by evangelical and other churches, getting kicked out or altogether leaving. Dr. David Gushee offers a powerful, inspiring message of hope and healing by helping Christians to return to Bible study, prayer, and reflection in a way that creates a vision for a more inclusive church.

Also available in audio (English), Spanish, and Korean.

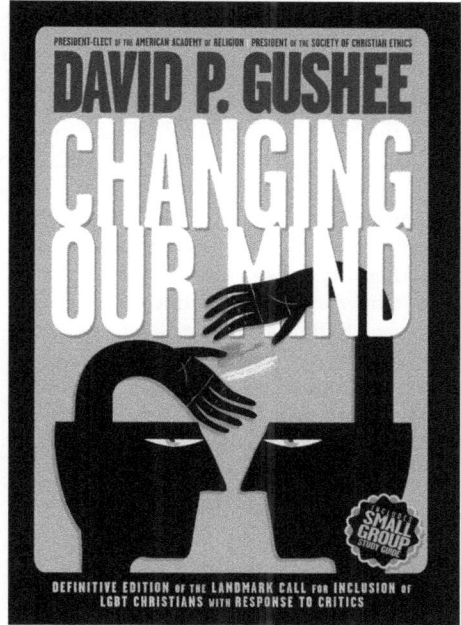

Introducing Christian Ethics

Dr. David P. Gushee

"A comprehensive one-stop manual on what it means to live Christianly."

Peter Enns, author of *The Bible Tells Me So*

What does it mean to be a Christian in today's turbulent world? After every disillusionment and debate, what convictions survive? Dr. David P. Gushee is an influential voice in American religious life as an ethicist, pastor, and activist. In this ambitious new book, Gushee sums up his many years of teaching and experience to provide a definitive, comprehensive vision of the Christian moral life.

Also available in audio.

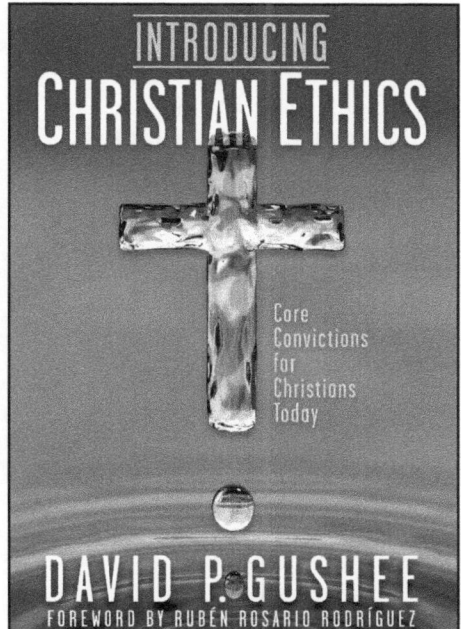

Related Books

A Letter to my Congregation

Ken Wilson

"This is a breakthrough work coming from the heart of evangelical Christianity and offered into the heart of evangelical Christianity. It is unlike other books that demand revision of traditional Christian sexual ethics but do so primarily by rejecting the authority of the Bible. That is not how evangelicals think, and it is not what Ken Wilson does here. Instead Wilson shows how God has led him on a journey toward a rethinking of what the fully authoritative and inspired Bible ought to be taken to mean in the life of the church today."

David P. Gushee, prolific Christian author and Director of the Center for Theology and Public Life at Mercer University

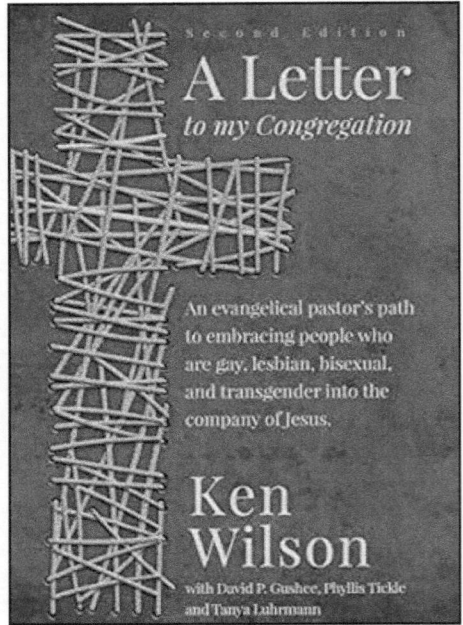

Solus Jesus

Emily Swan and Ken Wilson

If you read one book this year about the future of Christianity, then choose this book. Five hundred years ago the Protestant Reformation claimed the Bible as the authoritative guide for Christian living (*"Sola Scriptura!"* Only Scripture!). In this groundbreaking work, Emily Swan and Ken Wilson claim the authority of the church is shifting back to where it should be: in Jesus (*Solus Jesus!*). As co-founders of Blue Ocean Faith, Swan and Wilson are pioneering what it means to be post-evangelical—post-Protestant, even—in a time when such re-imagining is desperately needed.

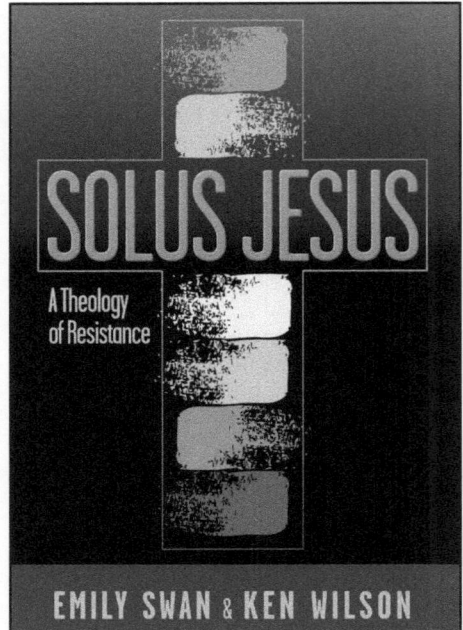

Related Books

The Word Made Fresh

George A. Mason

For three decades, George Mason's weekly messages have inspired those who attend Wilshire Baptist Church in Dallas, Texas, as well as George's followers nationwide. Now, this unique multimedia book collects 80 of George's most memorable and thought-provoking sermons along with links to videos of many of them. This collection covers timely themes ranging from the welcoming love of God and the basics of the Christian faith to such vital issues as the stewardship of our planet, the importance of interfaith relationships, the need to include the most vulnerable in our community life, and the importance of peacemaking.

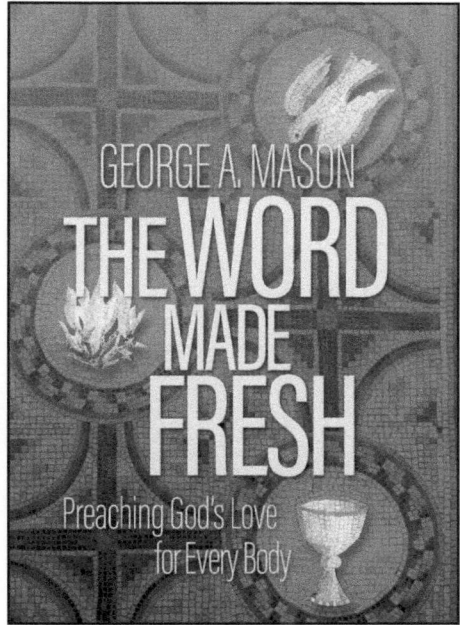

100 Questions and Answers about Sexual Orientation

&

100 Questions and Answers about Gender Identity

Michigan State University School of Journalism

This paired set of guides from the Bias Busters cultural competence series from the Michigan State University School of Journalism answer 100 basic questions about sexual orientation 100 basic questions about gender identity. The guides are written for family and friends, as well as government and community leaders, who want to get to know LGBTQ+ people and are looking for a starting point for deeper conversations.

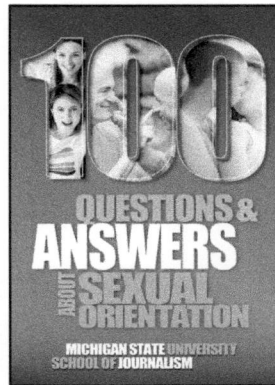

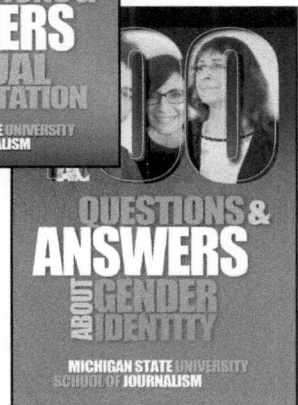

Milton Keynes UK
Ingram Content Group UK Ltd.
UKHW042139201024
449848UK00005B/31

9 781641 801850